LATINOS AND AMERICAN LAW

For
reference

Not to be taken
from the room.

Latinos and American Law

Landmark Supreme Court Cases

CARLOS R. SOLTERO

UNIVERSITY OF TEXAS PRESS

AUSTIN

Requests for permission to reproduce material from this work
should be sent to: Permissions, University of Texas Press
P.O. Box 7819, Austin, TX 78713-7819

www.utexas.edu/utpress/about/bpermission.html

∞ The paper used in this book meets the minimum requirements of
ANSI/NISO Z39.48-1992 (R1997) (Permanence of Paper).

LIBRARY OF CONGRESS CATALOGING-IN-PUBLICATION DATA

Soltero, Carlos R., 1969–
    Latinos and American law : landmark Supreme Court cases involving
Latinos/Hispanics / Carlos R. Soltero.
        p.   cm.
    Includes bibliographical references and index.
    ISBN-13: 978-0-292-71310-9 (cl. : alk. paper)
    ISBN-10: 0-292-71310-X
    ISBN-13: 978-0-292-71411-3 (pbk. : alk. paper)
    ISBN-10: 0-292-71411-4
    1. United States. Supreme Court—History.   2. Hispanic
Americans—Legal status, laws, etc.—United States—Cases.   I. Title.
    KF4757.5.L38A52   2006
    342.7308'73—dc22

                                        2006015018

To my love and wife, Jane,

and to my boys,

Antonio René, John Carlos, and Joseph Ramón

Contents

Acknowledgments

In 1993, I collected materials to teach a class on some of the subjects in this book for the spring semester of 1994 at Yale. While I was at Yale, and after I moved back to Texas, many people contributed to my study of issues related to Latinos in the American legal system. I hope I can explicitly acknowledge most of those who helped me compile and complete this work.

Among those whose academic mentorship helped me explore these issues, and to whom I am particularly grateful, is Rogers Smith, who mentored me as a college student, allowed me to work with him as a teaching assistant, and developed my interest in legal history, political philosophy, and American constitutional law. I am also grateful to Akhil Amar, who supervised my research into issues related to the rights of those in the American territories (which I incorporated into Chapter 2), the relationship of rights in American history, and of course, the Bill of Rights. I am deeply thankful for the Honorable Guido Calabresi's help in supervising research into this area and for his personal contributions to making my law school experience an outstanding one. I am similarly grateful for Natalia Martín's support and advice.

I am also thankful to others who have written about some of these issues and from whom I have been fortunate to have learned, including the Honorable José Cabranes, the Honorable Juan Torruella, the Honorable Guadalupe Salinas, Juan Perea, Juan Manuel García Passalacqua, Gerald Torres, and Mario García.

I would like to thank my friend Walter Taché for our friendship, ongoing discussions of some of these issues through the years, and in particular, his help in connection with my work on Chapter 13. Similarly, I would like to thank my friends Tom Saenz and Christina Duffy Burnett.

I also wish to thank those who have mentored me in the practice of law, including particularly René Barrientos, Craig Smyser, Lee Kaplan, Larry Veselka, Pat Lochridge, Lin Hughes, and Rick Milvenan. I am especially grateful to Craig for reviewing a chapter of this book and providing me insightful, thoughtful suggestions to improve the content.

Theresa May of the University of Texas Press has been outstanding to work with in bringing this work forward, and I thank her for her time, thoughts, contributions, and support. I am likewise grateful to Leslie Tingle and Sue Carter.

I am grateful to Yale University and the University of Texas at Austin for allowing me to teach some of these topics and for their human and research material resources.

I owe special thanks to Joan O'Mara and Madalina Hinojosa for assisting me in obtaining materials and for their service to the law firm. Similarly, Dee Elliott has been an invaluable source of support for years, and I thank her for her contributions toward making this book a reality.

Finally, I am most grateful for the constant support and education from all my family, particularly my wife, Jane, my father, Ramón Soltero, and my mother, Diana Barrientos. Jane's love, commitment, dedication, sacrifices, and conversations with me were necessary for me to have the opportunity to complete this book. I am especially grateful to my mother, as well as Michele Martise and Jane, for taking time to review and make suggestions for portions of this book.

Any and all errors that may remain in the text are solely mine.

LATINOS AND AMERICAN LAW

Introduction

Latinos and American Law discusses the historical significance of some landmark cases of the country's highest court involving Latinos/Hispanics. Of interest are not only the rulings themselves, but also the interaction between Latino/Hispanic individuals and communities in the United States and the American legal system. Through areas such as education, the administration of criminal justice, voting rights, employment, and immigration, those legally trained as well as non-lawyer readers will gain a greater appreciation of the subtle complexities of the issues facing Latinos and their interactions with the American legal system. Relatively few books have addressed how the legal system has impacted Hispanics, although in recent years the topic has received greater attention, and law review articles and other academic disciplines have more developed studies of Latinos.

The Supreme Court considers only a small number of cases appealed to the Court. These are a fraction of all cases filed in federal and state courts throughout the United States. Obviously missing from this discussion are tens of thousands of cases involving Latinos in the American legal system, the vast majority of which, while directly affecting lives, are decided by state courts, lower federal courts, or other courts. While these include cases generally unknown to the vast majority of Americans or people in law schools, some are very well known, such as *Gonzalez v. Reno* (11th Cir. 2000). Instead, this book is confined to legal dramas played out at the summit of the American legal system. Focusing on the Supreme Court makes sense because the Supreme Court is a unique institution in the United States, with a unique role in American history and the legal system. The names of landmark Supreme Court cases such as *Scott v. Sandford* (1856) (aka the *Dred Scott* case), *Plessy v. Ferguson* (1896), *Brown v. Board of Education* (1954), *Miranda v. Arizona* (1966), and *Roe v. Wade* (1973) are widely known and form the basis for discussions about issues in American society. The Supreme Court is at the pinnacle of the American legal system's judiciary branch. All federal courts are subservient to the Supreme Court, and matters involving constitutional or other federal issues are also reviewed from the courts of the states and other jurisdictions.

The American legal system developed from the British common law system, and therefore traces its roots to a source different from that of the legal systems of most European and Latin American countries, commonly referred to as civil law jurisdictions, where the Napoleonic codes form the basis of substantive law. At a theoretical level, this distinction is significant because the American legal system, like its other common law counterparts throughout the former British Empire and Commonwealth countries, tends to focus more on case law, precedents, judicial reasoning, and *stare decisis*, while the systems related to civil law jurisdictions focus more on the language of the codes and works of legal scholars interpreting the codes. *Black's Law Dictionary* defines *stare decisis* as "the doctrine of precedent, under which it is necessary for a court to follow earlier judicial decisions when the same points arise again in litigation."[1] In reality, and in practice, over time these two polar theoretical extremes have blended. For instance, every one of the United States' jurisdictions now have statutes that are functionally the equivalents of the codes and which "codify" common law rulings or other legislative enactments. Similarly, in part due to technological advancements making information easier to obtain and in part due to the influence of the American legal system, civil law countries have increasingly used prior rulings in making judicial determinations of particular legal disputes.[2]

Latinos and American Law analyzes issues of particular significance to Latinos as well as cases involving legal issues that are important to the American legal system generally and where Latinos were key participants. *Latinos and American Law* tries to promote understanding and to further the great ideals of the United States legal system: liberty, equality, and a government of laws and rules. *Latinos and American Law* is generally organized chronologically and divided according to the Supreme Court's various historical eras by reference to the Chief Justice at the time (e.g., the Warren Court, the Rehnquist Court, etc.). The introduction provides a historical backdrop for understanding the general role of Latinos in the American society and legal system. Each chapter focuses on one landmark Supreme Court case of significance to Latinos in the American legal system, beginning with a discussion of background factors, including relevant general legal issues. Then, each chapter walks through the opinion, or opinions, since in many of these cases the Court was divided and some justices wrote opinions separate from the Court's official opinion, either agreeing or disagreeing with the Court's ruling. The chapters then conclude with a brief analysis of the opinion's significance and post-decision events of note. While many cases involve constitutional issues, others do not. Some involve interpretations of legal statutes such as Title VI or Title VII of the Civil Rights Act of 1964 and provisions of the Voting Rights Act of 1965. This distinction is significant because the Court is the final arbiter on constitutional issues, but not of non-constitutional laws, which a subsequent Congress may choose to amend if Congress disagrees with a ruling from the Court on statutory issues. A ruling from the Court on constitutional issues generally can only be challenged either (1) by a subsequent case before the Supreme Court seeking to overrule or modify that decision, or (2) by constitutional amendment.

The legal issues and each chapter of the book describe legal situations as diverse as the groups comprising Latinos, including ethnic, geographic, and other differences.[3] The Court's rulings reflect the times, including the politics of the times. Frequently, the Court's rulings were pro-government. Of the cases in this book, the only "pro-government" ruling that involved legislation made for the benefit of Latinos is *Katzenbach v. Morgan* (1966), a case whose ruling has been subject to extensive criticism. Also noteworthy is the gap between the Court's rhetoric and the results of its holdings. Several cases highlight how narrow and formal construction of anti-discrimination laws can render them virtually meaningless in protecting relatively politically powerless groups. Portions of the book involve aliens'/immigrants' rights, an issue that frequently came to the Court's attention during the Burger Court (1969–1986). The first two chapters, as well as the cases from the Warren Court (1952–1968), highlight the fact that the roots or origins of Latinos/Hispanics in the United States stand independently and apart from immigration, or alienage, issues. *Botiller v. Dominguez* (1889) reflects the role of the Court as part of a conquering government in the Southwest after the U.S.-Mexican War of 1846. *Balzac v. Porto [sic] Rico* (1922) reflects the Court's role as co-governing colonial institution over Puerto Rico. Some of the opinions in *Latinos and American Law* reflect that the Court, at times, applies laws and constitutional protections differently depending on the places (specifically the U.S.-Mexican border region, other immigration points, and Puerto Rico). These places are largely inhabited by Latinos/Hispanics. *Hernandez v. Texas* (1954) challenged the American legal system's general binary white/black views of race and ethnicity. The Warren Court served as an instrument of social change during the post–World War II, Cold War, and Civil Rights eras.

"Latino" and "Hispanic" are used interchangeably in this book to refer to the people in the historical context of their existence within the United States who are characterized as having a Spanish surname and/or who emigrated from (or whose ancestors originated in) a predominantly Spanish-speaking country.[4] The terms "Hispanic" or "Latino" include not only members of the three largest ethnic groups generally characterized by people having a Spanish surname and/or who speak Spanish as a primary language in the country of their origin—Mexican-Americans, Puerto Ricans, and Cubans—but also Dominicans, Guatemalans, and other Central Americans, as well as Colombians, Argentinos, and other South Americans. Many have questioned whether these terms make any sense at all.[5] Until the United States government and the governments of subdivisions of the United States began using these terms, no one had been born a "Hispanic" or a "Latino," and the terms lack the precision of being born a woman or a man or even, to a lesser extent, black or white. Earl Shorris writes, "there are no Latinos, only diverse peoples struggling to remain who they are while becoming someone else."[6] Most people would agree that those born and raised in Latin America would not conceive of themselves as "Latino" or "Hispanic" as those terms are used in the United States, as opposed to *boliviano, ecuatoreano, mexicano,* or *nicaraguense,* for example. Linda Chavez makes the point with a slightly different perspective: "Before the affirmative action age, there were no *Hispanics,* only Mexicans, Puerto Ricans, Cubans, and so on."[7]

Not all Latinos/Hispanics speak Spanish. For some, English is the only language. Not all Latinos/Hispanics have Spanish surnames or first names. In light of all of the differences across subgroups of Latinos, one might wonder if we should even use these characterizations. From a legal perspective, however, such terms have come to have some import. Justice William Douglas provided a persuasive rationale in a dissenting opinion when the United States Supreme Court refused to accept *certiorari* (the writ most commonly used by people who seek to have the Supreme Court accept the discretionary review of their case from a lower court) in a class action suit brought on behalf of "Indo-Hispano" children seeking publicly funded bilingual education in New Mexico's public schools, *Tijerina v. Henry* (1970). In *Tijerina,* the federal district court refused to recognize the putative or proposed class because its membership was too vague. According to Justice Douglas, "One thing is not vague or uncertain, however, and that is that those who discriminate against members of this and other minority groups have little difficulty in isolating the objects of their discrimination."[8]

Joan Moore and Harry Pachón, in *Hispanics in the United States,* note also that the geographical spread beyond the "traditional" population zones (Cubans in Florida, Mexican-Americans in the Southwest, and Puerto Ricans in the Northeast) and the increasing number of Hispanics in the United States via immigration and high fertility rates have created a convergence of interests at some levels. Since the first census of the twenty-first century, Latinos/Hispanics are now considered "the largest minority group" in the United States. In the context of the American legal system, the Supreme Court in *Hernandez v. New York* (1991) recognized Latinos/Hispanics as a group in that it used those categories to consider a challenge to the fairness of jury selection where all the Hispanic/Latino jurors were struck from a criminal jury.

The flip side of classifying people is defining those not in the classified group. The two most important groups in relation to Hispanics are white Americans and black Americans because the United States as a society has viewed itself predominantly as bi-racial (black or white). The legal system has reflected this bi-racial view of the United States, and Hispanics (like Asian-Americans and others) do not neatly fit in one category or the other. Also, white Americans are the "majority" in the United States and are most heavily represented in the power structure; traditionally, black Americans have been the largest "minority" group in the United States and were the leaders and focus of the Civil Rights movement of the 1950s and 1960s as well as anti-discrimination laws passed in the nineteenth century. Other relevant groups to Latinos in the American political reality include Asian-Americans and Native Americans. Of particular importance is the fact that Asian-Americans and Native Americans are found in great preponderance in the West and Southwest, much like Mexican-Americans.

Legal systems generally mirror the societies in which they exist, since laws are in essence the rules governing societal norms. The American legal system is no exception, and whereas race has played a central role in aspects of the American legal system, until recently, Latinos/Hispanics were largely considered an anomaly or an afterthought within the black-white legal and societal structure. Additionally, norms generally applicable to nationals of other countries (foreign nationals) have at times been applied to Latinos, even when those Hispanics are citizens, such as in the case of Puerto Ricans.

Peter Skerry describes Mexican-Americans as "ambivalent" in deciding whether they should be considered a "minority" or an "ethnic group." These two terms are loaded with connotations, and he suggests that "minority group" means "a victimized racial claimant group" while "ethnic group" means a cultural immigrant group. Skerry refers to blacks as the prototypical "minority" and non-Hispanic Anglos like the Irish as "ethnics." Mexican-Americans and other Latinos are not ambivalent. Rather, the fact that Hispanics do not fit neatly into the black-white binary of American society and the legal system creates what may be perceived by some as ambivalence. Indeed, the very composition of Latinos/Hispanics—a mixed racial and ethnic background, whether it be mestizo, mulatto, or ladino—was one thing American society and the legal system sought to prevent since the seventeenth century through laws such as those forbidding mixed marriages, which the Supreme Court only declared unconstitutional in *Loving v. Virginia* (1967).[9] Whereas in the American context, mixed marriages and the children of mixed couples have been traditionally viewed as exceptions or aberrations, in Latin America, after five hundred years of Spanish colonialism and miscegenation, people of mixed ancestry are common, if not the norm. Throughout the history of United States, interactions with Latin America and with Latin Americans have traditionally reflected conflicts at the cultural level, involving different predominant religious views, as well as at the economic or political level. How this group has interacted with the highest level of the American legal system is the focus of this book.

While focusing on some landmark cases, *Latinos and American Law* does not discuss, highlight, or exhaust every significant or landmark Supreme Court case involving Latinos/Hispanics in the American legal system. Nor does the book attempt to address every issue involving Latinos/Hispanics in the American legal system. Rather, *Latinos and American Law* seeks to open a dialogue and provide a one-volume resource, not conclusive, definitive answers.

A

1. *Botiller v. Dominguez* (1889), Mexican Land Grants, and the Treaty of Guadalupe Hidalgo

Botiller v. Dominguez (1889),
Mexican Land Grants,
and the Treaty of Guadalupe Hidalgo

A. Background

Nemecio Dominguez and Domingo Carrillo, Mexican citizens, obtained a land grant dated October 1, 1834, from the Mexican government over a tract of land in Los Angeles County known as Rancho Las Virgenes. The land title transferred to Apolonio Dominguez, who died and left the ranch to his daughter, Dominga Dominguez. Sixty-five years after the initial land grant, Ms. Dominguez fought at the United States Supreme Court to keep the land she had inherited from her ancestors in the landmark case involving Latinos in the American legal system, *Botiller v. Dominguez* (1889).

In 1889, the United States celebrated the centennial of the Constitution of 1789, which at the time had been amended only five times after the ratification of the Bill of Rights on December 15, 1791. Less than forty years earlier the Court had ruled in its landmark *Scott v. Sandford* (aka *Dred Scott*)[1] (1856) decision that black Americans were not citizens and that slavery could not be abolished in the territories of the United States, which according to David O'Brien, had "left the Court at low ebb for two decades."[2] The Supreme Court's ruling in *Scott* further escalated sectional and philosophical divisions in the United States, culminating in the Civil War of 1861–1865, which ripped the country apart. Slavery was abolished in the Reconstruction era and the Reconstruction Congress passed laws to protect the constitutional rights of African-Americans, particularly the Civil Rights Act of 1866 and the Ku Klux Klan Act of 1871.

Meanwhile, laws enacted after the Mexican War of 1846–1848 created other types of divisions in the Western United States. Mexico ceded half of its national territory (when considered together with the annexation of Texas in 1845) to the United States, which became the American Southwest. The

Mexican War also became a formative event in relation to the role of Mexicans in the American legal system. The Treaty of Guadalupe Hidalgo legally ended the hostilities between Mexico and the United States in 1848.[3] Article VIII of the Treaty of Guadalupe Hidalgo stated in part that

> Mexicans in territories previously belonging to Mexico, and which remain for the future within the limits of the United States, as defined by the present Treaty, shall be free to continue where they now reside, or to remove at any time to the Mexican Republic, retaining the property which they possess in the said territories, or disposing thereof and removing the proceeds wherever they please; without their being subjected, on this account, to any contribution, tax or charge whatever.

Article IX further provided that Mexicans choosing to remain in the territories acquired by the United States would be

> incorporated into the Union of the United States and be admitted, at the proper time (to be judged of by the Congress of the United States) to the enjoyment of all the rights and citizens of the United States according to the principles of the Constitution; and in the meantime shall be maintained and protected in the free enjoyment of their liberty and property, and secured in the free exercise of their religion without restriction.

Shortly after the Mexican-American War ended, disputes over property and displacements of Mexicans in the former northern territories of Mexico and the Southwest of the United States occurred. The character of these disputes differed on the basis of both the particular circumstances of the persons and properties involved and the region. California became a state in 1850. Texas had been admitted to statehood in 1845 after almost a decade as an independent republic. New Mexico remained a territory until 1912. Richard Griswold del Castillo, who has written a book on the history of the Treaty of Guadalupe Hidalgo, estimates that the treaty's provisions relating to persons formerly under the Mexican government prior to the Mexican War impacted approximately one hundred thousand people at that time.[4]

On March 3, 1851, in part to create a standardized manner to provide good land title, Congress passed the California Land Settlement Act of 1851 ("the Act of 1851"). The Act of 1851, which formed a board of commissioners, required the registration of private land claims in California and created rights of appeal in various courts. Cases disputing land ownership and Mexican land grants became common, particularly in California. In the late 1840s, the discovery of large gold reserves led to the "gold rush." One historian estimates that more than one hundred thousand people migrated to California in 1849 alone.[5] Among those migrating to California to work in the mining industry were Chileans, Peruvians, Mexicans, and others from Latin America.

Several land grant disputes reached the Supreme Court before *Botiller*. Among these was the landmark case of *Fremont v. United States* (1854), cited by the Court in *Botiller*. That case involved a claim by Colonel John Charles Fremont (for whom Fremont, California was named). Colonel Fremont led the Bear Flag Rebellion of 1846 against Mexican rule prior to the war with Mexico. Fremont became senator from California in 1850 and unsuccessfully ran for president of the United States as a Republican in 1856. Fremont purchased Rancho Mariposa from José Alvarado (who had sold the ranch to pay creditors) in February of 1847, while American forces occupied California. The Mexican government had given Mr. Alvarado a land grant for that property in 1844. The United States challenged Fremont's claim to the land on the grounds that he had failed to meet several requirements of Mexican law, including failing to include a survey of the land grant. The Supreme Court ultimately affirmed the Mexican land grant from which Fremont's claim had derived, securing Colonel Fremont's property rights. Chief Justice Roger Taney, who was appointed by President Andrew Jackson and who had also authored the *Scott* decision, authored the opinion in *Fremont*. By the time the Supreme Court considered *Botiller*, in the wake of *Scott* and the Civil War, it was relatively reserved and conservative in tone.

The *Botiller* lawsuit began in California when Dominga Dominguez sued Brigido Botiller and others to eject them from, and recover possession of, the Rancho Las Virgenes. Ms. Dominguez asserted her land grant from the Mexican government to her ancestors. No one had presented a claim to the board of commissioners established by the Act of 1851 in California after the Mexican War. Sometime after the war, Mr. Botiller and others occupied and squatted on portions of the Rancho Las Virgenes. Ms. Dominguez filed suit in the Los Angeles County superior court, where a jury rendered a verdict in her favor, ordering Mr. Botiller and the others off the ranch. On April 26, 1887, the California Supreme Court affirmed the judgment based on the jury verdict. Brigido Botiller appealed to the United States Supreme Court, claiming that Ms. Dominguez was not the rightful owner because neither she (nor anyone else) had filed a claim with the commission in accordance with the Act of 1851 establishing her entitlement to the Rancho Las Virgenes based on the 1834 land grant.

B. *Botiller v. Dominguez* (1889): The Opinion

The Supreme Court issued its opinion on April 1, 1889. J. M. Gitchell represented Botiller and A. L. Rhodes represented Ms. Dominguez. Justice Samuel Freeman Miller, appointed by President Abraham Lincoln in 1862, wrote the opinion on behalf of a unanimous Supreme Court. In 1880, in a speech delivered before the University Law School of Washington, D.C., Justice Miller had proclaimed that "our Constitution, unlike most modern ones, does not contain any formal declaration or bill of rights".[6] Justice Miller is best known for writing the 5 – 4 majority opinion in the landmark *Slaughterhouse Cases* (1873), which took a narrow view of the post – Civil War constitutional amendments as being solely to "provide former slaves a measure of equality before the law with whites, not to expand the liberties of the general population."[7] Akhil Amar has correctly described Justice Miller's opinion in the *Slaughterhouse Cases* as being "generally thought today to have rendered the privileges-or-immunities clause [of the Fourteenth Amendment] utterly meaningless."[8]

Mr. Gitchell, Mr. Botiller's counsel, argued that the California courts had wrongly found that not everyone with a claim to real property in California "by virtue of any right or title derived from the Spanish or Mexican governments" was required to present their claims to the board of land commissioners appointed under the Act of 1851. Justice Miller characterized the question at issue in the case as "an important one in reference to land titles in [California], and [one] entitled to our serious consideration." Justice Miller noted that although "it has been generally supposed that nearly all the private claims to any of the lands acquired by the United States from Mexico by the treaty of peace made at the close of the Mexican War have been presented to and passed upon by the board of commissioners," claims were still in 1889 "often brought forward which have not been so passed upon by that board, and were never presented to it for consideration." Accordingly, this case would be precedent for other similar cases that continued to be brought even forty years after the U.S.-Mexican War. Justice Miller characterized the opinion of the California Supreme Court as holding that the board constituted under the Act of 1851 had no jurisdiction over, and could not by decree affect "in any manner, a title which had been perfected under the laws of the Mexican government prior to the transfer of the country to the United States." Therefore, it would be "impossible to tell to what extent such claims of perfected titles may be presented, even in cases where the property itself has by somebody else been brought before that board and passed upon."

Justice Miller also noted that the Mexican government, in connection with the Treaty of Guadalupe Hidalgo and the cession of the territories to the United

States, "caused to be inserted" provisions "intended for the protection of private property owned by Mexicans within this territory at the time the treaty was made." According to Justice Miller, California in 1846 was "in a wild state of nature, with very few resident white persons, and very little land cultivated within its limits." As supporting evidence, Justice Miller cited Article XI of the treaty, which refers to large parts of the ceded territory as "now occupied by savage tribes, who will hereafter be under the exclusive control of the government of the United States, and whose incursions within the territory of Mexico would be prejudicial in the extreme." Under Article XI, the United States committed to preventing incursions into Mexico by people who were part of these "savage tribes."

Then Justice Miller stated: "Very soon after the American army took possession of California, in 1846, it was discovered that rich mines of the precious metals were abundant in that country, and a rush of emigration almost unparalleled in history to that region commenced, which was continued from that time on for many years." All types of people in mining, ranching, and other industries, as well as settlers under Mexican church authorities and other claimants under Mexican land grants disputed ownership of the rich resources of California. Justice Miller quoted the provisions of the Act of 1851 in order to address the issue in the case: whether Ms. Dominguez had good title to the land under the 1834 grant although no one had filed a claim with the commission.

Ms. Dominguez' attorney, Mr. Rhodes, urged two points in response. First, he argued that the Act of 1851 was invalid to the extent that it conflicted with provisions of the Treaty of Guadalupe Hidalgo. Second, he contended that Congress had intended to limit the scope of the board of commissioner's inquiries under the Act of 1851 to imperfect, inchoate (which means partial or unfinished), and equitable claims without a strict legal title. In other words, Mr. Rhodes argued that Congress did not intend the Act of 1851 to apply to people holding clearly valid legal title.

Justice Miller first addressed the conflict between the Act of 1851 and the treaty, indicating that the government of Mexico, not private Mexicans in the courts of the United States, should complain about any alleged violations of the treaty between two sovereign countries since a treaty violation would involve a "matter of international concern." According to Justice Miller's opinion, the Court, in cases like Ms. Dominguez', "has no power to set itself up as the instrumentality for enforcing the provisions of a treaty with a foreign nation which the government of the United States, as a sovereign power, chooses to disregard." The role of the Court was only supposed to follow "statutory enactments of its own government," not international treaties.

As to what Justice Miller referred to as "the more important question," the Court began by analyzing the language of the Act of 1851, concluding that there was "nothing in the language of the statute to imply any such exclusion of perfected claims from the jurisdiction of the commission." The title or name of the Act of 1851, according to Justice Miller, further suggested that it meant to apply to *all* land claims, and "repels" any distinction between legal claims and other imperfect claims. The Court then quoted a portion of the act, including language in Chapter 8 that "each and every person claiming lands in California by virtue of any right or title derived from the Spanish or Mexican government shall present the same to the said commissioners when sitting as a board." From this, the Court concluded that "there is no hint or attempt at any distinction, as to the claims to be presented, between those which are perfect and those which are imperfect." Justice Miller found the language in Chapter 8 to be "as precise and comprehensive as it could well be made." Nor did the Court find any policy reasons for adopting a distinction. According to the Court, the purpose of the Act of 1851 was not to adjust or settle titles between private citizens, but rather to distinguish between lands the United States owned from those lands belonging "either equitably or legally, to private parties under a claim of right derived from the Spanish or Mexican governments."

Justice Miller wrote that no one could state "that there is anything unjust or oppressive in requiring the owner of a valid claim, in that vast wilderness of lands unclaimed and unjustly claimed, to present his demand to a tribunal possessing all the elements of judicial functions, with a guaranty of judicial proceedings" to have the validity of the title determined. The Court saw no injustice, constitutional violation, or treaty violation in how the United States "undertook to separate the lands in which it held the proprietary interest from those which belonged, either equitably or by a strict legal title, to private persons." In part, the reason for this view was that every person owning land or other property "is at all times liable to be called into a court of justice to contest his title to it" regardless of whether the challenge is from another individual or a government.

Rather than apply any exacting scrutiny to Ms. Dominguez' claim that the interpretation of Congress' Act of 1851 was dispossessing her of her private property, the Court applied what might be considered a "rational review" analysis: did Congress act rationally or reasonably? The Court found Congress' choice in the manner it set forth the claims as reasonable and based on the United States' experience in dealing with "a somewhat similar class of cases arising under the treaties for the purchase of Florida from Spain and of the territory of Louisiana from France." The Court, in an interesting choice of words, found it "not profitable" to "go into the details of the various acts of congress passed upon the subject."

The Court compared the Act of 1851 with prior laws seeking to incorporate newly acquired territories and found that Congress in the Act of 1851 had acted wisely. Justice Miller then referred to prior rulings from the Court, including the *Fremont* case, which distinguished the Act of 1851 from the Act of 1824. That act limited the jurisdiction of the Court to inchoate equitable titles, which required some other act of the government to vest in the party full legal title and ownership. The Court also cited *More v. Steinbach* (1888), where the Court ruled that even in cases where title under the grant was perfect, the grantee still had to present his claim to the commission for examination. Justice Miller rejected Ms. Dominguez' counsel's contention that the quoted language was *dicta* (meaning that the language was not central to the decision in that case, but merely a superfluous statement). Justice Miller also claimed that an examination of California Supreme Court cases either agreed with the Court's ruling in *Botiller* or at least were "not inconsistent."

Finally, the Court stated it was "quite satisfied" and without doubt that no title to land in California dependent on Spanish or Mexican grants could "be of any validity" unless it had been submitted to, and confirmed by, either the board/commission or a subsequent court that considered a claim brought first before the board/commission and then ruled that the grant was valid. Accordingly, the U.S. Supreme Court reversed the California Supreme Court's judgment in favor of Ms. Dominguez and instructed the lower courts to follow its ruling in further proceedings to enforce that ruling.

C. The Significance of *Botiller* and Post-*Botiller* Developments to Latinos in the American Legal System

Many Hispanics/Latinos live in areas of the United States that were once under Spanish and/or Mexican control. Absent territorial expansion throughout the nineteenth century, in all likelihood the United States would not have as large (in whole numbers or percentages) a population of Latinos. Accordingly, the various land grant cases, and the Supreme Court's interpretation of treaty obligations, are significant. Disputes over citizenship rights also were common in the period after the Mexican-American War, notwithstanding the Treaty of Guadalupe Hidalgo.

Additionally, *Botiller* exemplifies one of several ways in which Mexican landowners and others were displaced and dispossessed during the nineteenth century, a subject covered by many historians, particularly those who have written about Western history and Mexican-American/Chicano history. Some commentators have asserted that together *Fremont* and *Botiller* indicate a double standard depending on the ethnicity (or relative influence) of the claimant.[9] Chief Justice Taney's view of the requirements to perfect claims under Mexican land grants in *Fremont,* where Colonel Fremont stood to gain on a questionable land grant title, was very lax. And the Court rejected Ms. Dominguez' undoubtedly perfect claims under Mexican law in *Botiller* because she failed to comply with the Act of 1851.[10] While the Court clearly showed antipathy to some claims, particularly to *ejido* (communal land) claims, there were cases where the Supreme Court did rule in favor of Mexican claimants.[11] *Botiller* was by no means the last Mexican land grant case or the last case asserting rights under the Treaty of Guadalupe Hidalgo appealed to the Supreme Court. Apart from other nineteenth-century cases, some parties continued to make claims under the Treaty of Guadalupe Hidalgo and Mexican land grants, some as recently as *Tijerina v. Henry* (1970), a class action claim involving Reies Lopez Tijerina, a Chicano activist from the 1960s in New Mexico involved in the Tierra Amarilla raids, as lead plaintiff.[12]

Apart from claims made by Mexicans, or people of Mexican descent residing in the United States, the Mexican government historically made claims under the Treaty of Guadalupe Hidalgo against the United States government, seeking to redress perceived injustices to Mexican nationals in the United States. Some were made shortly after the end of hostilities and the signing of the treaty.[13] Other instances of these claims include negotiations during the 1923 Bucareli conferences, where the United States and Mexico negotiated outstanding disputes between them, and the Mexican government at one point made a claim for $245 million on behalf of residents of the Southwest United States, which the United States rejected.

The Court's discussion of its rejection of the claim that the Act of 1851 conflicted with the Treaty of Guadalupe Hidalgo in *Botiller* fails to discuss a series of prior cases from the Court that stand generally for the proposition that since a treaty involves an act of Congress, which is also true when Congress enacts a statute, the more recent in time (the treaty or the statute) prevails, regardless of the form in which Congress acted. *Botiller* reflects the rulings of the Court favoring the conquering government's statute over treaty obligations and provisions which, in part, were intended to protect the rights (including property rights) of Mexicans living in the United States after the war. The Supreme Court would have other opportunities in the early twentieth century to consider issues from other territorial acquisitions, including *Balzac v. Porto [sic] Rico* (Chapter 2).

B

THE TAFT COURT (1921–1930)

2. *Balzac v. Porto [sic] Rico* (1922), the *Insular Cases* (1901), and Puerto Rico's Status in the American Legal System

Balzac v. Porto [sic] Rico (1922), the Insular Cases (1901), and Puerto Rico's Status in the American Legal System

A. Background

On July 25, 1898, during the Spanish-American War, the United States Navy invaded Puerto Rico. The United States has owned Puerto Rico ever since. United States troops met minimal resistance when invading Puerto Rico. Some referred to it as a "military picnic."[1] The Treaty of Paris, signed on December 10, 1898, formally and legally ended the Spanish-American War and ceded Puerto Rico to the United States.[2] Unlike the Philippines, Puerto Rico saw comparably little or no "guerilla" warfare after the invasion.

From the U.S. perspective, the most serious and bloodiest chapter in America's decisive, successful, and bloody military history, the Civil War, had concluded just thirty-three years prior to the invasion of Puerto Rico, when Robert E. Lee surrendered to Ulysses S. Grant at Appomattox in 1865. Shortly after that surrender, in 1868, in one of Spain's two remaining colonial outposts in the Americas, Puerto Ricans declared their independence from Spain in a revolt led by Ramón Emeterio Betances called the Grito de Lares, which Spanish authorities swiftly and bloodily quashed.[3]

In 1893, Puerto Rico "celebrated" four hundred years of colonial rule under Spain; Columbus had landed on Puerto Rico on November 19, 1493, during his second voyage to the Americas. By 1897, after the Lares revolt and a series of independence movements throughout Latin America, Puerto Rico had succeeded in obtaining greater autonomy and self-government within the Spanish system of government.[4] In 1898, when war broke out between Spain and the United States, Cuba and the Philippines were the largest territories in dispute. Puerto Rico, although small, appealed strategically to American naval officers and scholars, including the highly influential Alfred T. Mahan.[5]

The racial and cultural characteristics of the inhabitants of the newly acquired possessions of the United States (Puerto Rico and the Philippines) were, and have been, key issues affecting how the United States has governed those territories.[6] Racial considerations had long played a role in United States expansionism, including the many wars with the Native American nations of North America, the U.S.-Mexican War, and the Civil War. The larger number of people from "alien races and cultures" made the newly acquired territories in 1898 "unfit" for ultimate statehood.[7] Unlike prior territorial acquisitions, these territories were destined to be colonial dependencies for varying periods of time. The *Balzac* case questioned the coexistence of the Bill of Rights with colonial rule. Specifically, in *Balzac v. Porto*[8] *[sic] Rico,* the Supreme Court considered whether a newspaper publisher criminally accused of defaming a political figure (the military governor of Puerto Rico at the time) was entitled to a trial by jury as guaranteed by the Sixth Amendment to the United States Constitution.

B. The Academic Debate, the Genesis of the Territorial Incorporation Doctrine, and the *Insular Cases* (1901)

For long-standing monarchies and other imperial powers like France, England, Germany, and even Japan, nineteenth-century colonialism raised fewer problems than it did for the United States, with its democratic history and institutions, including a written constitutional tradition. The constitutional issue at the beginning of the twentieth century was the status of the territories (and the people who lived in them) in the American legal system. Stated differently, the most prevalent constitutional issue of the times involved the constitutionality of American imperialism/colonialism. As Chief Justice Taft wrote in *Balzac:*

> Few questions have been the subject of such discussion and dispute in our country as the status of our territory acquired from Spain in 1899. The division between the political parties in respect to it, the diversity of views of the members of this court in regard to its constitutional aspects, and to the constant recurrence of the subject in the House of Congress, fixed the attention of all on the future relation of this acquired territory to the United States.

In the period from 1898 to 1902, at least twenty-nine law review articles were published by prominent constitutional legal scholars in the *Yale Law Journal, Harvard Law Review,* and *Columbia Law Review* dealing with the territories acquired as a result of the Spanish-American War.[9] The academic debates involved four main constitutional issues concerning the newly acquired territories: (1) Does the Constitution "follow the flag" and therefore automatically apply wherever the federal government governs? (2) Are the inhabitants of the newly acquired territories "citizens" under the Fourteenth Amendment, which states in part that "[A]ll persons born or naturalized in the United States and subject to the jurisdiction thereof, are citizens of the United States and of the State wherein they reside"? (3) From what source does the United States derive its power to acquire, hold, and govern colonies? (4) How do the acquisitions of 1898 differ from, or conform with, the terms governing prior territorial acquisitions? These issues arose because the two main purposes of the Constitution are the political structure of the federal government and the protection of individual liberties from undue encroachment by the federal government. The structure of the national government was based on federalist principles and promoting local self-government. The Bill of Rights was based on the experiences of persons who had been under British colonial rule. As such, the provisions of the Bill of Rights are deeply rooted in Anglo-Saxon legal principles and are strongly anti-colonialist.

Before the Spanish-American War of 1898, the United States recognized only four possible statuses in relation to the United States (apart from the District of Columbia): a full-fledged state on equal footing with others; territories where the Constitution applied in full, and which were on the path to eventual statehood, such as Utah in 1898; foreign countries that were sovereigns; and Native American tribal governments, which were "domestic dependent sovereigns." Prior to 1900, the applicability of the Bill of Rights in United States territories was settled law. Throughout the nineteenth century, the United States expanded the territory to which the Constitution and the Bill of Rights applied. Everywhere the United States flag went, the Constitution and its judicial interpretations followed. Territories were acquired and governed under the Territory Clause[10] and admitted to statehood on an equal footing under the Constitution via the Statehood Admission Clause.[11] As late as 1898, a Supreme Court opinion stated that it was "beyond question" that the Bill of Rights "followed the flag" and applied in the territories of the United States.[12]

However, in the *Insular Cases* (1901), a judicially activist Supreme Court refused to follow its precedents and created the Territorial Incorporation Doctrine. The term *"Insular Cases"* refers to cases, primarily involving tariff disputes, that the Supreme Court decided early in the twentieth century relating to the status of the territories acquired after the Spanish-American War. In the *Insular Cases*, the Supreme Court reconsidered this issue and determined that the Constitution *did not* fully apply in the new territories, legally sanctioning their colonial status.[13]

For the first time in United States constitutional history, the Supreme Court's Territorial Incorporation Doctrine created a distinction between "incorporated" and "unincorporated" territories by "judicial fiat."[14] The chief difference between an incorporated and an unincorporated territory is that one is on track toward statehood while the other is not. Under the Territorial Incorporation Doctrine, Chief Justice Taft said, "[i]ncorporation has always been a step, and an important one, leading to statehood."[15] The distinctions manifested in the Territorial Incorporation Doctrine were created as legal rationalizations for American colonialism. As Supreme Court Chief Justice Melville Weston Fuller (appointed by President Cleveland) stated in 1901 in one of the *Insular Cases*:

> That theory [Territorial Incorporation Doctrine] assumes that the Constitution created a government empowered to acquire countries throughout the world, to be governed by different rules than those obtaining in the original States and territories, and substitutes for the present system of republican government, a system of domination over distant provinces in the exercise of unrestricted power.[16]

Territorial expansion played an important role in American politics and American constitutional history prior to 1898. However, the 1898 Spanish-American War brought the United States into the imperialists' club for the first time. The acquisition and permanent occupation of Puerto Rico, the Philippines, and other Spanish colonies by the United States after the Spanish-American War raised new political issues. The acquired territories involved significant numbers of people of different races and cultures. The racial component of the colonies' inhabitants was framed in the academic debate just as it was in the political debates. According to one *Harvard Law Review* article written by Simeon Baldwin:

> Our Constitution was made by a *civilized and educated people.* It provides guarantees of personal security which seem ill adapted to the conditions of society that prevail in many parts of our new possessions. To give the *half-civilized Moros of the Philippines, or even the ignorant and lawless brigands that infest Puerto Rico, or even the ordinary Filipino of Manila, the benefit of such immunity* from the sharp and sudden justice—or injustice—which they have been hitherto accustomed to expect, would, of course, be a serious obstacle to the maintenance there of an efficient government.[17]

Another law professor, Talcott H. Russell, authored an article in the *Yale Law Journal*, stating:

> Its inhabitants are some of them at such *a low stage of human development as to be beyond the pale of constitutional guarantees.* Though belonging in some sense to the United States, they cannot be for a moment considered as

citizens of the United States . . . [w]e have been engaged for the last year in a war [which] can scarcely be dignified by that name. *We have had an army chasing savages* around the swamps of the Philippines.[18]

C. The *Balzac* Supreme Court, the Times, and Changes to U.S.–Puerto Rican Relations from the Time the Supreme Court Decided the *Insular Cases* in 1901 until 1922

The *Balzac* Supreme Court must be considered first by examining the Chief Justice of the Supreme Court at the time, William Taft, whom President Warren G. Harding appointed to that position in 1921. Chief Justice Taft played a big role on the Court generally, and particularly in the unanimous *Balzac* opinion, which he authored. Throughout his career in public service and public life, Taft rose to the highest levels of all three branches of the American government. Prior to becoming Chief Justice, Taft served as President from 1908 until 1912, served in Congress as a representative from Ohio, and had been Secretary of War under President Theodore Roosevelt. While Taft was president, his foreign policy toward Latin America was known as "Dollar Diplomacy," which comprised two basic principles: encouraging U.S. investments in overseas generally and in Latin America specifically, and protecting those investments by "establishing financial protectorates in nations noted for their financial inefficiency."[19] Taft lost his re-election bid in 1912 to Woodrow Wilson when his former boss, Theodore Roosevelt, splintered the Republican party by forming the Progressive "Bull Moose" party and running for president against him, thereby providing Wilson a margin of victory.[20]

Among the other justices on the Taft Court at the time of *Balzac* were two well-regarded jurists in American legal history, Oliver Wendell Holmes and Benjamin Cardozo. While Taft was Chief Justice, he worked hard to obtain unanimous opinions.[21] Accordingly, the Taft Court, compared to the Supreme Court in other eras, had a large number of unanimous opinions.[22]

By 1922, the issue of the United States' colonial possessions no longer occupied the center of the political, legal, or academic stage as it had when the Supreme Court considered the *Insular Cases* in 1901. By then, other international crises, such as World War I, had occurred. The United States debated isolationism versus entanglements in Europe. Revolutions erupted in Russia, Mexico, and Turkey that changed the international political landscape for the United States in very significant ways. Anti-Communism began to emerge, as did social strife. Moreover, overt racism had resurfaced in the second half of the 1910s in part as a backlash to Reconstruction, including the re-emergence of the Ku Klux Klan.[23]

By the time *Balzac* reached the Supreme Court, Puerto Rico had been under American rule for over twenty years. Congress passed the Foraker Act in 1900, providing for the establishment of a government in Puerto Rico, but, despite the expressed concerns of Puerto Ricans, was silent on the issue of citizenship. Puerto Ricans were no longer Spanish citizens, but they were not American citizens either. Between 1901 and 1922, the Supreme Court considered and decided several cases involving the Philippines and Puerto Rico, including *Gonzales v. Williams* (1904), where the Court held that Puerto Ricans were not "aliens," but also ruled that they had not been naturalized. The rights of Puerto Rico's inhabitants were in limbo. In 1917, Congress passed the Jones Act, granting citizenship to Puerto Ricans by statute. Mr. Balzac therefore at least had recourse to a different argument: that by 1917, the status of Puerto Rico, and the rights of its inhabitants, had changed, and that the *Insular Cases* were no longer the law. The Supreme Court considered that argument in *Balzac*.

In addition to the Sixth Amendment's provisions regarding jury trial rights in criminal cases, there were First Amendment (free press, free speech) issues and other circumstances of *Balzac* which juxtaposed the anti-colonial history of the United States during its struggles against England as a burgeoning nation in the late eighteenth century with the colonial policies the United States adopted toward Puerto Rico and other possessions in the late nineteenth and early twentieth centuries. This situation highlighted the conflicts between, on the one hand, the anti-colonial, pro-democratic political system that developed in colonial America, including the U.S. Constitution and the Bill of Rights, and, on the other, the new political realities of the twentieth century. The most glaring similarities between unincorporated territories and the American colonial experience regarding the importance of criminal juries are found in cases involving a core First Amendment right—political speech.

The facts of *Balzac* are similar to those of a famous case from colonial American history where British colonial authorities prosecuted the publisher of a newspaper in the American colonies for seditious libel, the *Zenger* case.[24] John Peter Zenger was a German immigrant who published the *New York Weekly Journal,* the first major independent opposition newspaper in the United States. The British colonial authorities tried Zenger for seditious libel in connection with some articles criticizing the contemporary colonial governor of New York, William Cosby. Zenger was prosecuted for seditious libel, by indictment, without a grand jury considering the charges. The jury in *Zenger* acquitted Zenger, and that case is a preeminent example of jury nullification in American Colonial history. The *Zenger* trial allowed a local jury to determine whether written articles constituted libel against the colonial government, and although Zenger was technically "guilty" because his conduct violated the law as written, the jury disregarded or "nullified" the existing law. Like Zenger, Mr. Balzac was indicted without a grand jury considering the charges, and like Zenger his prosecution involved political speech. However, unlike Zenger (who had a jury trial), a local judge appointed by colonial authorities tried Balzac's case without a jury. Like Peter Zenger over a hundred years earlier, Jesús M. Balzac, the editor of a daily newspaper in Puerto Rico, was criminally prosecuted for allegedly libelous statements made about the colonial governor. Balzac is also factually similar to *Dorr v. United States* (1904), which involved criminal prosecution against two editors of a Filipino newspaper for making allegedly libelous statements against members of the colonial government.[25]

D. *Balzac v. Porto [sic] Rico* (1922): The Opinion

Jesús Balzac published a newspaper called *El Baluarte* in Arecibo, Puerto Rico. On April 16, 1918, and April 23, 1918, Mr. Balzac wrote editorials about then governor of Puerto Rico Arthur Yager, who had been appointed by his Princeton classmate, President Woodrow Wilson. At that time, Puerto Rican governors were selected by the United States, not locally elected. The district attorney brought two misdemeanor criminal prosecutions against Mr. Balzac (one for each newspaper article) based on seditious libel. Although these offenses were not felonies at the time in Puerto Rico, they carried a potential penalty of up to two years in jail and up to $500 in fines. The district attorney brought the claims based on "information" rather than following a grand jury indictment. In Puerto Rico at the time of the prosecution, no statute provided for a jury trial in misdemeanor offenses. Puerto Rico's civil code provided for a jury in felony trials, but not misdemeanors. A felony was defined as a crime punishable by death or imprisonment. Every other crime was considered a misdemeanor.

On July 29, 1918, the district judge in Arecibo, Puerto Rico, found Mr. Balzac guilty on both counts and sentenced him to jail for nine months and to pay costs. On March 4, 1920, the Puerto Rico Supreme Court affirmed the convictions. Mr. Balzac's constitutional complaints were that, as an American citizen, he was entitled to a jury as guaranteed by the Sixth Amendment, and that imprisoning him based on his newspaper publications violated his free speech and free press rights as guaranteed by the First Amendment. Regarding the statements, the Puerto Rican Supreme Court (all appointed by the American colonial government) said:

> The article transcribed in the information in this case is so violent in its invective that we do not see fit to reproduce it for the purposes of our records.

Not only did a simple reading of it show that the Governor of Porto [sic] Rico was the subject of the attack, but that in half a dozen or more places of the article there were phrases that, if true would necessarily expose Arthur Yager to public hatred, contempt, or ridicule.

Similarly, Chief Justice Taft, writing for a unanimous United States Supreme Court in a decision handed down on April 10, 1922, dismissed the First Amendment claim in that case in a single paragraph:

A reading of the two articles removes the slightest doubt that they go far beyond the "exuberant expressions of meridional speech" . . . Indeed they are so excessive and outrageous in their character that they suggest the query whether their superlative vilification has not overleapt itself and become unconsciously humorous. But this is not a defense.

After addressing a jurisdictional issue where the Court concluded that Mr. Balzac had properly preserved his rights to complain on appeal, the Court turned its attention to the jury trial issues. The Sixth Amendment requirement that in all criminal prosecutions, the accused shall enjoy the right to a speedy and public trial, by an impartial jury of the state and district wherein the crime shall have been committed, applied to Puerto Rico. Article 3 of the Constitution also provides that the trial of all crimes be by jury, except in cases of impeachment. Chief Justice Taft started his opinion favorably to Mr. Balzac's position: "It is well settled that the provisions for jury trial in criminal and civil cases apply to the territories of the United States." The opinion then takes a nosedive, relying on the *Insular Cases,* and concludes that the constitutional guarantee to a trial by jury does not apply to "unincorporated territories" like Puerto Rico, relying on the Territorial Incorporation Doctrine of Justice White's opinion in the *Insular Cases* and various subsequent cases including *Dorr.*

While Chief Justice Taft stated that the *Insular Cases* "revealed much diversity of opinion in this Court as to the constitutional status of the territory acquired by the Treaty of Paris ending the Spanish War . . . the Dorr Case shows that . . . Justice White['s opinion] in *Downes v. Bidwell,* has become the settled law." *Balzac* reaffirmed the Territorial Incorporation Doctrine, agreeing with *Dorr* that

the power to govern territory, implied in the right to acquire it, and given to Congress in the Constitution in article 4, § 3, to whatever other limitations it may be subject, the extent of which must be decided as questions arise, does not require that body to enact for ceded territory, not made part of the United States by congressional action, a system of laws which shall include the right of trial by jury, and that the Constitution does not, without legislation and of its own force, carry such right to territory so situated.

In other words, the Territorial Clause in the Constitution is the source of congressional authority over Puerto Rico. Chief Justice Taft in *Balzac* then presented the question before the Supreme Court as follows: "Has Congress, since the Foraker Act of April 12, 1900 enacted legislation incorporating Porto Rico into the Union?" Jackson Ralston, a well-known international and labor lawyer, represented Mr. Balzac. Mr. Ralston became a law professor at Stanford University Law School, and yearly a prize is awarded in his name. The gist of Mr. Ralston's argument was that the Jones Act had "incorporated" Puerto Rico. The Supreme Court rejected that argument because neither the Foraker Act nor the Jones Act contained a specific congressional statement indicating incorporation. Chief Justice Taft stated that if Congress meant to take "the important step" of incorporating Puerto Rico, Congress would have done so unambiguously by plain declaration, and "would not have left it to mere inference." Chief Justice Taft also stated that incorporation only became "acute" after the United States acquired the territories as a result of the Spanish-American War, including Puerto Rico and the Philippines. Chief Justice Taft found that the Foraker Act's inclusion of a section called a "Bill of Rights" including all of the guarantees of the Constitution, except those relating to indictment by a grand jury and the right of trial by jury in civil and criminal cases, meant that Puerto Rico was not incorporated. Chief Justice Taft rejected Mr. Balzac's contention that the Jones Act "incorporated" Puerto Rico, and referred to Puerto Rico's status as "anomalous." The *Balzac* opinion states that the only additional rights the Jones Act gave Puerto Ricans was to enable them "to move into the continental United States and becom[e] residents of any State there to enjoy every right of any other citizen of the United States, civil, social and political." By contrast, in Puerto Rico, U.S. citizens including Puerto Ricans do not have the constitutional right to a trial by jury.

Chief Justice Taft feared that recognizing a constitutional right to trial by jury in Puerto Rico could "provoke disturbance" rather than aid the "orderly administration of justice."[26] What "disturbances" could arise from juries presiding over criminal cases? Chief Justice Taft stated that in Puerto Rico, a long-established system of jurisprudence existed with fair and orderly trials without juries. Accordingly there was no need to impose jury trials. This culturally sensitive position had some intuitive force in suggesting that federal constitutional requirements should not be mechanically applied where not appropriate. Furthermore, Chief Justice Taft noted that since Puerto Rico's legal system was founded on the civil law tradition, imposing this "Anglo-Saxon" requirement would disrupt the local legal system.[27] These are ironic and hypocritical rationales for not applying the constitutional criminal jury trial guarantees to the colonies. While the Supreme Court claimed respect and sensitivity to the colony's culture and traditions by not applying the right to trial by jury, other parts of the Constitution, United States laws generally, and laws particularly invidious to the colonies such as restrictions on speaking the native language or putting up the colony's local flag were unilaterally imposed on Puerto Rico and its inhabitants during the early twentieth century.[28]

Efficiency in administering justice appeared a tantamount concern to Chief Justice Taft and the Court. Forcing the jury system into "unincorporated" territories would force the courts to go through the cumbersome steps of jury selection and jury deliberations. However, the same concerns applied with equal force to juries within the fifty states. Most on point are Florida, Louisiana, Texas, California, and other states that at one point were civil code jurisdictions without juries. When they became part of the United States, these entities were forced to adopt the right to a jury trial. As the first Justice Harlan commented during one of the *Insular Cases,* "such inconveniences are of slight consequences compared with the dangers to our system of government arising from judicial amendments of the Constitution."[29] Chief Justice Taft's hypocritical opinion claimed to respect local self-government where in fact local self-government was being systematically denied. This rationale appears particularly insufficient to justify depriving a defendant of his or her constitutionally guaranteed rights as a United States citizen in a U. S. jurisdiction.

The Court's opinion also reasoned that jury duty requires participation in self-governance and since the territories are unfit for self-government, the jury system does not really fit either. In Chief Justice Taft's words:

> the jury system postulates a conscious duty of participation in the machinery of justice which it is hard for people not brought up in fundamentally popular government at once to acquire. One of its greatest benefits is in the security it gives the people that they, as jurors, actual or possible, being part of the judicial system of the country, can prevent its arbitrary use or abuse. Congress has thought that a people like the Filipinos, or the Porto Ricans, trained to a complete judicial system which knows no juries, living in compact and ancient communities, with definitely formed customs and political conceptions, should be permitted themselves to determine how far they wish to adopt this institution of Anglo-Saxon origin, and when.

According to Chief Justice Taft: "In common-law countries centuries of tradition have prepared a conception of the impartial attitude jurors must assume." While Puerto Ricans and others may not have had centuries of training in "common law notions of fairness and impartiality," by that time Puerto Rico's colonial inhabitants had served in juries in federal courts and in felony cases since September 20, 1899.[30] Even Stanley Laughlin, who has advocated restrictions on jury trials in the name of permitting "diversity" and cultural preservation, finds this rationale "rather farfetched" because many "mainland Americans never see the inside of a courthouse before being called for jury duty, and they or their ancestors may have emigrated from civil-law countries."[31]

Mr. Balzac's attorney compared Puerto Rico to Alaska, but the Supreme Court stated that was a "very different case" because Alaska

> was an enormous territory, very sparsely settled, and offering opportunity for immigration and settlement by American citizens. It was on the American continent and within easy reach of the then United States. It involved none of the difficulties which incorporation of the Philippines and Porto Rico presents, and one of them is in the very matter of trial by jury.

Chief Justice Taft's opinion also stated that the United States District Court in Puerto Rico is not "a true United States court established under Article III of the Constitution to administer the judicial power of the United States" but rather a court created by Congress under the Territory Clause in Article IV of the Constitution. Finally, and most importantly for Mr. Balzac, the Supreme Court affirmed Mr. Balzac's conviction and imprisonment.

E. The Significance of *Balzac* and Subsequent Developments regarding Puerto Rico's Status and the Territorial Incorporation Doctrine

Balzac is even more important for Puerto Rico's status and rights of citizens of Puerto Rico than the *Insular Cases* for at least three reasons. First, the Taft Court in *Balzac* *unanimously* approved the Territorial Incorporation Doctrine of Justice White's famous plurality (not majority) opinion from the *Downes* case (which was one of the *Insular Cases*) and solidified it as part of the American legal system. Second, *Balzac* involved one of the most fundamental and core political rights in the American legal system, the right to a jury trial in a criminal case and the right of citizens to participate politically in the administration of justice in Puerto Rico. While the *Insular Cases* also involved important, fundamental economic rights of importation and taxation, jury rights are central to the Bill of Rights. Third, the greater inclusion of Puerto Ricans into the American system through the granting of citizenship in 1917 distinguished the legal landscape in 1922 from that in 1901. Chief Justice Taft's arguments on behalf of the Court in *Balzac* were simply legal rationalizations for perpetuating colonialism. If the goal of the United States was to improve the capacity for self-governance of the natives and to bring to Puerto Rico the "blessings of liberty," [32] one could hardly imagine a more appropriate populist institution, apart from the voting booth, than the jury box.[33] A jury trial serves not only the particular interests of the defendant in a criminal case, but also the participatory needs of citizens in self-government by dispensing justice.

As a result of the Territorial Incorporation Doctrine, congressional power over the unincorporated territories has remained plenary and limited only by "fundamental rights" which have been recognized on an ad hoc basis rather than a finding that all constitutional provisions apply, as would be the case from a "Total Incorporation," or *ex propio vigore,* perspective. There are many parallels between the debates surrounding the Territorial Incorporation Doctrine and the incorporation debate throughout the mid-twentieth century, where the justices of the Supreme Court debated how many (if all, any, or some) of the provisions of the Bill of Rights applied as limitations to the powers of state governments after the passage of the Fourteenth Amendment. As in the context of the incorporation controversy involving the states, the Court only recognized "fundamental rights" under established constitutional law. The Supreme Court alone determines which constitutional rights are "fundamental" enough, resulting in a legal limbo for colonial inhabitants governed under the plenary power of Congress similar to that for Native Americans.[34] Sarah Cleveland convincingly traces the origins of the "inherent powers" doctrine to the plenary power doctrine, which the Supreme Court has used in the context of the colonies, Native Americans, and aliens. The plenary powers in these areas share an origin in "a peculiarly unattractive, late-nineteenth-century nationalist and racist view of American society and federal power."[35] This selective approach proceeds from the premise that "fundamental rights" would exist even without constitutional provisions, while rights like the right to a jury trial are "merely" remedial. As the second Justice Harlan stated in the Incorporation Debate context, due process requires only that criminal trials be fundamentally fair, not that they be jury trials.[36] Although the right to a jury trial is remedial, throughout American history jury trials have been considered fundamental. Since *Balzac,* the Supreme Court has recognized that juries are crucial to the fair administration of justice based on American political history. Indeed, the opinion of the Supreme Court in *Duncan v. Louisiana* (1968) stated:

> The guarantees of jury trial in the Federal and State Constitutions reflect a profound judgment about the way in which law should be enforced and justice administered. A right to jury trial is granted to criminal defendants in order to prevent oppression by the Government. Those who wrote our constitutions knew from history and experience that it was necessary to protect against unfounded criminal charges brought to eliminate enemies and against judges too responsive to the voice of higher authority.[37]

The *Duncan* decision's language on the fundamental nature of juries discredits the view that criminal jury trials are not fundamental. *Balzac,* like *Duncan,* involved the right to a jury trial in "marginal" criminal cases, where the defendants were being tried neither for capital offenses nor for petty offenses, but where both defendants faced actual prison time. According to at least one scholar, the "overwhelming probability" is that the Court would overrule *Balzac* if presented with the issue because not "to do so would require a justification, explaining why Puerto Rico could deny a fundamental right which no state can deny."[38] Without question, the language in *Duncan,* an Incorporation Debate case that emphasizes the fundamental nature of jury trials in criminal cases, and other cases, such as *Reid v. Covert* (1957), have cast doubt on *Balzac*. In 1979, four Supreme Court Justices repudiated the *Insular Cases, Balzac,* and the Territorial Incorporation Doctrine.[39] However, Chief Justice Rehnquist approvingly cited *Balzac* in *United States v. Verdugo-Urquidez* (1990) (Chapter 11), and more recent federal circuit cases have followed *Balzac,* meaning that more likely than not *Balzac* remains good law.[40]

During the twentieth century, the United States allowed Puerto Ricans increasing autonomy and self-government. In 1946, President Harry Truman appointed the first native Puerto Rican, Jesus Piñero, as governor of the island. In 1952, Congress passed a law which allowed Puerto Rico to adopt a local constitution, which Puerto Rico did. Prior to 1952 Puerto Rico undoubtedly remained an "unincorporated" territory.

The 1952 Puerto Rican Constitution generated considerable legal and political debate. To summarize one side of the debate, since the constitution was an act of Congress, the source of governance remains the Territory Clause of the Constitution, and if Congress in its sole discretion (where Puerto Rico has never had a voting representative) chooses to amend or repeal the Puerto Rican Constitution, it can do so. To summarize the other side of the debate, in 1952 a "compact" between the Congress and the Puerto Rican voters created the "Estado Libre Asociado" (literally, "free associated state," but loosely and badly translated as "commonwealth"). Two important post-*Balzac* Supreme Court opinions involving economic assistance to Puerto Rico are particularly significant, *Califano v. Torres* (1978) and *Harris v. Rosario* (1980). These cases made their way to the Supreme Court in the late 1970s in the context of three relevant trends: the expansion of federal entitlements during the "war on poverty" begun by President Lyndon Johnson in the mid-1960s, the expansion of "rights" flowing from the opinions of the liberal Warren Court, and the industrialization of Puerto Rico and Puerto Rico's corresponding economic dependence on federal economic assistance and the U.S. economy. One book summarized Puerto Rico's developmental model as "factories and foodstamps."[41] In *Harris*, the Supreme Court found that Congress could treat Puerto Rico differently from the states "as long as there is a rational basis for its action" under the Territorial Incorporation Doctrine (TID). The *Harris* case involved economic assistance under the Aid to Families with Dependent Children (AFDC) program.

Distinctions made on the basis of place usually depend on the degree of United States dominion and control over the locality or physical territory. At one end of the spectrum are the states comprising the United States, where the Constitution applies in full against the federal government and selectively against state governments. At the other end are aliens in foreign countries, where the Bill of Rights does not generally apply. Between those extremes are places where the applicability of the Bill of Rights is less clear, including military bases, coaling stations, territories (incorporated and unincorporated), and Indian tribal nations. Among these "places," the denial of trial by jury in the unincorporated territories is the least justifiable. In cases involving crimes committed by military personnel on military bases, the Fifth Amendment excludes the applicability of the Sixth Amendment.[42] Similarly, the fact that "guano islands" are uninhabited, or at best slightly populated, provides a compelling reason not to apply trial by jury in those "places." Regarding crimes committed abroad, sovereign nations may have an interest in trying in their own legal systems those criminal matters related to crimes committed within their country. However, in the case of colonies of the United States, none of these concerns exist. In the colonies, there are substantial numbers of civilians who are not under the power of another sovereign. In the colonies, there are United States courts, United States prosecutors, United States judges, and United States interests at stake. Yet the Supreme Court, through the TID, has unjustifiably exempted portions of the Bill of Rights from application in the territories. To borrow from the first Justice Harlan's dissent regarding the rejection of the application of the constitutional right to a jury trial in criminal cases, the constitutional provision should read: "The trial of all crimes, except in cases of impeachment, and except where [Puerto Ricans and others residing in the unincorporated territories] are concerned, shall be by jury."[43] With regard to unincorporated territories, the case for applying the Bill of Rights in full is stronger since there is no competing "sovereign," as is the case with state governments.

The issue of race or national origin goes to the very essence of the TID since the colonial inhabitants were, and remain, overwhelmingly not Anglos. Their constitutional rights have traditionally been devalued, and correspondingly there has been less concern about self-government by those "people" in those "places." Even citizenship in the territories is devalued and "second class," since "aliens" in the United States and U.S. citizens overseas in sovereign countries like Japan and England have more rights than citizens in the territories, based on the *Reid* decision.

The Incorporation Debate and the debates over the TID raise significant issues about the Supreme Court in American constitutional law, history, and politics. Does the text of the written United States Constitution, including the Bill of Rights, mean what it says, or does it contain precatory declarations that should be selectively applied? Incorporation against the states has been about protecting individual rights, federalism, and race. The same concerns show up in this debate. According to the first Justice Harlan, it

> will be an evil day for American liberty if the theory of a government outside of the supreme law of the land finds lodgment in our constitutional jurisprudence. No higher duty rests upon [the U.S. Supreme] court than to exert its full authority to prevent all violation of the principles of the Constitution.[44]

Despite those concerns, for inhabitants of Puerto Rico and other territories, that "evil day" began in 1901 and has continued for over a century. If the Supreme Court ever reconsidered *Balzac* or the TID, it would have the opportunity to close a dark chapter in American constitutional history.

In recent years, newspapers, television news reports, and magazines have covered protests against the United States Navy's bombings and other actions in one of Puerto Rico's islands, Vieques. Adding to the complexities of the consequences of Puerto Rico's colonial status are two opinions from federal district judges in Puerto Rico in 2000. In one, a federal district judge held that U.S. citizens in Puerto Rico were entitled to vote in the 2000 presidential election (although the First Circuit promptly reversed the ruling).[45] In the other, the federal judge held that the Puerto Rican Constitution trumps federal law and makes the federal death penalty act "locally inapplicable."[46] At their core, these issues are symptoms of the true problem: Puerto Rico's status, which, according to one federal district judge, has "enslaved" Puerto Ricans.[47]

C

THE WARREN COURT (1953–1969)

3. *Hernandez v. Texas* (1954)
and the Exclusion of Mexican-Americans from Grand Juries

4. *Katzenbach v. Morgan* (1966)
and Voting Rights of Puerto Ricans with
Limited English Proficiency

5. *Miranda v. Arizona* (1966)
and the Rights of the Criminally Accused

Hernandez v. Texas (1954)

and the Exclusion of

Mexican-Americans from Grand Juries

A. Background

In 1954, the Supreme Court, under the leadership of Earl Warren, whom President Eisenhower appointed as Chief Justice in 1953, rendered its most significant opinion of the twentieth century, *Brown v. Board of Education. Brown* held that separate, segregated public schools could not be equal and that state-sponsored segregated schools violated the Constitution's Equal Protection Clause. This chapter focuses on the case that literally and physically precedes *Brown* in the official Supreme Court reporter, *Hernandez v. Texas* (1954). Like *Brown, Hernandez* involved an equal protection challenge, and like *Brown* the Court spoke unanimously through Chief Justice Warren.

The Warren Court began charting a new path in American legal history that has frequently been described as "revolutionary." According to Lucas A. Powe, "Scholars seem agreed that the Warren Court consisted of a group of powerful, talented men who were more sympathetic to claims of individual liberty while being simultaneously more egalitarian than their predecessors, more willing to intervene in contentious controversies, more prone to ignore the past, and more convinced that national solutions were superior to local solutions."[1] Only fifteen years earlier, the Supreme Court had a confrontation with President Franklin D. Roosevelt over the Court's systematic striking down of "New Deal" legislation. Roosevelt threatened to expand the number of justices from nine to fifteen, through what became known as the "court packing plan," leading to the infamous phrase "a switch in time saves nine." In other words, the Court became more deferential to the political branches and their liberal economic policies. The Court moved toward the left, increasingly approving laws expanding the role of the federal government in American life. This trend would continue throughout the Warren Court. Earl Warren became Chief Justice in 1953 after having been a career politician, including governor of California.

Hernandez is a landmark Supreme Court opinion for Latinos in the American legal system, and while its holding would impact subsequent lower court opinions in the context of public school education, *Hernandez* also involved the exclusion of Mexican-Americans from serving as jurors, which, like voting, is a primary duty and privilege of U.S. citizenship. In contrast to the Court's reasoning in *Brown*, in *Hernandez* the Court applied a simple, linear analysis based on the Court's precedents, not on "social science" or other changed circumstances. Jury trials (notwithstanding their inapplicability in Puerto Rico and other unincorporated territories, as discussed in Chapter 2) are a hallmark of the American legal system.[2] In one case the Supreme Court stated that the choice to have juries reflects "a profound judgment about the way in which law should be enforced and justice administered."[3] Over two hundred years ago, the French scholar Alexis de Tocqueville praised the role of the American jury system in promoting civic participation among the American colonists. The American jury system is not without critics, however. Some assert that juries are not accountable for their conclusions; juries waste time and money; and many citizens purposely avoid jury duty because of the disadvantages in terms of not getting paid for missing work and taking substantial time away from their lives.

Unlike "grand" juries, which convene in secret with a prosecutor and preliminarily investigate alleged criminal activity, "petit" juries (composed of people different from those in a grand jury in a given case) sit in open court. They consider the evidence presented and the arguments of counsel, and render verdicts.

Unsurprisingly, in light of the important role of juries (grand and petit) in the American legal system, one of the first major equal protection cases the Supreme Court considered after the 1868 passage of the Fourteenth Amendment (which amended the Constitution to explicitly provide for equal protection to individuals from actions by state governments) involved discrimination in jury service. In *Strauder v. West Virginia* (1879), the Supreme Court struck down a West Virginia statute excluding African-Americans from serving as jurors because it violated the Equal Protection Clause. The landmark *Strauder* ruling established that members of a "protected class" could not be systematically excluded from jury service. The Supreme Court later extended its *Strauder* ruling in what became known as "the rule of exclusion." The rule of exclusion was at the heart of Mr. Hernandez' case. Under the rule of exclusion, even if a jury selection system was not discriminatory as written in the books, if a defendant could prove that state officials *applied* the otherwise fair system in a discriminatory manner, the defendant could establish a violation of the Equal

Protection Clause. This reasoning is analogous to the distinction between *de facto* and *de jure* segregation challenges on education. But the *Hernandez v. Texas* opinion, for Latinos in the American legal system, is far more significant than merely being "*Strauder* for Mexicans," as discussed below.

B. *Hernandez v. Texas* (1954): The Opinion

A farmworker, Pete Hernandez, was accused of killing Joe Espinosa. A grand jury in Jackson County, Texas (in Southeast Texas, inside the triangle made by Houston, Corpus Christi, and San Antonio), indicted Mr. Hernandez for the murder in September of 1951. Then, a Jackson County jury convicted Mr. Hernandez and sentenced him to life imprisonment. Mr. Hernandez appealed his conviction. On June 18, 1952, the Texas Court of Criminal Appeals (the highest court in Texas to consider criminal matters) wrote its opinion affirming the conviction and sentence. Describing Mr. Hernandez as "a Mexican, or Latin American," the Texas Court of Criminal Appeals stated that he claimed "he was discriminated against upon the trial of this case because members of the Mexican nationality were deliberately, systematically, and willfully excluded from the grand jury that found and returned the indictment in this case and from the petit jury panel from which was selected the petit jury that tried the case." Texas' highest criminal court rejected his appeal in part because it found that Mexicans "are not a separate race but are white people of Spanish descent" and since other white people served on the juries, the absence of people of Mexican ancestry did not violate equal protection. The Texas court's opinion also raised the specter that a contrary ruling might require proportional ethnic representation on juries.

On January 11, 1954, the United States Supreme Court heard argument in Mr. Hernandez' case and on May 3, 1954, issued its unanimous decision. As Lucas A. Powe noted, unanimity mattered to the Warren Court at the time the Court announced its opinion in *Hernandez*.[4] The sole issue the Court considered in *Hernandez* was whether Mr. Hernandez' conviction and life sentence should be reversed based on his claim that otherwise fully qualified Mexican-Americans were systematically excluded from service as jury commissioners, grand jurors, and petit jurors in Jackson County in violation of the Fourteenth Amendment's Equal Protection Clause. As set forth in footnote 1 of the Supreme Court's opinion, the Texas jury selection system in the 1950s provided that at each term of court, the judge appointed three to five jury commissioners, who selected from the county assessment roll the names of sixteen grand jurors from different parts of the county. These names were placed in a sealed envelope and delivered to the clerk. Thirty days before the court convened, the clerk delivered a copy of the list to the sheriff, who summoned the jurors. The jury commission also selected the general jury panel.

Gus Garcia, a lawyer affiliated with the League of United Latin American Citizens (LULAC), a civic organization committed to promoting the civil rights of Latinos in the United States, law professor Carlos Cadena from St. Mary's Law School, and James DeAnda (who would later become a bankruptcy judge) represented Mr. Hernandez before the Supreme Court. Other Latinos had challenged the systematic exclusion of Mexican-Americans from jury service since the early 1930s, without success at the state court level.[5]

Chief Justice Warren began the opinion with the broad proposition that the Court's precedent held that criminal prosecutions in cases where persons of the defendant's race or color have been systematically excluded from the grand or petit jury violate equal protection, regardless of whether the state acts through its legislature, courts, or through officials like prosecutors. The opinion referenced *Strauder* and subsequent cases in the context of African-Americans before turning to the crux of the opinion: "The State of Texas would have us hold that there are only two classes—white and Negro—within the contemplation of the Fourteenth Amendment. The decisions of this Court do not support that view." In support, Chief Justice Warren cited cases where the Court had previously ruled that the Fourteenth Amendment applies to prevent discrimination based on ancestry, specifically the Japanese internment cases during World War II. Warren also noted that "except where the question presented involves the exclusion of persons of Mexican descent from juries, Texas courts have taken a broader view of the scope of the equal protection clause." That statement referenced, as set forth in footnote 6, cases where Texas courts had previously ruled that equal protection prevented the systematic exclusion of Roman Catholics from a jury (interestingly the defendant in that case, Juárez, had a Spanish surname) and that a court in Texas had, prior to 1954, invalidated restrictive covenants prohibiting the sale of land to persons of Mexican descent.

Justice Warren then stated the language from the *Hernandez* opinion that has been frequently cited:

> Throughout our history differences in race and color have defined easily identifiable groups which have at times required the aid of the courts in securing equal treatment under the laws. But community prejudices are not static, and from time to time other differences from the community norm may define other groups which need the same protection. Whether such a group exists within a community is a question of fact. When the existence of a distinct class is demonstrated, and it is further shown that the laws, as written or as applied, single out that class for different treatment not based

on some reasonable classification, the guarantees of the Constitution have been violated. The Fourteenth Amendment is not directed solely against discrimination due to a "two-class theory"—that is, based upon differences between "white" and Negro.

The Court noted that Mr. Hernandez' attorney acknowledged that the Texas system of selecting grand and petit jurors by jury commissions *could* be used without discrimination. The Court then referenced prior cases involving challenges to the Texas system (there had been several), stating that "the system is susceptible to abuse and can be employed in a discriminatory manner." The Court then continued that the "exclusion of otherwise eligible persons from jury service solely because of their ancestry or national origin is discrimination prohibited by the Fourteenth Amendment." Mr. Hernandez' challenge, based on the rule of exclusion, was that those applying the law, not the law itself, discriminated against people of Mexican descent.

The Court indicated that Mr. Hernandez had to prove two things in order to prevail in reversing his conviction. First, that persons of Mexican descent constituted a separate class in Jackson County, distinct from "whites." Second, he needed to prove discrimination against Mexicans. Mr. Hernandez' attorney had proved the first point at the trial court through testimony in the record concerning the "attitude of the community," which in that case revealed that officials distinguished between "white" and "Mexican." According to the Court:

> The participation of persons of Mexican descent in business and community groups was shown to be slight. Until very recent times, children of Mexican descent were required to attend a segregated school for the first four grades. At least one restaurant in town prominently displayed a sign announcing "No Mexicans Served." On the courthouse grounds at the time of the hearing, there were two men's toilets, one unmarked, and the other marked "Colored Men" and "Hombres Aqui" ("Men Here"). No substantial evidence was offered to rebut the logical inference to be drawn from these facts, and it must be concluded that petitioner succeeded in his proof.

Thus, Mr. Hernandez had established, to the satisfaction of the Supreme Court, that Mexicans were a distinct cognizable group, at least in Jackson County. Relying on the rule of exclusion, Chief Justice Warren then indicated that Mr. Hernandez had met his burden of proving discrimination by relying on statistics and stipulations from the State of Texas. Although 14% of the population of Jackson County were persons with Mexican or Latin American surnames, Texas stipulated that "for the last twenty-five years there is no record of any person with a Mexican or Latin American name having served on a jury commission, grand jury or petit jury in Jackson County." The parties also stipulated that there were in fact male persons (women were systematically excluded from jury service) of Mexican or Latin American descent in Jackson County who were eligible to serve on these juries. The Court found that jury commissioners could discriminate based on Spanish surnames gleaned from the lists of eligible prospective jurors: "just as persons of a different race are distinguished by color, these Spanish names provide a ready identification of the members of this class."

The primary basis the State of Texas used to challenge the claims of discrimination and rebut the *prima facie* case of the denial of equal protection came from the testimony of five jury commissioners that they had not discriminated against persons of Mexican or Latin American descent in selecting jurors, but instead sought those they thought were best qualified. The Court rejected the commissioners' conclusory testimony, stating that when faced with a history of exclusion from jury service, as in the case of black people in Alabama, lack of discriminatory intent "could not be met by mere generalities" or conclusory statements that they did not discriminate. Otherwise, according to Chief Justice Warren's opinion for the Court, the Equal Protection Clause's guarantee "would be but a vain and illusory requirement."

The Court stated that while circumstances or chance may dictate that no persons in a certain class will serve on a particular jury or during some particular period, "it taxes our credulity to say that mere chance resulted in their being no members of this class among the over six thousand jurors called in the past 25 years. The result bespeaks discrimination, whether or not it was a conscious decision on the part of any individual jury commissioner."

Chief Justice Warren's last paragraph responded to Texas' straw man argument of a "quota" requirement in the jury box or that the Court's ruling would require proportional representation of all the ethnic groups in a given community on every jury. Specifically, Mr. Hernandez, according to the Court,

> did not seek proportional representation, nor did he claim a right to have persons of Mexican descent sit on the particular juries which he faced. His only claim is the right to be indicted and tried by juries from which all members of his class are not systematically excluded—juries selected from among all qualified persons regardless of national origin or descent. To this much, he is entitled by the Constitution.

In other words, Mr. Hernandez and others are entitled to a fair process and system, not a particular result. Because Texas' system and procedures were discriminatory and not fair, the Supreme Court reversed Mr. Hernandez' conviction.

C. The Significance of *Hernandez v. Texas* and Post-*Hernandez* Developments to Latinos in the American Legal System

Hernandez v. Texas is one of the most significant legal cases for Latinos in the American legal system for several reasons. First, the Court established that Mexican-Americans constituted a protected class for equal protection purposes, which was necessary for any serious consideration of a constitutional challenge to discriminatory practices based on race, national origin, or ethnicity. *Hernandez* became the leading authority used by Mexican-Americans, and later other Latinos, to challenge discriminatory practices. *Hernandez* also details specific instances of discrimination against Mexican-Americans, rendering statements suggesting that Mexican-Americans have never been subject to state sanctions and discrimination in the United States at best factually inaccurate.

Second, historically, *Hernandez* symbolizes the positive results of litigation and other civic efforts by Mexican-Americans of what Mario García calls "The Mexican-American Generation" to secure equal civil rights for Latinos and persons of Spanish surnames. Mexican-Americans, like African-Americans in the post–World War II era who had served or otherwise participated in the war effort against fascism and who were in the midst of urbanization and economic recovery, refused to tolerate second-class status. This struggle, which somewhat parallels the struggles by African-Americans at the time, was perhaps most evident in attempts to desegregate the "Mexican schools" that permeated the Southwest. Together with the Court's ruling in *Brown*, *Hernandez* helped eradicate this form of discrimination against Mexican-Americans, as extensively described elsewhere.[6] Among those groups were LULAC and the American GI Forum, established by Dr. Hector Garcia, who paid for Mr. Hernandez' attorney in this case. The practice of discrimination and exclusion against Mexican-Americans in Texas was widespread and well known. Other cases establish *de facto* segregation of Mexican children to "Mexican schools" throughout this time period.[7] Pauline Kibbe, executive secretary of the Good Neighbor Commission from 1943 to 1947, estimated that by 1946 fifty counties in Texas with significant Mexican origin populations (over 15%) had never called a Mexican-American for jury duty.[8] Although people in Texas had challenged the exclusion of Mexican-Americans from juries since the 1930s, the state courts had routinely denied any relief until the Warren Court's ruling in *Hernandez*.

Third, the Supreme Court rejected Texas' limited bi-racial view of the Equal Protection Clause. Not only does *Hernandez* say (through a unanimous Supreme Court) that the Fourteenth Amendment transcends a black/white view of the Constitution, but also that because "community prejudices are not static," the identity of a group entitled to protection under the Equal Protection Clause may change over time. This also makes the Texas Court of Criminal Appeals holding that "Mexicans are white people" legally irrelevant. The Warren Court was more interested in trying to abolish classifications and segregation in public services, facilities, and accommodations, rather than figuring out whether Mexican-Americans were "white" or "black." One well-regarded treatise cites *Hernandez* as the first case where the Supreme Court cited constitutional authority to strike down a jury selection process discriminating on a basis other than race.[9]

Fourth, *Hernandez* involves a challenge to systemic or "indirect" discrimination, as opposed to a case involving direct evidence of discrimination. The Court accepted Mr. Hernandez' contention based not on the notion that his jury was particularly flawed or that he proved intentional discrimination by any particular official against Mexican-Americans, but that the system *as applied* was discriminatory. An example of direct evidence of discrimination involving state action would be a law stating that "no person of Mexican descent may serve on a jury." "Direct" evidence proves discrimination without inferences or presumptions. A party proving discrimination may sometimes rely on indirect means by showing that the alleged discriminator's stated reasons are false. Although there had been no law "on the books" discriminating against Mexican-Americans from serving on juries in Texas, in *Hernandez* the Supreme Court made the practice of informal or *de facto* discrimination against Mexicans from serving on juries illegal and unconstitutional.

Years later, the Supreme Court again considered a claim from a Mexican-American seeking to reverse a conviction based on an argument that Mexicans were systematically excluded from grand juries in Texas, this time in Hidalgo County, on the Texas-Mexico border. In that case, *Castañeda v. Partida* (1977), the Supreme Court stated that "it is no longer open to dispute that Mexican-Americans are a clearly identifiable class" and that persons with Spanish surnames are "readily identifiable." In a 5–4 decision, the Court rejected the contention that because Mexican-Americans in Hidalgo County were a "governing majority" that included 80% of the population in that county, there could be no discrimination against Mexican-Americans in jury selection, and ruled that there had been discrimination in violation of equal protection. Also of interest is the following quote from the Court's *Castañeda* opinion, referencing the opinion of the Texas Court of Criminal Appeals, which was "particularly revealing" as to the lack of rebuttal evidence in the record:

How many of those listed in the census figures with Mexican-American names were not citizens of the state, but were so-called "wet-backs" from the south side of the Rio Grande; how many were migrant workers and not residents of Hidalgo County; how many were illiterate and could not read and write; how many were not of sound mind and good moral character, how many had been convicted of a felony or were under indictment or legal accusation for theft or a felony; none of these facts appear in the record.

Castañeda, like *Hernandez v. Texas* and several other cases, was part of the Supreme Court's erosion of Texas' "key man" system, which relied on jury commissioners to select prospective grand jurors from the community at large rather than random selection of grand jurors. Texas was far from unique in using the "key man" system. In fact the United States Commission on Civil Rights in 1970 noted that the four Southwestern states of Texas, Arizona, New Mexico, and California all used that system. By contrast, other states have traditionally used a random method of juror selection similar to the federal system. In 1979, Texas amended its manner for selecting grand jurors to include an optional method of random selection used in civil cases, at the discretion of the state district court judge.[10] Challenges to the grand jury system have continued. For instance, in 2000, the Texas Court of Criminal Appeals considered similar challenges and noted the difficulties in precisely defining the group now referred to as "Hispanics."[11]

Fifth, *Hernandez* reaffirmed the case law stating that no one is entitled to a proportionally ethnic representation on a jury. Although people use the phrase "jury of one's peers," and even the Supreme Court stated that the proper functioning of the jury system requires the jury to be composed of a body which is truly representative of the community and not the organ of any special group or class, there is no constitutional requirement that any particular "type" of person be on a jury. Nowhere in the Constitution will one find requirements relating to the size, unanimity in reaching a verdict, or composition (e.g., cross section of society) of a jury. Civic participation on a jury also has a greater proportionate impact on a particular decision than choices at a voting booth. Does the composition of juries matter? Certainly many critics of the jury's verdict in the criminal trial of *California v. O. J. Simpson* think so. Beatriz De la Garza posits that the exclusion of Mexican men (women were also still excluded) contributed to the acquittal of an Anglo man who killed two Mexicans on land they owned near Laredo, Texas, in the early twentieth century.[12] Are a criminal defendant's "peers" persons of the same race, gender, ethnicity, or other persons accused of a crime? The answer to these questions lies in the fact that jury selection deals more with excluding prospective jurors than with "placing" any juror in the box. This issue, as it relates to Latinos, arose again before the Supreme Court in *Hernandez v. New York* (1991) (Chapter 12).

Notwithstanding the Texas Court of Criminal Appeals' statement that adoption of Mr. Hernandez' position "would destroy our jury system," the jury system continues to function as of 2005.

Finally, at the same time that the Supreme Court's ruling required Jackson County, Texas, to revamp the application of its jury selection to include Mexican-Americans, it also overturned the conviction of the murder of a *Mexican-American victim*, Joe Espinosa. Thus, while *Hernandez* has been widely praised for helping Latinos, it is also an example of a major problem Latinos face in the criminal justice system, the *underprosecution* of crimes against Mexican-American victims.[13]

As for Mr. Hernandez, the State of Texas chose not to re-try him, although it could have. According to one of the lawyers who assisted Mr. Hernandez in his challenge to the Supreme Court, Mr. Hernandez had a physical disability that made it too costly for the local authorities to keep him incarcerated. After the Supreme Court's decision was final, Mr. Hernandez was released from prison.

Despite the Supreme Court's ruling in the *Hernandez* case, discrimination against Mexican-Americans in the administration of criminal justice in the Southwest continued. In 1970, the U.S. Commission on Civil Rights (USCCR) found that Mexican-Americans were still underrepresented in petit and grand juries. The USCCR concluded in its transmittal letter to the president of the United States, the president of the Senate, and the speaker of the House of Representatives:

Under authority vested in this Commission by the Civil Rights Act of 1957, as amended, we have appraised allegations that American citizens of Mexican descent in five Southwestern States are being denied equal protection of the law in the administration of justice. We have found, through extensive field investigations during 1967 and 1968, three State Advisory Committee meetings in 1968, and a Commission hearing in 1968, all in that section of the country, that there is widespread evidence that equal protection of the law in the administration of justice is being withheld from Mexican Americans.

Our investigations reveal that Mexican American citizens are subject to unduly harsh treatment by law enforcement officers, that they are often arrested on insufficient grounds, receive physical and verbal abuse, and penalties which are disproportionately severe. We have found them to be deprived of proper use of bail and of adequate representation by counsel. They are substantially underrepresented on grand and petit juries and excluded from full participation in law enforcement agencies, especially in supervisory positions.[14]

Throughout the report, the USCCR cited excessive force by officials, political interference in political and labor organizations, misconduct by the Texas Rangers, and vigilantism as contributing to unequal justice for Mexican-Americans in the Southwest. In sum, Mexican-Americans received harsher treatment at all stages of the criminal justice system. Claims of unequal treatment and administration of justice involving Latinos/Hispanics continue.[15]

Katzenbach v. Morgan (1966)

and Voting Rights of Puerto Ricans

with Limited English Proficiency

A. Background

The right to vote in elections and participate in electing representatives is a hallmark of citizenship in the United States. The history of voting rights in the United States can fairly be characterized as a slow expansion of including the categories of people entitled to full and equal status to participate in American democracy. Remarkably, there have only been twenty-seven amendments to the Constitution since its enactment in 1789, over two hundred years ago. Of those twenty-seven amendments, eight relate to voting issues,[1] three of which were necessary to establish as part of the fundamental, constitutional law of the land that no state could deny the right to vote on the basis of race, sex/gender, or being between the ages of eighteen and twenty-one years of age. Apart from formal ways by which people were denied the right to vote, many informal ways have existed throughout American history to cajole, threaten, or otherwise impede the right to participate in electing the representatives of the American governments at the local, state, and federal levels. Common mechanisms included the poll tax, literacy requirements, and attempts to exclude voting in primaries. The stories of struggles to expand suffrage have been well documented elsewhere, and those struggles make the relatively low voter turnout in many modern elections that much more unfortunate.

In addition to constitutional amendments, Congress passed federal laws seeking to ensure access to the voting booth to those denied unimpeded access. For instance, in the nineteenth century, Congress passed enforcement legislation in 1870 and 1871, including the Civil Rights Act of 1871, making the obstruction of voting and other civil rights criminal.[2] One of the major legislative results of the Civil Rights movement of the 1960s was the passage of the

Voting Rights Act of 1965. *Katzenbach v. Morgan* (1966) was one of the early challenges to the validity of the Voting Rights Act, particularly as it impacted Puerto Rican citizens with limited English language proficiency who were otherwise qualified voters in New York. Just a month before the Court heard argument on *Katzenbach v. Morgan*, the Court had considered and rejected South Carolina's challenge to different provisions of the Voting Rights Act in *South Carolina v. Katzenbach* (1966). In *South Carolina*, the Court upheld the provision in section 2 which suspended literacy tests and similar voter qualifications for five years based on a formula where the attorney general of the United States would determine that there was a "test or device," that fewer than 50% of the voting-age residents were registered on November 1, 1964. The Court also upheld the "preclearance" provision of section 5, which required the Department of Justice to approve any changes that would create any new "standard, practice, or procedure with respect to voting." Years earlier, the Court had concluded in *Lassiter v. North Hampton County Board of Elections* (1959) that North Carolina's English literacy requirement was constitutional and not an irrational requirement for voting.

By 1965, the Puerto Rican migration, or "diaspora" as some have called it, to New York and other parts of the United States had been a significant social issue for about two decades. In many ways, Puerto Rican migration to the mainland of the United States resembled the migration of many others from all over the world. Literary works including Piri Thomas' *Down These Mean Streets* and Rene Marquez' *La Carreta* tell stories of new migrants from Puerto Rico, as does the more mainstream and well-known *West Side Story*. While the Puerto Rican migration was similar to migrations from Europe, Asia, and other parts of the world, there were differences as well. For one thing, unlike other migrants, the newly arrived Puerto Ricans were already U.S. citizens due to the Jones Act of 1917. Additionally, their place of origin, certainly by the 1950s, was readily accessible for return trips by airplane, the so-called *guagua aerea* (air bus). Like other migrants, and like other Latinos, Puerto Ricans faced discrimination in various aspects of life. For example, written laws limited access to the voting booth to those that were literate in English.

New York's election law 150 at the time required Puerto Ricans and other "new voters" to present, as evidence of literacy,

a certificate or diploma showing that he has completed the work up to and including the sixth grade of an approved elementary school or of an approved higher school in which English is the language of instruction or a certificate or diploma showing that he has completed the work up to and including the sixth grade in a public school or a private school accredited by the Commonwealth of Puerto Rico in which school instruction is carried on predominantly in the English language or a matriculation card issued by a college or university to a student then at such institution or a certificate or a letter signed by an official of the university or college certifying to such attendance.

A prior version of the law required the successful completion of the eighth rather than the sixth grade in an English language school.

The Supreme Court considered *Katzenbach* and the companion case of *Cardona v. Power* (1966), which involved a challenge by Ms. Cardona, a Puerto Rican living in New York who tried to register to vote "but was refused registration because she failed to meet the New York English literacy requirement." Ms. Cardona sued, complaining that although she could not read or write English, New York's English literacy test was "an arbitrary and irrational classification" that violated the Equal Protection Clause at least as applied to someone like herself, who had grown up in Puerto Rico and was literate in Spanish.

B. *Katzenbach v. Morgan* (1966): The Opinions

Senator Robert Kennedy of New York had introduced section 4(e) of the Voting Rights Act as a floor amendment without committee hearings or report. Shortly after the passage of the Voting Rights Act of 1965 (VRA), non-Hispanic New Yorkers went to court to challenge the VRA's provision making New York's English literacy tests illegal. John P. Morgan and Christine Morgan, registered voters in New York, filed suit in the District Court for the District of Columbia (as required by Congress as the exclusive court to file these kinds of challenges) to challenge the constitutionality of 4(e) because of its conflict with the New York laws restricting voting to those literate in English.

The full text of section 4(e) provided that

(1) Congress hereby declares that to secure the rights under the fourteenth amendment of persons educated in American-flag schools in which the predominant classroom language was other than English, it is necessary to prohibit the States from conditioning the right to vote of such persons on ability to read, write, understand, or interpret any matter in the English language.

(2) No person who demonstrates that he has successfully completed the sixth primary grade in a public school in, or a private school accredited by, any State or territory, the District of Columbia, or the Commonwealth of Puerto Rico in which the predominant classroom language was other than

English, shall be denied the right to vote in any Federal, State, or local election because of his inability to read, write, understand, or interpret any matter in the English language, except that in States in which State law provides that a different level of education is presumptive of literacy, he shall demonstrate that he has successfully completed an equivalent level of education in a public school in, or a private school accredited by, any State or territory, the District of Columbia, or the Commonwealth of Puerto Rico in which the predominant classroom language was other than English.[3]

Mr. and Ms. Morgan sought a declaration that this provision of the VRA was unconstitutional and an injunction prohibiting the attorney general of the United States, then Nicholas Katzenbach, from either enforcing or complying with the VRA. Once the New York City Board of Elections declared an intention to comply with section 4(e) of the VRA, Mr. and Ms. Morgan joined the board members, James M. Power, Thomas Maller, Maurice J. O'Rourke, and John R. Crews, as defendants in the case. The attorney general of New York, Louis J. Lefkowitz, participated as *amicus curiae* together with the Morgans in seeking to declare section 4(e) unconstitutional, and the United States intervened as a defendant. *Amicus curiae*, translated as "friends of the court," is a term used for those who submit briefs as being interested in the outcome of the case although they are not actually parties to the case. Also appearing as *amicus curiae*, but on the side of supporting the constitutionality of the VRA and urging reversal, was Rafael Hernández Colón, attorney general of Puerto Rico, who argued on behalf of the Commonwealth of Puerto Rico. Mr. Hernández Colón would be elected governor of Puerto Rico in 1972, 1984, and 1988.

In accordance with the portion of the VRA providing for the appointment of a special three-judge panel to consider challenges at the federal district court level, a three-judge panel was assembled, consisting of judges Holtzoff, McGarraghy, and McGowan. The panel split 2–1. On November 15, 1965, they rendered their opinions on the cross-motions for summary judgment (a mechanism by which legal claims involve disputes solely over the interpretation of legal issues, not the facts, and which are decided by judges without the necessity of a jury trial to determine any fact issues which are not genuinely in dispute) filed by the parties. Judges Holtzoff and McGarraghy agreed with the Morgans that the VRA was unconstitutional because it conflicted with New York's statute imposing English literacy as a voting requirement. The gravamen of their opinion was that states have traditionally been the ones to determine voter eligibility. Judge Holtzoff rejected the contention that discrimination against "Spanish-speaking citizens" in the form of exclusion from voting was a motive for New York's literacy requirement since the "requirement was originally

adopted in 1921—long before the large influx of Puerto Ricans into New York."
Judge Holtzoff also noted:

> Much of the oral argument and of the written material submitted in behalf
> of the Government, is intended to demonstrate what is claimed to be the
> unfairness of excluding from the right to vote in New York, those Puerto
> Ricans who can read and write Spanish, but are not literate in English. No
> matter how weighty and cogent such an argument may be, and we express
> no opinion on this subject, it should be addressed to the Legislature of
> New York State, rather than to the Courts.

In dissent, Judge McGowan discussed the "controversies rampant at the time
about the acquisition of Puerto Rico," which "need not be raked over again,"
and referenced the *Insular Cases* (1901) (Chapter 2), the Jones Act, and the 1952
Puerto Rican Constitution. Judge McGowan noted aspects of testimony and
discussions before the U.S. Senate about legislation to draft the Puerto Rican
Constitution, stating that Puerto Rico is "the only Latin-American area under the American flag, which is a focal point of inter-American relations" and
that "in view of the importance of 'colonialism' and 'imperialism' in the anti-
American propaganda, the Department of State feels that S. 3336 would have
great value as a symbol of the basic freedom enjoyed by Puerto Rico, within the
larger framework of the United States."

Attorney General Nicholas Katzenbach appealed the ruling of the three-
judge court directly to the Supreme Court, as provided for in the VRA. The
Supreme Court heard argument on April 18, 1966, and issued its opinions on
June 13, 1966. Justice Brennan wrote the majority opinion for seven justices on
the Court; he began by stating that *Morgan v. Katzenbach*, together with a par-
allel case, *Cardona*, concerned the constitutionality of 4(e) of the VRA, which
in the portions relevant to the cases provided that no person who completed
the sixth grade in an accredited school in Puerto Rico in which the language of
instruction was other than English shall be denied the right to vote because of
an inability to read or write English. According to the majority's opinion, under the New York election laws "requiring an ability to read and write English
as a condition of voting . . . many of the several hundred thousand New York
City residents who have migrated there from . . . Puerto Rico had previously
been denied the right to vote." Mr. and Ms. Morgan had challenged the right of
these non-English literate Puerto Rican citizens to vote, contrary to the laws of
New York prior to the enactment of the VRA's section 4(e). The Supreme Court
reversed the ruling of the three-judge panel in New York, stating that the VRA
was a proper exercise of congressional powers under section 5 of the Fourteenth

Amendment, and that because of the Supremacy Clause, federal law trumped and prevailed over the New York English literacy requirement. Section 5 of the Fourteenth Amendment authorizes Congress to pass any appropriate legislation to enforce the other provisions of the Fourteenth Amendment.

Justice Brennan acknowledged that under article I, section 2 of the Constitution and the Seventeenth Amendment, "the States establish qualifications for voting for state officers, and the qualifications established by the States for voting for members of the most numerous branch of the state legislature also determine who may vote for United States Representatives and Senators." However, according to the Supreme Court's opinion, the States cannot "grant or withhold the franchise on conditions that are forbidden by the Fourteenth Amendment, or any other provision of the Constitution." Justice Brennan noted that New York had "acted" by limiting the right to vote based on English literacy, an important fact because the Equal Protection Clause of the Fourteenth Amendment has a "state action" requirement, meaning that a violation of equal protection by private individuals without governmental action will not support a claim of a constitutional violation. Then Justice Brennan limited the Court's "task" to determining whether the New York English literacy requirement as applied to deny the right to vote to a person who successfully completed the sixth grade in a Puerto Rican school violated the Equal Protection Clause. Justice Brennan and the majority chose to distinguish *Lassiter* rather than overrule *Lassiter*, the case where the Court had previously upheld an English literacy requirement, by stating that an English literacy requirement is "not in all circumstances prohibited by the first sections of the Fourteenth and Fifteenth Amendments."

Justice Brennan stated that those who drafted section 5 of the Fourteenth Amendment intended to confer on Congress "the same broad powers expressed in the Necessary and Proper Clause" of the Constitution. The Court then cited the "classic formulation of the reach of those powers," citing Chief Justice Marshall's opinion in *McCulloch v. Maryland* (1819): "Let the end be legitimate, let it be within the scope of the constitution, and all means which are appropriate, which are plainly adapted to that end, which are not prohibited, but consist with the letter and spirit of the constitution, are constitutional." After citing additional authority for that view, Justice Brennan concluded, "There can be no doubt that 4(e) may be regarded as an enactment to enforce the Equal Protection Clause." As far as the reasons, Justice Brennan noted that Congress explicitly declared that it enacted 4(e) "to secure the rights under the fourteenth amendment of persons educated in American-flag schools in which the predominant classroom language was other than English." That category of persons included those who migrated from Puerto Rico to New York and those who had been denied the right to vote because of their inability to read and write English. According to Justice Brennan, section 4(e) "may be viewed as a measure to secure for the Puerto Rican community residing in New York non-discriminatory treatment by government—both in the imposition of voting qualifications and the provision or administration of governmental services, such as public schools, public housing and law enforcement." Congress had thus prohibited states from denying to the Puerto Rican community the right to vote, which serves as the basis to preserve all other rights. Flowing from this, Justice Brennan articulated the hope that Puerto Ricans, as a minority in New York, could, by having the right to vote, obtain nondiscriminatory treatment in public services and better obtain "perfect equality of civil rights and the equal protection of the laws." In other words, Justice Brennan had shifted the focus from discrimination in voting to discrimination in the delivery of government services that might be impacted by the results of exercising the right to vote.[4] Justice Brennan, a New Jersey Supreme Court justice before President Eisenhower appointed him to the United States Supreme Court, probably had a particular insight into the treatment of Puerto Ricans in the Northeast at the time. Additionally, while Republican President Eisenhower sought a moderate Catholic for the Court when he appointed Justice Brennan, many knew at the time that in fact Justice Brennan was a longtime liberal. Justice William Douglas, Chief Justice Earl Warren, Justice Thurgood Marshall, and Justice Brennan formed the liberal heart of the Warren Court. Justice Brennan would later be a vocal dissenter in many Burger Court and Rehnquist Court opinions.

Justice Brennan then showed a particularly unusual deference to the legislative branch for liberal judges during the Warren Court era, indicating that Congress had authority to make the judgment that section 4(e) was necessary after weighing the "various conflicting considerations." According to Justice Brennan and the Court's opinion, the considerations were

> the risk or pervasiveness of the discrimination in governmental services, the effectiveness of eliminating the state restriction on the right to vote as a means of dealing with the evil, the adequacy or availability of alternative remedies, and the nature and significance of the state interests that would be affected by the nullification of the English literacy requirement as applied to residents who have successfully completed the sixth grade in a Puerto Rican school.

Justice Brennan indicated that the Court would have reached the same conclusion if it had confined its inquiry to "whether 4(e) was merely legislation aimed at the elimination of an invidious discrimination in establishing voter

qualifications." The Court was "told that New York's English literacy requirement originated in the desire to provide an incentive for non-English speaking
immigrants to learn the English language and in order to assure the intelligent exercise of the franchise." However, Justice Brennan reasoned that Congress might well have questioned the literacy requirement in light of the many
exemptions provided (citing a grandfather clause applying to registered voters regardless of literacy prior to the passage of the law in 1921 as the primary
exemption in footnote 13). Brennan noted "some evidence suggesting that prejudice played a prominent role in the enactment of the requirement," citing in
footnote 14 a speech at the New York State Constitutional Convention where a
person spoke of the danger of voting and the need to "check" voting by people
from the "valuable and necessary infusion of Southern and Eastern European
races." Brennan then stated:

> Congress might have also questioned whether denial of a right deemed so
> precious and fundamental in our society was a necessary or appropriate
> means of encouraging persons to learn English, or of furthering the goal
> of an intelligent exercise of the franchise [or] Congress might well have
> concluded that as a means of furthering the intelligent exercise of the fran-
> chise, an ability to read or understand Spanish is as effective as ability to
> read English for those to whom Spanish-language newspapers and Spanish-
> language radio and television programs are available to inform them of elec-
> tion issues and governmental affairs.

The Court then reiterated that "the application of New York's English literacy
requirement to deny the right to vote to a person with a sixth grade education
in Puerto Rican schools [taught in Spanish] constituted an invidious discrimination in violation of the Equal Protection Clause."

In the famous footnote 10, Justice Brennan took issue with the dissent's concern that Congress could jeopardize constitutional protections if it interpreted
the Constitution differently from the Court, as the dissent implied it had given
the Court's ruling in *Lassiter,* by stating that Congress' power only worked in
one direction, to expand rights. According to footnote 10, Congress could not
go beyond the "floor" set by the Constitution. Of course in the area of voting
rights, which might have more of a "zero-sum" quality, expanding one person
or group's rights may limit another's.

Justice Brennan then concluded that section 4(e) of the VRA complied with
"the letter and spirit of the constitution," and that the fact that the VRA could
have gone further and eradicated other laws that denied the right to vote to

people educated in "non American-flag schools" did not render it unconstitutional. The Court's justification for this aspect of the decisions was

> Congress' greater familiarity with the quality of instruction in American-flag schools, a recognition of the unique historic relationship between the Congress and [Puerto Rico], an awareness of the Federal Government's acceptance of the desirability of the use of Spanish as the language of instruction in Commonwealth schools, and the fact that Congress has fostered policies encouraging migration from the Commonwealth to the States.

Accordingly, the Court reversed the three-judge panel's ruling, finding section 4(e) of the VRA constitutional, and ruling that New York could not prevent Puerto Ricans from voting because of lack of English language literacy. Justice Douglas filed a two-sentence concurring opinion, joining the majority on everything except the discussion of "whether the congressional remedies adopted in 4(e) constitute means which are not prohibited by, but are consistent with 'the letter and spirit of the constitution.'"

Two justices dissented. The first was Justice John M. Harlan, Illinois Republican and grandson of Justice John Marshall Harlan, who had authored famous dissents against segregation in *Plessy v. Ferguson* (1896) and who also wrote a dissenting opinion in the *Insular Cases* (1901) (Chapter 2). Unlike his grandfather, the second Justice Harlan is generally regarded as a conservative and advocate of judicial restraint during the Warren Court era. Justice Potter Stewart, an Ohio Republican, joined the second Justice Harlan's dissent. Justice Harlan wrote the dissenting opinion, which began with the statement, "Worthy as its purposes may be thought by many, I do not see how 4(e) of the Voting Rights Act of 1965 can be sustained except at the sacrifice of fundamentals in the American constitutional system—the separation between the legislative and judicial function and the boundaries between federal and state political authority." Starting his opinion by analyzing the *Cardona* case, Justice Harlan, like Justice Brennan in his opinion for the majority, observed that voting is a matter generally left to the states, subject to the various constitutional provisions. There, the opinions part ways. According to Justice Harlan, all classifications inherently discriminate between different classes of persons, and the test Justice Harlan believed applied to this alleged violation of the Equal Protection Clause was a rational review analysis of whether the classification is "reasonably designed to serve a legitimate state interest." Applying that standard, Justice Harlan would have found that New York's law satisfied that standard; he would have found no constitutional violation in the *Cardona* case based on the North

Carolina literacy test case *Lassiter* in 1959, which held that states had "wide scope" for qualifications of that sort without violating constitutional standards.

Justice Harlan conceded that the *Cardona* case was a closer call because, unlike the North Carolina law discriminating between illiterates and literates, the New York law discriminated between those literate in English and those not literate, as well as those literate in other languages. Justice Harlan noted that Ms. Cardona

> alleges that she is literate in Spanish, and that she studied American history and government in United States Spanish-speaking schools in Puerto Rico . . . that she [regularly read] the New York City Spanish-language daily newspapers and other periodicals, which . . . provide proportionately more coverage of government and politics than do most English-language newspapers, and that she listens to Spanish-language radio broadcasts in New York which provide full treatment of governmental and political news.

However, Justice Harlan would still have found New York's distinction constitutionally permissible: "Although to be sure there is a difference between a totally illiterate person and one who is literate in a foreign tongue, I do not believe that this added factor vitiates the constitutionality of the New York statute." Justice Harlan's stated reasons were that "the range of material available to a resident of New York literate only in Spanish is much more limited," that "the business of national, state, and local government is conducted in English," that propositions, amendments, and offices for which candidates are running listed on the ballot are in English, and "that most candidates . . . make their speeches in English." In Justice Harlan's view, New York justifiably could require "its voters to be able to understand candidates directly, rather than through possibly imprecise translations or summaries," or New York could justifiably seek to promote and safeguard the "intelligent" use of the ballot. Justice Harlan also alluded to "New York's long experience with the process of integrating non-English-speaking residents into the mainstream of American life." Further, Justice Harlan noted that the federal government required English literacy as a prerequisite to naturalization, which he viewed as attesting to the national view of the importance of English language proficiency "as a prerequisite to full integration into the American political community."

Justice Harlan's dissent then turned to the *Morgan* case; after restating the procedural aspects, he observed that although section 4(e) of the VRA "is framed in general terms, so far as has been shown it *applies in actual effect only to citizens of Puerto Rican background*" (emphasis added). Again, Justice Harlan (and Stewart) would have applied a judicial review of rationality: "was Congress acting rationally in declaring that the New York statute is irrational?" Justice Harlan took issue with the majority as having "confused the issue of how much enforcement power Congress possesses under 5 with the distinct issue of what questions are appropriate for congressional determination and what questions are essentially judicial in nature."

Justice Harlan contrasted the Court's ruling in *Katzenbach v. Morgan* with the Supreme Court's upholding of the constitutionality of other portions of the VRA in *South Carolina v. Katzenbach* (1966). Specifically, Justice Harlan contrasted Congress' "detailed investigation of various state practices that had been used to deprive Negroes of the franchise," a "voluminous legislative history" and "judicial precedents supporting the basic congressional finding that the clear commands of the Fifteenth Amendment had been infringed by various state subterfuges" with the enacting of section 4(e), which according to Justice Harlan did not have that kind of a record, and he found that no "factual data provide a legislative record supporting 4(e) by way of showing that Spanish-speaking citizens are fully as capable of making informed decisions in a New York election as are English-speaking citizens." Justice Harlan found no legislative record or "any showing whatever to support the Court's alternative argument that section 4(e) should be viewed as but a remedial measure designed to cure or assure against unconstitutional discrimination of other varieties, e.g., in public schools, public housing and law enforcement . . . to which Puerto Rican minorities might be subject in such communities as New York." In addition to contrasting the record in *Katzenbach v. Morgan* with *South Carolina v. Katzenbach,* he also compared it to a more detailed record supporting the Civil Rights Act of 1964 in *Heart of Atlanta Motel, Inc. v. United States* (1964), one of the cases in which the Court used an expansive reading of the Commerce Clause to eradicate racial discrimination.

Justice Harlan believed, based on the Court's holding in *Lassiter,* that English literacy tests were constitutionally permissible. By contrast, he considered Congress' attempt to supersede the Court's interpretation of the Constitution as unconstitutional, and he would have upheld the lower court's ruling. Justice Harlan challenged the majority's deference to congressional expression of policy, on the basis that just as the judiciary gives "congressional enactments a presumption of validity . . . state statutes are given a similar presumption." Because of the direct conflict between the two legislative enactments, one automatically had to give. According to Justice Harlan, "to hold, on this record, that 4(e) overrides the New York literacy requirement seems to me tantamount to allowing the Fourteenth Amendment to swallow the State's constitutionally ordained primary authority" in voting, which would have limitless implications in other fields of their exclusive primary competence as well. Accordingly, the dissenters would have affirmed the judgments in the cases, upheld the literacy requirements, and found section 4(e) unconstitutional.

C. The Significance of *Katzenbach* and Post-*Katzenbach* Developments to Latinos in the American Legal System

For several reasons, *Katzenbach* is one of the most significant cases involving Latinos in the American system. First, at issue was access to the voting booth, one of the most fundamental rights in the American legal system. Second, during the Civil Rights movement, Congress had affirmatively passed a law, the VRA, which made New York's *de jure* discrimination against Puerto Ricans illegal. Latinos did not initiate the *Katzenbach* litigation (although Ms. Cardona did initiate the companion case); rather, other New Yorkers who sought to continue the discriminatory, exclusionary practices filed the case. As a practical matter, *Katzenbach* resulted in breaking down barriers to the voting booth for many Latinos, and ultimately led to bilingual ballots, further enfranchising non-English-speaking citizens.

Katzenbach provided strong support for the power of Congress to adopt remedial legislation to vindicate civil rights violations, and has not been without its critics. One stated that *Katzenbach* "stood *Marbury v. Madison* on its head by judicial deference to congressional interpretation of the Constitution."[5] According to Laurence Tribe, "*Katzenbach* remains the leading case" on the power of Congress to enforce the Fourteenth Amendment.[6] According to Tribe, Justice Brennan's conclusions were based on two alternative theories: (1) "Congress could reasonably conclude that, by granting Puerto Ricans the right to vote, it would be providing this group with a political weapon which its members could use to gain nondiscriminatory treatment in the distribution of political services," and (2) Congress "could reasonably have concluded that the English language literacy test itself violated the fourteenth amendment's equal protection clause, notwithstanding the previously stated contrary view of the Supreme Court."[7] The Court later considered other voting rights issues in *Oregon v. Mitchell* (1970), where it upheld a federal law granting the vote to eighteen-year-olds in connection with the Voting Rights Act Amendments of 1970, but found that Congress could not do so with respect to state elections.

Section 4(e) is but one part of the VRA. In 2005, the VRA turned forty years old. Over that time period, Hispanics have made claims and filed lawsuits under other portions of the VRA as well. The Mexican American Legal Defense and Education Fund (MALDEF), formed in 1968, has frequently been involved in these efforts, as has the Puerto Rican Legal Defense and Education Fund

(PRLDEF) and other groups. Voting initiatives such as the Southwest Voter Registration Project were created to increase the number of registered voters and encourage Latinos to exercise their right to vote, political action that together with the legal and demographic changes has expanded Latino voters. Latinos have had proportionately fewer eligible votes than other groups, partially because of the number of non-citizen immigrants in some of the communities. As Barry Goldwater noted on the floor of Congress, many Hispanics in the United States, particularly prior to 1970, were not citizens, and citizenship has always been a requirement to vote.[8]

The VRA was amended in 1970, among other things, to eliminate all literacy tests across the United States, a change which Congress made permanent in 1982. The VRA was also amended in ways that are significant to Latinos in 1975 and 1982. The 1975 amendments added a section prohibiting discriminatory voting practices based on language. Specifically, no state or political subdivision can legally deny or abridge the right of any citizen to vote because the person is a member of a language minority group.[9] In part to address the dissent in *Katzenbach v. Morgan*, Congress made findings that "voting in discrimination against citizens of language minorities is pervasive and national in scope" and that "in many areas of the country, [the language] exclusion is aggravated by acts of physical, economic, and political intimidation."[10] A covered state or its political subdivisions "must provide voting notices, forms, instructions, assistance, or other materials and ballots in the minority language as well as in the English language."[11] According to a 1992 amendment, a governmental entity is "covered" if either more than 5% of the citizens of voting age are members of a single language minority and are limited English proficient or there are more than ten thousand people in that category. Amendments to the VRA sought to alter rulings from the Burger Court that had interpreted an "intent" requirement into dilution claims, which was at issue in *Johnson v. DeGrandy* (1994) (Chapter 13).

Miranda v. Arizona (1966)
and the Rights of the
Criminally Accused

A. Background

Miranda v. Arizona (1966), or at least its central holding, is the most widely known Supreme Court opinion featured in this book. Anyone having seen a movie or television series depicting an arrest after 1966 has probably heard what has become widely known as the "*Miranda* warnings": the arrested person has the right to remain silent, anything the arrested person says can and will be used against that person in a court of law, the arrested has the right to an attorney, and if that person cannot afford one, the state will provide one. Apart from the warnings themselves, *Miranda* is a landmark case because it is one of the main triumphs (or travesties, depending on point of view) of the Warren Court. *Miranda* is a core case for almost all criminal procedure classes in law school, and thousands of written articles, texts, cases, and other materials discuss *Miranda*.

Although *Miranda* is actually one of four consolidated cases, it has become the leading case for those propositions. *Miranda*, a case originating from a criminal prosecution for a rape in Phoenix, involved Ernesto Miranda's confession to the crime while in police custody. According to Chief Justice Warren, the four cases were similar in having "incommunicado interrogation of individuals in a police-dominated atmosphere, resulting in self-incriminating statements without full waiver of constitutional rights." That of the four confession cases considered by the Supreme Court in 1966 in this consolidated opinion, the one from Arizona would involve a person of Mexican origin is of no surprise, for several reasons. Historically, the largest number of Latinos in the United States have lived in the Southwest, largely because of the region's proximity to Mexico and because the Southwestern states were at one time part of Mexico (and previously Spanish colonial provinces in New Spain). The historical acquisition of the Southwest by the United States as a result of the Mexican-American War of 1846 and the conquest of the "Wild West" provided for a law-and-order culture in the Southwest that often focused more on order than on law. The Southwest has a history quite different from the history of the states that were previously British colonies. Military and physical force secured the Midwest, Florida, and the Southwest for the migrants from the eastern United States in the nineteenth century. In the Southwest during the second half of the nineteenth century and for much of the twentieth century, people of Mexican origin were frequently relegated to an inferior position based on their ancestry, and the criminal justice system reflected the societal biases.

Conflict, discrimination, and tension fairly characterize the relationship between Mexicans and the criminal justice system in the Southwest during this time period. For instance, while the Texas Rangers are generally seen as an important, positive influence in American history,[1] the Texas Rangers' interaction with the Mexican community has also been documented as being negative and repressive.[2] Under the Treaty of Guadalupe Hidalgo (Chapter 1), Mexicans were allowed to remain in the United States with a pledge that their civil rights and property rights would be protected.[3] The post-1848 history revealed breaches of these pledges by formal, institutionalized means,[4] as well as by less formal, private, unofficial means.[5] Mexicans were relegated to an inferior position in the United States and were excluded from the legal and political structure.[6] Peonage was a common practice. In short, the experience of Mexicans in the Southwest somewhat resembled that of antebellum blacks in the South. The criminal justice system was no exception. Double standards existed in the case of justice toward Mexicans.[7] This double standard, which some have referred to as "gringo justice," was manifest not only in disproportionate and harsh treatment of Mexican defendants, but also in the lack of prosecution of crimes against Mexicans and violations of Mexicans' rights.[8] One recent book detailed how excluding all Mexicans from a Webb County jury in the early twentieth century resulted in the failure to convict an Anglo person who had killed two Mexicans. According to Amado Morales, "The problem of conflict between the Mexican-American community and law enforcement agencies is only symptomatic of much broader social problems seen in the historical and contemporary American scene."[9] One often cited example involved the "Sleepy Lagoon Case" of the World War II era, where in a trial for a murder resulting from gang warfare in Los Angeles, the trial judge characterized the gang members as being part of a biologically inferior people, "the brown, Spanish-speaking descendants of the savage and bloodthirsty Aztecs." And, in Los Angeles during World War II, Zoot Suiters (Mexican-American youths who wore the local style of the times) were attacked by Navy soldiers awaiting their tours in the Pacific.[10] Mexican youths were

> dragged from theaters, stripped of their clothing, beaten, and left naked on the streets. Youngsters were dragged out of restaurants and off streetcars, mauled and beaten by the yelling mob. [Meanwhile] police officers stood by doing little or nothing to thwart the rioting servicemen.[11]

Several days of violence ensued, which came to be known as the Zoot Suit Riots. According to *Time* magazine, the strategy of the police was to accompany the sailors in police cars, watch the beatings, and jail the victims.[12] These events can be seen in the popular movies *L.A. Confidential* and *American Me*. Years later, in the 1960s, riots would again erupt in part due to perceptions of unfair treatment at the hands of law enforcement by members of the Mexican-American, or, as they were generally known by some, Chicano, community.

Miranda is based on the right against self-incrimination found in the Fifth Amendment to the U.S. Constitution. The relevant language of the clause provides that "No person . . . shall be compelled to be a witness against himself." Unlike other constitutions, like those of socialist countries, the U.S. Constitution is primarily based on "negative" rights, or on rights that people have preventing excessive governmental intrusion rather than on "positive" rights such as "a right to a job." The founders of the Constitution conceived of the federal government as one of limited powers, although throughout the twentieth century the powers and reach of the federal government increased tremendously. *Miranda* involved a prosecution by a state government (Arizona), not the federal government. Nevertheless, the federal Constitution applies to prevent overreaching by state governments as well because of the Due Process Clause of the Fourteenth Amendment, enacted in 1868, and the so-called Incorporation Doctrine. For the hundred years or so following the passage of the Fourteenth Amendment, Supreme Court justices debated how much, if any, of the Bill of Rights was "incorporated" against the states by the Due Process Clause. Some justices, primarily Justice Hugo Black, an Alabama Democrat appointed by President Roosevelt who had been a member of the Ku Klux Klan, championed the position that all of the Bill of Rights should be considered totally incorporated. By contrast, Justice Felix Frankfurter, also an FDR appointee, but of sharply different judicial philosophies and views, rejected the notion of incorporation altogether, and believed that the only requirement of the Due Process Clause was that states provide the process due based on notions of "fundamental fairness." Regardless, by the time *Miranda* reached the Court in 1966, the Court had decided that the Fifth Amendment's right against self-incrimination applied to the states to the full extent that it prevented the federal government from coercive statements.

In *Balzac v. Porto [sic] Rico* (1922) (Chapter 2) and *Hernandez v. Texas* (1954) (Chapter 3), the Supreme Court was unanimous. Not so in *Miranda*. Instead, apart from Chief Justice Warren's opinion for a majority of five justices, four justices dissented, and *Miranda* generated three spirited dissenting opinions. In total, *Miranda* occupies over one hundred pages in the official Supreme Court reporter.

B. *Miranda v. Arizona* (1966): The Opinions

On March 13, 1963, Phoenix police arrested Ernesto A. Miranda (then twenty-three years old) for kidnapping and raping an eighteen-year-old girl. According to the reported case accounts, the following happened. On March 3, 1963, the eighteen-year-old girl had left her job at a concession stand at the Paramount Theater in downtown Phoenix, taken a bus near her home, and started to walk home when she noticed Mr. Miranda's car, which was parked behind a ballet school. Mr. Miranda pulled his car "out of the lot and came so close to her that she had to jump back to prevent being hit." He then parked the car across from some apartments in the same block, walked toward her, grabbed her, and covered her mouth, instructing her not to scream. He then tied her hands and ankles and placed her in the back of his car, drove her to another location about twenty minutes away, and raped her. Phoenix police took Mr. Miranda into custody at a police station. After the rape victim identified Mr. Miranda, the police officers took Mr. Miranda into interrogation room number 2 of the detective bureau. After two hours of questioning by two police officers, Wilfred Young and Carroll Cooley, Mr. Miranda signed a typed and written confession to the crimes. As Chief Justice Warren further noted, the police officers "admitted at trial that Miranda was not advised that he had a right to have an attorney present." Mr. Miranda was also convicted in a separate trial for committing another crime, an unrelated robbery. Not only did Mr. Miranda match the victim's description, but Mr. Miranda also had a "lengthy criminal record, including charges of attempted rape." [13]

In 1963, a Phoenix jury found Mr. Miranda guilty of the kidnap and rape and he was sentenced to prison for twenty to thirty years for each crime. The sentences were to run concurrently (they run at the same time and thus overlap). Mr. Miranda had a court-appointed lawyer who was paid $100 and called no witnesses. [14] According to the Arizona Supreme Court, Mr. Miranda "offered no evidence in his defense at the trial of his case." Mr. Miranda appealed his convictions to the Arizona Supreme Court, complaining of a number of procedural technicalities, including a defective indictment; prejudicial jury argument by the prosecutor, who stated that the victim acquiesced in the rape due to fear; and violation of his constitutional rights in the manner in which his confession was obtained. On April 22, 1965, the Arizona Supreme Court rejected Mr. Miranda's appeal. Mr. Miranda then appealed to the United States Supreme Court, which heard argument on February 28, 1966, and issued its landmark ruling on June 13, 1966.

The Warren Court's rulings in the 1960s regarding the criminal justice system have been fairly described as "revolutionary." According to Lucas Powe, the Warren Court that issued *Miranda* in 1966 was different from the Warren Court that had issued the *Hernandez* ruling in 1954 because the composition of the Court had changed. Generally, the Warren Court is perceived as having been liberal for the entire sixteen years under Chief Justice Earl Warren; however, the Warren Court's tendency to safeguard the constitutional rights of those accused of a crime developed over the term of the Court.[15] At the time the Court heard argument and wrote its opinions in *Miranda*, it had issued a series of landmark decisions in the area of criminal procedure and the rights of the accused, all of which had the general effect of providing greater protections to those accused of criminal activity and of making prosecutions more difficult. Before *Miranda*, the Warren Court ruled among other things that the exclusionary rule prohibited the admission of evidence obtained in violation of the Fourth Amendment's protection against unreasonable and/or warrantless searches and seizures;[16] the scope of Sixth Amendment guarantees provided for greater protections than previously interpreted;[17] and indigents had the right to receive assistance of counsel, at state expense if the accused could not afford one.[18] Through selectively incorporating the Bill of Rights guarantees and expanding the substantive protections to criminal defendants, the Warren Court helped eradicate some grievous ills of the American criminal justice system, while creating new ones. Chief Justice Warren's opinion in *Miranda* primarily relied on, and referred to, the *Escobedo v. Illinois* (1964) decision pertaining to an accused having a constitutionally guaranteed right to stop a custodial interrogation under the Sixth Amendment's right to counsel provision. In other words, the Supreme Court had reversed Mr. Escobedo's conviction based on his confession because he had requested a lawyer, but was denied access to a lawyer, prior to the interrogation.

John Flynn, an experienced criminal lawyer recruited by the ACLU, argued the case for Mr. Miranda. Interestingly, in one of the companion cases to *Miranda* involving a federal prosecution in California, Thurgood Marshall, then solicitor general and soon to join the Court as the first black Supreme Court Justice, argued the case on behalf of the United States government at the

Supreme Court. At oral argument, Mr. Flynn described Mr. Miranda as a twenty-three-year-old from "Spanish-American extraction." Showing a keen appreciation of his audience, Mr. Flynn made class-based arguments predicated on not only his client's ethnicity but also his eighth-grade education, poverty, and history of mental illness. In response to questioning from Justice Potter Stewart as to the rights of a suspect when the investigation has focused on him, Mr. Flynn argued that a man has the right to assert his Fifth Amendment right at that point "if he's rich enough, and if he's educated enough." [19] The gravamen of the argument made by Gary Nelson, assistant attorney general of Arizona, was that no constitutional violation had occurred in the case of Mr. Miranda, and that the voluntariness of confessions ought to be viewed on a case-by-case basis, considering the totality of the circumstances. Duane Nedrud, on behalf of the National District Attorney's Association, also argued to the Court on February 28, 1966, but he had a sharper tone, understandably in his capacity as *amicus* as opposed to representing a party. Mr. Nedrud stated early in his argument that "if we are talking about equality between the rich and the poor, we are striving for a worthy objective. If we are talking about equality between the policeman and the criminal, we are on dangerous ground." [20] Mr. Nedrud defended the tough job of police officers and argued that limiting the use of confessions in criminal cases would be "taking from the police the most important piece of evidence in every case they bring before a court of justice. Police officers are public servants. They are not attempting to put innocent people in jail." [21] At oral argument, Chief Justice Warren asked Mr. Nedrud if lawyers, particularly criminal defense lawyers, were a "menace to our administration of justice," which Mr. Nedrud answered by stating that the job of defense attorneys is to attempt to free the defendant, and if retained before an interrogation, they would "prevent a confession from being obtained." Mr. Nedrud argued that without confessions, there would be fewer convictions, the obvious implication being that criminals would go free.

Three and a half months after oral argument, on June 13, 1966, the Supreme Court issued its opinions. Chief Justice Warren began the opinion for a five-member majority of the Court with this broad proposition:

> The cases before us raise questions which go to the roots of our concepts of American criminal jurisprudence: the restraints society must observe consistent with the Federal Constitution in prosecuting individuals for crime. More specifically, we deal with the admissibility of statements obtained from an individual who is subjected to custodial police interrogation and the necessity for procedures which assure that the individual is accorded his

privilege under the Fifth Amendment to the Constitution not to be compelled to incriminate himself.

The entire *Miranda* opinion, including this first sentence, was extensively edited, according to Supreme Court historians. According to David O'Brien, a prior version of this paragraph read "the role society must assume" instead of "the restraints society must observe," and that Justice Brennan suggested that revision.[22] Chief Justice Warren then referenced *Escobedo* and the subsequent "spirited legal debate" in the two years since the Court had issued that ruling, and the lower courts' inconsistent decisions interpreting *Escobedo*. In part of his opinion, Chief Justice Warren clarified that *Escobedo* (Mr. Escobedo's request for an attorney had been denied), together with the *Miranda* ruling, did not mean, "as some have suggested, that each police station must have a 'station house lawyer' present at all times to advise prisoners." Consistent with Mr. Nedrud's argument, much of the criticism about the Court's *Escobedo* and other contemporary decisions was that the Court was handcuffing police by placing criminal defense lawyers in the way of criminal investigations. The *Miranda* opinion responded to that criticism with the statement that "[o]ur decision is not intended to hamper the traditional function of police officers in investigating crime."

Chief Justice Warren stated that the Court began "with the premise that our holding is not an innovation in our jurisprudence, but is an application of principles long recognized and applied in other settings." The clear implication was that the Court did not radically alter the Constitution, but rather clarified its requirements. Chief Justice Warren then summarized the holding as follows:

> Our holding will be spelled out with some specificity in the pages which follow but briefly stated it is this: the prosecution may not use statements, whether exculpatory or inculpatory, stemming from custodial interrogation of the defendant unless it demonstrates the use of procedural safeguards effective to secure the privilege against self-incrimination. By custodial interrogation, we mean questioning initiated by law enforcement officers after a person has been taken into custody or otherwise deprived of his freedom of action in any significant way.

Chief Justice Warren discussed the procedural safeguards that must be employed. The accused may waive these rights, only if "the waiver is made voluntarily, knowingly and intelligently." If at any time the suspect indicates "in any manner and at any stage of the process that he wishes to consult with an attorney before speaking there can be no questioning. Likewise, if the individual is alone and indicates in any manner that he does not wish to be interrogated, the police may not question him." Answering some questions or volunteering some statements does not waive the right to refrain from answering any further inquiries until after consultation with an attorney. According to Chief Justice Warren, the Fifth Amendment's privilege against self-incrimination covers both direct confessions and statements that constitute admissions.

Sensitive and aware of the criticism of the Court following *Escobedo,* Justice Warren manifested a need to tie the decision to the roots of the American system. Part of the opinion states, "We sometimes forget how long it has taken to establish the privilege against self-incrimination, the sources from which it came and the fervor with which it was defended. Its roots go back into ancient times." While stating that abusive techniques are "undoubtedly the exception now," they are "sufficiently widespread to be the object of concern." The Court noted that the modern practice of in-custody interrogation, which is "psychologically rather than physically oriented," even without employing brutality or the "third degree," can exact "a heavy toll on individual liberty and trades on the weakness of individuals." Chief Justice Warren's lengthy opinion discusses torture, the Star Chamber, and psychological coercion. The opinion cites materials from prosecutors, police training manuals, law review articles, a study by the Commission on Civil Rights from 1961, and other materials. Apart from the findings of the Civil Rights Commission in 1961 indicating that police continue to use physical force in obtaining confessions, footnote 7 of the opinion cites several published cases where the accused had been coerced, whether by broken bones, use of lighted cigarette butts on the back of a witness to secure an incriminating statement about a third party's guilt, strapping a person in the nude to a chair during questioning, and other dubious practices. The Court also noted that information from the 1930s, including the Wickersham Report to Congress, showed that police violence and the so-called third degree flourished at that time in American history. Chief Justice Warren cited other Supreme Court cases even after that time where "the police resorted to physical brutality—beatings, hanging, whipping—and to sustained and protracted questioning incommunicado in order to extort confessions." According to Chief Justice Warren, all these policies point to one overriding thought: the constitutional foundation underlying the privilege is the respect a government must accord to the dignity and integrity of its citizens, and that in order to maintain a "fair state-individual balance," the government should "shoulder the entire load."

Chief Justice Warren clarified that confessions were not forbidden, and that they would even be admissible in court against a criminal defendant as long as the incriminating statement or confession was freely and voluntarily given, once the suspect was warned of his or her rights. To cite an extreme example: even under Chief Justice Warren's ruling, the police are not required to "stop a person who enters a police station and states that he wishes to confess to a crime, or a person who calls the police to offer a confession or any other statement he desires to make." Toward the end of the opinion, Chief Justice Warren, who had served as California's attorney general and governor before his appointment to the Court, expressed sympathy for officers: "In announcing these principles, we are not unmindful of the burdens which law enforcement officials must bear, often under trying circumstances. We also fully recognize the obligation of all citizens to aid in enforcing the criminal laws." The opinion then points to the FBI as a role model for the states to follow because of its

> exemplary record of effective law enforcement while advising any suspect or arrested person, at the outset of an interview, that he is not required to make a statement, that any statement may be used against him in court, that the individual may obtain the services of an attorney of his own choice and, more recently, that he has a right to free counsel if he is unable to pay.

Chief Justice Warren also noted that such safeguards hold in several other common law jurisdictions, namely Scotland, England, India, and Ceylon.

Chief Justice Warren then addressed each of the four consolidated cases individually, and in the case of Mr. Miranda found that from the testimony of the officers and by Arizona's admission, Mr. Miranda was not "in any way apprised of his right to consult with an attorney and to have one present during the interrogation, nor was his right not to be compelled to incriminate himself effectively protected in any other manner." Therefore his confessions and statements were inadmissible, notwithstanding the typed-in clause in the statement he signed stating that he had "full knowledge" of his "legal rights." Accordingly, the Supreme Court reversed Mr. Miranda's conviction.

There were four dissenters, and three separate dissenting opinions. Justice Tom Clark, a former Dallas district attorney who had also served in the Justice Department under President Franklin D. Roosevelt, wrote one of the dissents. President Harry Truman appointed Tom Clark as his attorney general, then appointed him to the Court in 1949. Justice Clark disagreed with "the Court's criticism of the present practices of police and investigatory agencies as to custodial interrogations." Justice Clark noted that the record did not reflect that any of the "police manuals" were actually in use by the police department, or that they were universally used in the United States. Justice Clark stated that the majority's opinion had no support in prior case law and that he would have continued to follow the case-by-case "totality of the circumstances" approach to challenged confessions and statements under a due process analysis. He would have affirmed Mr. Miranda's rape and kidnapping convictions.

The second, longer, dissent was authored by Justice John M. Harlan, appointed to the Court by President Dwight D. Eisenhower. Justice Potter Stewart and Justice Byron White joined Justice Harlan's dissenting opinion. Like Justice Clark, these dissenters would have affirmed Mr. Miranda's conviction and would have continued to evaluate the admissibility of confessions or statements based on considerations of due process. Justice Harlan characterized the majority's opinion as a "new constitutional code of rules for confessions. The foremost requirement, upon which later admissibility of a confession depends, is that a fourfold warning be given to a person in custody before he is questioned." Justice Harlan described the Court's ruling as being based on a utopian concept of voluntariness which required a "strained reading of history and precedent and a disregard of the very pragmatic concerns that alone may on occasion justify such strains." Justice Harlan's detailed dissent is divided into several sections.

In the first section, he takes issue with Chief Justice Warren's "constitutional premises" and concludes that over the twenty-five-year period preceding the *Miranda* opinion, the Court had developed "an elaborate, sophisticated, and sensitive approach to admissibility of confessions," considering them on a case-by-case basis, and that prior case law had recognized the value in "suspect questioning as an instrument of law enforcement." Quoting from Judge Friendly's 1965 *California Law Review* article, which resonates with the Cold War political language of the time, Justice Harlan criticizes the Court's citation of precedent as a "domino method of constitutional adjudication . . . wherein every explanatory statement in a previous opinion is made the basis for extension to a wholly different situation."

In the next section of Justice Harlan's dissent, entitled "Policy Considerations," he contends that the Court's new ruling shifts the role of the Constitution from preventing undue pressure to preventing the obtaining of confessions, as a tool of law enforcement. According to Justice Harlan, "There can be little doubt that the Court's new code would markedly decrease the number of confessions." Over the course of this section, Justice Harlan's dissent becomes more stinging and poignant, stating that the degree of harm by the decision cannot be predicted with accuracy, and that the "social costs of crime are too great to call the new rules anything but a hazardous experimentation."

Examining Mr. Miranda's case specifically, Justice Harlan recounts the facts of the brutal crime, Mr. Miranda's eighth-grade education, his schizophrenia (although he was oriented, sane, and competent to stand trial), and notes that the Phoenix officers obtained a detailed oral confession followed by a written statement, in less than two hours of questioning, in the daytime, "without any force, threats, or promises." Given these circumstances, Justice Harlan claimed to be "astonished" that the Court's new reading of the Constitution mandated throwing out confessions such as Miranda's, produced without "any of the traditional indicia of coercion." According to Justice Harlan,

> They assured a conviction for a brutal and unsettling crime, for which the police had and quite possibly could obtain little evidence other than the victim's identifications, evidence which is frequently unreliable. There was, in sum, a legitimate purpose, no perceptible unfairness, and certainly little risk of injustice in the interrogation. Yet the resulting confessions, and the responsible course of police practice they represent, are to be sacrificed to the Court's own finespun conception of fairness which I seriously doubt is shared by many thinking citizens in this country.

Justice Harlan also disputes Chief Justice Warren's arguments based on the law of other countries or the FBI's practices as being irrelevant or incorrect. In the final section of Justice Harlan's dissent, he speaks for the rights of the victims, a point which foreshadowed the trend whereby proponents of victims' rights initiatives sought to curb or overrule perceived excesses of the Warren Court.

Justice White also wrote a dissenting opinion, which Justice Harlan and Justice Stewart joined as well. Justice White, a Democrat appointed by President John F. Kennedy, frequently voted with the government in matters of criminal procedure. In his dissent, Justice White assigns to the Court a "deep-seated distrust of all confessions" and acknowledges that the nub of his dissent is his disagreement with the Court's "not so subtle overtone of the opinion—that it is inherently wrong for the police to gather evidence from the accused himself." Justice White begins by stating that the clear waiver requirement, which is the heart of the Court's ruling in *Miranda,* has "no significant support in the history of the privilege or in the language of the Fifth Amendment." Justice White then notes that the common law history cited by Chief Justice Warren related to judicial, not police, interrogations. Apart from stating that the Court's opinion was not grounded in the law or precedents, Justice White writes that the majority's opinion did not cite even a "single transcript of a police interrogation, let alone the interrogation that took place in any of these cases which it decides today"; he concludes that as a matter of empirical investigation or social science, the opinion is "patently inadequate." Justice White's opinion notes that the Fifth Amendment does not forbid confessions, only those that are compelled.

Like the other governmental agencies and *amici* that argued to the Court, Justice White expressed concerns about the effects on criminals "going free," citing statistics on recidivism in the United States and stating that the "most basic function of any government is to provide for the security of the individual and of his property." Justice White's pitch for victims' rights is probably best summarized in the following quote from his dissent:

In some unknown number of cases the Court's rule will return a killer, a rapist or other criminal to the streets and to the environment which produced him, to repeat his crime whenever it pleases him. As a consequence, there will not be a gain, but a loss, in human dignity. The real concern is not the unfortunate consequences of this new decision on the criminal law as an abstract, disembodied series of authoritative proscriptions, but the impact on those who rely on the public authority for protection and who without it can only engage in violent self-help with guns, knives and the help of their neighbors similarly inclined. There is, of course, a saving factor: the next victims are uncertain, unnamed and unrepresented in this case. Nor can this decision do other than have a corrosive effect on the criminal laws as an effective device to prevent crime. A major component in its effectiveness in this regard is its swift and sure enforcement. The easier it is to get away with rape and murder, the less the deterrent effect on those who are inclined to attempt it. This is still good common sense. If it were not, we should posthaste liquidate the whole law enforcement establishment as a useless, misguided effort to control human conduct.

As a result of this 5–4 decision, Mr. Miranda's conviction was reversed, and the landscape for police in-custody interrogations changed.

C. The Significance of *Miranda* and Post-*Miranda* Developments to Latinos in the American Legal System

For several reasons, *Miranda* is one of the most significant legal cases for Latinos in the American legal system. *Miranda* changed how law enforcement and the criminal justice system have interacted with all citizens and others, including Latinos. Additionally, *Miranda* has had a widespread effect on American life. According to Lucas Powe, "If *Miranda* is not the most controversial decision by the Warren Court, it is close enough, and it is the most controversial criminal procedure decision hands down . . . *Gideon* required five backward states to change their laws and behavior. *Mapp* required half the states to change theirs. *Miranda* required *all* the states to change theirs." [23]

Police do dangerous and difficult work. Crimes ought to be punished and criminals brought to justice. Some studies, though, indicate that even without confessions, conviction rates of law enforcement agencies did not suffer after the *Miranda* decision.[24] However, concerns about overzealous police practices are exactly why the constitutional provisions of the Bill of Rights were enacted. Central to the concerns of the framers were tortured or coerced confessions of the kind that made the Star Chamber infamous. While police practices continue to improve, overzealous police practices and even forced confessions continue in the twenty-first century. A recent Supreme Court case, *Chavez v. Martinez* (2003), provides a grim and somber reminder of these concerns. In that civil suit, where a person who claimed to have been beaten in custody sued the police officer and the department under 42 U.S.C. section 1983, the Court ruled that Mr. Chavez' constitutional rights had not been violated. Notwithstanding the Court's holding, the transcript of the detention provides some evidence that these concerns remain. During the detention, the suspect, who later had to seek emergency medical attention, repeatedly stated that he was "dying" and that he was "choking."[25]

As recently as 2000, the Supreme Court, through Chief Justice Rehnquist, reaffirmed *Miranda*'s central ruling and explicitly rejected an attempt by Congress to overrule *Miranda*, reasoning that Congress had no power to overrule since *Miranda* involved a constitutional, not a legislative, issue.[26] However, in the almost forty years since the *Miranda* decision emanated from the Warren Court, the Burger Court and the Rehnquist Court have issued numerous rulings that have narrowed the scope of the holding in *Miranda*. For instance, the specific or particular language of *Miranda* is no longer always required. Similarly, confessions, even ones obtained involuntarily, may be admitted into evidence at trial for other purposes or at other quasi-criminal proceedings such as proceedings in tax court and/or immigration matters without violating the Fifth Amendment's privilege against self-incrimination. *Miranda* does not apply to non-citizens if the involuntary confession was obtained outside the United States.

Part of the right against self-incrimination found by the Warren Court decisions included a prohibition from district attorneys arguing at the trial court that the fact that a criminal defendant refused to "take the stand" and testify was an indicia of guilt.[27] More recently, in *Portuondo v. Agard* (2000), the Rehnquist Court found that a prosecutor's suggestion in closing argument that a criminal defendant accused of rape had the ability to craft his testimony because he sat through the trial did not violate the Sixth Amendment to the Constitution, which provides that a criminal defendant has a right to be present at trial and to be confronted with the witnesses against him in open court. In dissent, Justice

Ruth Bader Ginsburg (joined by Justice Stevens) stated that the Court's ruling in that case "transforms a defendant's presence at trial from a Sixth Amendment right into an automatic burden on his credibility." [28]

As for Mr. Miranda, the State of Arizona retried him *without the use of his confession* and another jury convicted him again of the rape and kidnapping of the eighteen-year-old victim for another twenty-year sentence. Mr. Miranda served prison time and was released in 1972. After his release, he returned to prison "a couple more times over the next few years." [29] According to Powe, he used to carry police cards with Miranda warnings and autographed them for $1 to $2. Years later, in a bar fight, a man stabbed and killed Mr. Miranda in connection with a dispute over a bet in a poker game. Commentators have noted the irony that police authorities read the *Miranda* warnings in Spanish and English to the man who killed Mr. Miranda; the man "chose to remain silent, and was released pending further investigation. He disappeared and has never been found." [30]

D

THE BURGER COURT (1969–1986)

6. *San Antonio ISD v. Rodriguez* (1973)
and the Search for Equality in School Funding

7. *Espinoza v. Farah Mfg. Co.* (1973)
and "National Origin" Discrimination in Employment

8. *United States v. Brignoni-Ponce* (1975),
Law and Order on the Border

9. *Plyler v. Doe* (1982)
and Educating Children of Illegal Aliens

San Antonio ISD v. Rodriguez (1973)
and the Search for
Equality in School Funding

A. Background

Rodriguez v. San Antonio Independent School District (1973) involves a constitutional challenge to inequitable public school financing in Texas. Unlike most other cases in this book, *Rodriguez* is frequently taught in law school constitutional law classes because of its central holdings that (1) poor people or people discriminated against on the basis of absence of wealth are not an identifiable class and (2) education is not a "fundamental right" for equal protection purposes.

Rodriguez appeared before the Court in 1973, almost two decades after *Brown*. Although the Court had been dealing with numerous school cases on how to implement *Brown*, desegregation was far from complete. In fact, the federal government had to resort to calling in the National Guard to forcibly integrate several public schools, leading to famous Supreme Court cases such as *Cooper v. Aaron* (1958) and *Baker v. Carr* (1962).

Many articles, law review articles, and even a few noteworthy books have chronicled the struggles of Mexican-Americans in overcoming inferior educational opportunities in public schools. Mexican-Americans faced discrimination in public education throughout the Southwest, including Texas, during the twentieth century. An early case from Texas, *ISD v. Salvatierra*, demonstrates that segregation was a way of life in parts of the Southwest for people of Mexican descent. In *Salvatierra*, parents of children segregated from the Anglo schoolchildren in public schools claimed an equal protection violation in a manner somewhat analogous to the struggles of African-Americans which culminated with the landmark *Brown v. Board of Education* (1954). The struggles to defeat segregation in public schools by African-Americans and Mexican-Americans has been extensively chronicled.[1] As discussed in Chapter 2, *Hernandez v. Texas* (1954) was a landmark case decided in the same term as *Brown,* which although involving jury selection in criminal cases became a leading authority to help equalize educational opportunities for Mexican-American children. Because *Hernandez* involved what some have termed the "other white" strategy, meaning that Mexicans are "white people" against whom non-Mexican whites discriminated in violation of the Equal Protection Clause, its use in the desegregation context led to interesting debates. If Mexicans are "white," then isn't a school that has a population almost exclusively African-American and Mexican-American "integrated" or unitary?

Constitutional law scholars have referred to another landmark case decided the same year as *Rodriguez: Keyes v. Denver School District No. 1* (1973), for the proposition that *Brown* and desegregation efforts "went North."[2] However, *Keyes* more properly reflects that *Brown* and desegregation efforts went to the Southwest, because *Keyes* involved "tri-ethnic desegregation": blacks, Mexican-Americans, and Anglos, and *Keyes* involved the Court's rejection of the argument that because there were both black and Mexican-American students in schools, they were "desegregated" or a "unitary" school district. Also of interest is that the Mexican-American community's representatives in that litigation fought less for full integration, and more for bilingual education in schools, which required a critical mass and therefore some degree of "segregation." *Keyes,* like *Rodriguez,* reflects a generation of conflicts in public education after *Brown.* In other words, after the litigation mandating the end of desegregation, litigation frequently addressed additional, different inequalities in public education.

The political setting in which the Court considered *Rodriguez* involved the last years of the Vietnam War, President Richard Nixon's landslide re-election in 1972, and a firm commitment to reversing the trends of the liberal Warren Court. Chief Justice Warren Burger (who replaced Earl Warren) had become a reliable conservative vote on the Court for President Nixon. Together with Chief Justice Burger was Harry Blackmun, a fellow Minnesota Republican who (at least in these early years of the Court) voted in line with Chief Justice Burger to the degree that the two justices earned the nickname "the Minnesota twins."[3] In addition to Justice Blackmun and Chief Justice Burger, President Nixon appointed William Rehnquist and Lewis Powell. In addition to Earl Warren's departure, two other liberals of the Warren Court had left by 1973: Abe Fortas and Hugo Black.

At the heart of *Rodriguez* was the question of how public school could be financed consistent with the Equal Protection Clause as applied to funding of public schools by states or state agencies. Texas has had responsibility for public education since 1836,[4] and funding public schools in Texas had been a political football for over 150 years. The 1845 Constitution required the legislature to establish free public schools throughout the state based on property taxes, as did the Reconstruction Constitution of 1869. The post-Reconstruction political situation involved a re-establishment of the "old system" and a demise of civil and political rights to blacks and Mexicans.[5] In this climate, the post-Reconstruction Constitution, which denied school funding based on local taxes, was passed in 1876.[6] Since then, Texas "lawmakers have stacked new financing schemes upon old, creating today's multi-layered school finance structure."[7] Among the provisions of Texas' state constitution that the Supreme Court cited in footnotes to its opinion are article X, 1 from 1845, stating, "A general diffusion of knowledge being essential to the preservation of the rights and liberties of the people, it shall be the duty of the Legislature of this State to make suitable provision for the support and maintenance of public schools" and provisions requiring that property taxes fund public education. Texas, like Florida and a handful of other states, has no state income tax as a source, or even potential source, of funding public schools.

The equal protection jurisprudence of the United States Supreme Court developed three "tiers/levels of scrutiny" under which it analyzed statutes or other state actions. Under the traditional rational review, applied mostly to economic and social regulation, the Court upheld a challenged statute if its purpose was rationally related to a legitimate state interest. If a statute discriminated on the basis of gender, then the Court applied an intermediate review which examined whether a statute was substantially related to an important state interest. Finally, if a classification discriminated on the basis of race, national origin, or another "suspect class," it would survive strict scrutiny only if the statute was directly related to a compelling state interest. In practical application, the tests became largely outcome-determinative. Strict scrutiny has been described as "strict in theory, but fatal in fact."[8] The Court also applied strict scrutiny when the issue at interest was deemed a "fundamental right."

In 1968, Demetrio Rodríguez filed suit in a federal district court in San Antonio, Texas, suing Edgewood Independent School District and the other districts in the county (Bexar), challenging Texas' system of public school financing. Mr. Rodríguez filed the suit as a class action on behalf of schoolchildren throughout the state (including his three boys) who were members of minority groups or who were poor and resided in school districts having a low property tax base. Mr. Rodríguez sued the State Board of Education, the Commissioner of Education, the State Attorney General, and the Bexar County (San Antonio) Board of Trustees. Interestingly, even though Mr. Rodríguez initially sued San Antonio Independent School District (the named defendant in the Court's opinion), after a pretrial conference, the district court dismissed the school districts from the case, and SAISD rejoined the lawsuit on the side of Mr. Rodríguez and supported the challenge to Texas' school finance system by filing an *amicus curiae* brief with the Supreme Court. Years later, Mr. Rodríguez, a sheet metal worker at Kelly Air Force Base in 1968, recalled that the conditions at Edgewood High School were that of "an old, two-story school which had been condemned." He recalled that there "was no air conditioning and they used fans bought by the PTA. The books were old."

In 1970, San Antonio was nearly 50% Mexican-American and had a segregated system with thirteen school districts in and around the San Antonio area, of which five were predominantly Mexican-American and eight were predominantly Anglo.[9] School financing in Texas in the 1970s was (and remains) a three-source structure with funding coming from the local district, the state, and the federal government. The chief claim of the class of Mexican-American children and parents was that Texas' heavy reliance on local property taxation for funding public schools violated the Equal Protection Clause of the Fourteenth Amendment since poorer property base districts were inferior to property rich districts.

The plaintiffs in *Rodriguez* argued that the Texas public school finance system was unconstitutional and that the Court should apply strict scrutiny. First, they argued that wealth was a suspect class and that Texas' school financing scheme discriminated against the "poor." Second, they argued that public education was a fundamental interest or a fundamental right and that the financing scheme violated equal protection by infringing on poor students' rights to public education.

As provided by a statute involving constitutional challenges, a three-judge federal district court panel considered the case, as in *Katzenbach v. Morgan* (1966) (Chapter 4). According to footnote 4 of the Supreme Court's opinion, "trial was delayed for two years to permit extensive pretrial discovery and to allow completion of a pending the Texas legislative investigation concerning the need for reform of its public school finance system." In other words, the federal district court gave the Texas legislature (which meets every other year) the opportunity to change the system without judicial intervention. On December 23, 1971, the three-judge panel unanimously ruled in favor of Mr. Rodríguez and the other plaintiffs, declaring the Texas school finance system unconstitutional under the Equal Protection Clause. The district court panel reached that conclusion based on a record establishing substantial inter-district disparities in school expenditures in San Antonio and in varying degrees throughout Texas, largely attributable to differences in the amounts of money collected through local property taxation. The district court held that the Texas system discriminated on the basis of wealth, a suspect classification, and that because education was a fundamental right, under strict scrutiny, Texas could not establish a compelling state interest. The district court could not even find a rational basis for Texas' school financing scheme. In accordance with specific procedural statutes, the Texas state defendants appealed to the Supreme Court.

B. *San Antonio Independent School District v. Rodriguez* (1973): The Opinions

Justice Powell wrote the majority's opinion in *Rodriguez,* and the other Nixon appointees joined him, as well as Justice Potter Stewart, who also wrote a concurring opinion. As Earl Maltz has indicated, Justice Powell "played an absolutely pivotal role on the Court during the Burger era. Indeed his jurisprudence largely defined that of the Court as a whole." He adds that "Powell's impact on the law reflected the simple fact that he was consistently the justice most likely to be in the majority during the Burger era."[10]

The Court heard argument on October 12, 1972. One of the most prominent law professors in the country, University of Texas School of Law professor Charles Allan Wright (co-author of the famous treatise on federal procedure, Wright and Miller), argued the case on behalf of the defendant Texas state governmental agents. Referring to Wright's arguments, Justice Powell stated that Texas "candidly admits" that "no one familiar with the Texas system would contend that it has yet achieved perfection" and that it had "defects" and "imperfections"; but he defended the system's rationality with vigor. Arthur Gochman, a San Antonio attorney, represented Mr. Rodríguez and the other parents.

The Court issued its opinion on March 21, 1973, through Justice Powell on behalf of a total of five justices. Justice Powell began with a description of the history of financing public schools in Texas, beginning in the nineteenth century, and referencing various restructuring dates and milestones, such as the 1918 increase in state property taxes to finance a program providing free textbooks throughout the state. Justice Powell noted the then-recent change in Texas from being "a predominantly rural State," with its population and property wealth spread relatively evenly across the state, to an increasingly urban state, with markedly increasing disparities in population and taxable property between districts, which accounted for "increasingly notable differences in levels of local expenditure for education." Justice Powell noted how the passage of legislation establishing the Texas Minimum Foundation School Program in the 1970s accounted for approximately half of the total educational expenditures in Texas. According to Justice Powell, Texas, through its general revenues, financed "approximately 80% of the Program, and the school districts are responsible—as a unit—for providing the remaining 20%." The district's share, known as the

Local Fund Assignment, was apportioned among the school districts under a formula designed to reflect each district's relative taxpaying ability. Every Texas school district imposes a property tax to raise revenues in excess of the amount necessary to satisfy its Local Fund Assignment.

The increases in expenditures for public education increased approximately 500% between 1949 and 1967. Justice Powell noted that throughout the litigation, the school district where Mr. Rodríguez lived, Edgewood Independent School District, was compared with Alamo Heights Independent School District, the most affluent district in the San Antonio area. This comparison illustrated "the manner in which the dual system of finance operates and to indicate the extent to which substantial disparities exist despite the State's impressive progress in recent years." A concrete comparison between two districts of comparable size in Bexar county (Alamo Heights and Edgewood) of the seven districts in the San Antonio area illustrates the inequities of the finance system, based on the figures provided in Justice Powell's opinion (see Table 1).

Justice Powell also noted that Edgewood is in the core-city sector of West San Antonio in a residential neighborhood that has little commercial or industrial property, and that the residents are "predominantly of Mexican-American descent: approximately 90% of the student population is Mexican-American and over 6% is Negro." By contrast, Alamo Heights, the most affluent school district in San Antonio, had a predominantly Anglo school population, with only 18% Mexican-Americans and "less than 1% Negroes."

TABLE 1. ALAMO HEIGHTS AND EDGEWOOD: FIGURES PROVIDED IN JUSTICE POWELL'S OPINION

	Alamo Heights	Edgewood
No. of students	5,432	22,862
Schools (elem./sec.)	6	25
Property value per pupil	$49,000	$5,960
Property wealth/student	$570,109	$38,854
Tax rate (per $100)	85¢	$1.05
Sources/tax revenue per pupil		
District	$333	$ 26
State	$225	$222
(Total state)	$558	$248
Federal	$ 36	$108
Total Funding	**$594**	**$356**

According to Justice Powell's opinion, the Texas officials "virtually concede[d] that its historically rooted dual system of financing education could not withstand the strict judicial scrutiny" that would apply to reviewing "legislative judgments that interfere with fundamental constitutional rights or that involve suspect classifications." In other words, if Texas had the traditional heavy burden of justification that its educational system was structured with precision and was "narrowly tailored" to serve legitimate objectives and that it selected the least drastic means, then, according to Justice Powell, "the Texas financing system and its counterpart in virtually every other State will not pass muster." Therefore, the result of the Court's ruling depended entirely on whether the Court applied its "strict scrutiny" or merely its "rational review." According to Justice Powell, if strict judicial scrutiny applied, the judgment of the district court would be affirmed. "If not, the Texas scheme must still be examined to determine whether it rationally furthers some legitimate, articulated state purpose and therefore does not constitute an invidious discrimination in violation of the Equal Protection Clause of the Fourteenth Amendment."

Justice Powell then provided a comprehensive analysis of prior rulings involving wealth discrimination and education. Justice Powell distinguished prior Supreme Court decisions dealing with the rights of indigents to equal treatment in the criminal trial and appellate processes and cases disapproving of wealth restrictions on the right to vote, characterizing *Rodriguez* as *sui generis* in significant aspects and unable to neatly fit "into the conventional mosaic of constitutional analysis under the Equal Protection Clause."

Justice Powell stated that the district court (and other lower courts) had an incorrect and "simplistic" analysis of wealth discrimination, which Justice Powell characterized as follows: "since, under the traditional systems of financing public schools, some poorer people receive less expensive education than more affluent people, these systems discriminate on the basis of wealth." The problem with this approach, according to Justice Powell, is that it "largely ignores the hard threshold questions, including whether it makes a difference for purposes of consideration under the Constitution that the class of disadvantaged poor cannot be identified or defined in customary equal protection terms, and whether the relative—rather than absolute—nature of the asserted deprivation is of significant consequence." In other words, the term "poor" is almost inherently relative and similarly relative is the deprivation resulting from having less money. According to Justice Powell the category of poor or of people discriminated on the basis of wealth was ambiguous in *Rodriguez* because Texas' public school financing scheme might be discriminating (1) against "poor" persons whose incomes fell below some identifiable level of poverty or who might be characterized as functionally "indigent," or

(2) against those who were relatively poorer than others, or (3) against all those who, "irrespective of their personal incomes, happen to reside in relatively poorer school districts." Justice Powell then concluded that none of these categories could be characterized as "suspect" classes under the Constitution. The key distinction with prior cases involving individuals or groups of individuals who were discriminated against on the basis of wealth shared two characteristics: "because of their impecunity they were completely unable to pay for some desired benefit, and as a consequence, they sustained an absolute deprivation of a meaningful opportunity to enjoy that benefit." As examples, Justice Powell noted criminal indigents who could not pay the fees required to transcribe their cases for appeal. By contrast, in the context of the Texas school-financing system at issue in *Rodriguez,* Justice Powell concluded that it would be fair to conclude that "the poorest families are not necessarily clustered in the poorest property districts." Rather than considering the facts in the record in Texas, Justice Powell relied on a "recent and exhaustive study of school districts in Connecticut" that concluded that poor people did not live in poor districts in Connecticut. Second, unlike prior Court controversies presented to the Court, Texas was not *absolutely* depriving poor children of an education. The only argument Mr. Rodríguez raised is that the children in Edgewood Independent School District and similar districts having relatively low assessable property were receiving an arguably inferior education. In the context of wealth, "the Equal Protection Clause does not require absolute equality or precisely equal advantages." Since Mr. Rodríguez and the other plaintiffs failed to rebut Texas' assertion that "every child in every school district [receives] an adequate education," there was not an absolute deprivation. Because of the lack of a defined category of "poor people" and the lack of absolute deprivation, Mr. Rodríguez' disadvantaged class was "not susceptible of identification in traditional terms."

Justice Powell also rejected a claim based on "a theory of relative or comparative discrimination based on family income" suggesting "a continuum, the poorer the family the lower the dollar amount of education received by the family's children," which relied primarily on an affidavit submitted by Joel S. Berke of Syracuse University's Educational Finance Policy Institute. Justice Powell found Berke's affidavit legally insufficient because the survey was based on only 10% of school districts in Texas and because of the facts in ninety-six of those district studies, composing almost 90% of the sample, against Mr. Rodríguez' claims: the districts that spent next to the most money on education were populated by families having next to the lowest median family incomes, while the districts spending the least had the highest median family incomes.

The Court concluded that "no factual basis exists upon which to found a claim of comparative wealth discrimination." The last claim rejected by Justice Powell involved what he called "district wealth discrimination," which the Court refused to recognize. Justice Powell objected to expanding equal protection analysis in this fashion, even assuming "a perfect correlation between district property wealth and expenditures from top to bottom," because the Court should not "extend its most exacting scrutiny to review a system that allegedly discriminates against a large, diverse, and amorphous class, unified only by the common factor of residence in districts that happen to have less taxable wealth than other districts" and which lacked "the traditional indicia of suspectness: the class is not saddled with such disabilities, or subjected to such a history of purposeful unequal treatment, or relegated to such a position of political powerlessness as to command extraordinary protection from the majoritarian political process." In conclusion, the Court rejected Mr. Rodríguez' claim of discrimination based on wealth.

Justice Powell in Section II.B then turned the Court's analysis to whether education is a "fundamental right." Justice Powell tackled the issue head-on, beginning with the unanimous Court's oft-cited pronouncement in *Brown* that "education is perhaps the most important function of state and local governments" and then citing a lengthy quote, which although made "in the context of racial discrimination has lost none of its vitality with the passage of time," about compulsory school attendance, the importance of education for democracy and good citizenship, and its role as the foundation for success in life in the United States. Justice Powell also noted that this "abiding respect for the vital role of education in a free society may be found in numerous opinions of Justices of this Court writing both before and after Brown," citing landmark cases involving religious free exercise and establishment issues, the right of teachers to teach foreign languages in public schools, which was recognized in *Meyer v. Nebraska* (1923), and other cases. The Court then stated its "complete agreement with the conclusion of the three-judge panel below that 'the grave significance of education both to the individual and to our society' cannot be doubted." Then, Justice Powell stated that the relative importance of a service performed by a state "does not determine whether it must be regarded as fundamental for purposes of examination under the Equal Protection Clause." The fundamental interests recognized by the Court include the right to interstate travel. However, the needs for shelter or housing, food, or public assistance, while as important or more so than education, have not been recognized as constitutionally "fundamental" rights. Justice Powell noted that legislatures, not courts, should address these issues and that the Court should not "create substantive constitutional rights in the name of guaranteeing equal protection." According to Justice Powell,

> the key to discovering whether education is "fundamental" is not to be found in comparisons of the relative societal significance of education as opposed to subsistence or housing. Nor is it to be found by weighing whether education is as important as the right to travel. Rather, the answer lies in assessing whether there is a right to education explicitly or implicitly guaranteed by the Constitution.

Using that framework, Justice Powell noted that education is not among the rights afforded explicit protection under the Constitution, and further concluded that the Court found no basis "for saying it is implicitly so protected." In *Rodriguez*, the Court rejected the argument made by Mr. Rodríguez' attorney, summarized by the Court's opinion as follows:

> [E]ducation is distinguishable from other services and benefits provided by the State because it bears a peculiarly close relationship to other rights and liberties accorded protection under the Constitution. Specifically, they insist that education is itself a fundamental personal right because it is essential to the effective exercise of First Amendment freedoms and to intelligent utilization of the right to vote.

According to Justice Powell's opinion, Mr. Rodríguez' attorney had argued that "the right to speak is meaningless unless the speaker is capable of articulating his thoughts intelligently and persuasively. The 'marketplace of ideas' is an empty forum for those lacking basic communicative tools"; similarly, the attorney argued, the right to vote is hollow in the absence of education. Justice Powell concluded that these values, though desirable, should not be forced by "judicial intrusion into otherwise legitimate state activities." Among the authorities cited to support this conclusion, Justice Powell referenced Justice Brennan's opinion for the Court in *Katzenbach v. Morgan* (1966) (Chapter 4). The Court cited *Katzenbach* for the proposition that every step Texas took leading to the establishment of its then existing system was implemented in an effort to extend public education and to improve its quality, but just because every reform benefits some more than others, and may be criticized for what it fails to accomplish, "the thrust of the Texas system is affirmative and reformatory" and, therefore, should be viewed under rational review. As in its analysis of wealth, the Court noted that Texas had not absolutely deprived Mr. Rodríguez' children and other children in property poor districts of an education, and that the claim was based only on a claim of relative differences in spending levels.

Since the Court concluded that strict scrutiny did not apply because there was no suspect class based on wealth and no fundamental interests at stake with education, the Court applied rational review to the challenge in the *Rodriguez* case. Before that, however, Justice Powell characterized *Rodriguez* as "far more than a challenge to the manner in which Texas provides for the education of its children. We have here nothing less than a direct attack on the way in which Texas has chosen to raise and disburse state and local tax revenues." Justice Powell then refused to condemn Texas' "judgment in conferring on political subdivisions the power to tax local property to supply revenues for local interests," consistent with deference traditionally shown to state legislatures on tax and fiscal policy issues. According to Justice Powell, the Court stood on "familiar ground" in acknowledging that the "Justices of this Court lack both the expertise and the familiarity with local problems so necessary to the making of wise decisions with respect to the raising and disposition of public revenues." Justice Powell added that all tax systems inherently have a discriminatory impact. As in the case of tax and fiscal policy, federal courts ought to defer to state agencies on issues of educational policy, which he stated involve "a myriad of intractable economic, social, and even philosophical problems." The Court questioned the assumption that more funding necessarily means a higher quality of education. The Court also noted debates about local control versus centralized control over education, as well as federalism issues involving state laws in a federal court. Accordingly, Justice Powell wrote that the judiciary "is well advised to refrain from imposing on the States inflexible constitutional restraints that could circumscribe or handicap the continued research and experimentation so vital to finding even partial solutions to educational problems and to keeping abreast of ever-changing conditions." The Court then analyzed whether Texas' financing structure was rational. First, the Court noted that Texas' system was comparable to those of other states in relying heavily on property taxes. The Court further noted that the history of education since the industrial revolution has involved a struggle between educational opportunities for all children and desires of individual families to provide the best education for their own children.

Analyzing Texas' system with this paradigm, the Court found that Texas' system was responsive to these two forces because it provided basic education for every child in the state, yet permitted and encouraged local control. The Court cited numerous opinions from its prior cases, both majority decisions and dissenting opinions, emphasizing the importance of local control. The Court then stated that merely because local control could be preserved and promoted using other financing systems did not mean that Texas' system was constitutionally infirm. In conclusion, Justice Powell stated that "to the extent

that the Texas system of school financing results in unequal expenditures between children who happen to reside in different districts, we cannot say that
such disparities are the product of a system that is so irrational as to be invidiously discriminatory." He noted that Texas' plan was not "the result of hur-
ried, ill-conceived legislation" but instead reflected decades of experience in
Texas and elsewhere and "in major part is the product of responsible studies by
qualified people." Therefore, the Court found Texas' scheme as satisfying the
rational review standard.

Finally, Justice Powell commented that the practical considerations he identified in his opinion "of course, play no role in the adjudication of the constitutional issues presented here. But they serve to highlight the wisdom of the
traditional limitations on this Court's function." Gratuitously, Justice Powell
stated that "this Court's action today is not to be viewed as placing its judicial
imprimatur on the status quo. The need is apparent for reform in tax systems
which may well have relied too long and too heavily on the local property tax."
However, according to the Court, any innovative thinking as to public education, its methods, and its funding must come "from the lawmakers and from
the democratic pressures of those who elect them." The theme of judicial restraint, voiced in contrast to the judicial activism of the Warren Court, became
a hallmark of the Burger Court, of which *Rodriguez* is a quintessential example.
Accordingly, the Supreme Court reversed the district court, ruling against the
challenge from Mr. Rodríguez and others, finding no violation of the United
States Constitution in Texas' public school financing scheme.

Justice Potter Stewart issued a concurring opinion, finding that while the
"method of financing public schools in Texas, as in almost every other State,
has resulted in a system of public education that can fairly be described as cha-
otic and unjust," it did not violate the United States Constitution. Justice Stewart also wrote that "any other course would mark an extraordinary departure
from principled adjudication under the Equal Protection Clause" and that "the
uncharted directions of such a departure are suggested" by Justice Marshall's
dissenting opinion. According to Justice Stewart:

> unlike other provisions of the Constitution, the Equal Protection Clause
> confers no substantive rights and creates no substantive liberties. The func-
> tion of the Equal Protection Clause, rather, is simply to measure the validity
> of *classifications* created by state laws. There is hardly a law on the books that
> does not affect some people differently from others. But the basic concern
> of the Equal Protection Clause is with state legislation whose purpose or ef-
> fect is to create discrete and objectively identifiable classes. And with respect
> to such legislation, it has long been settled that the Equal Protection Clause

is offended only by laws that are invidiously discriminatory—only by classifications that are wholly arbitrary or capricious.

Justice Stewart reiterated that legislatures are presumed to act constitutionally, even if their laws result in some inequality, and that conversely, regardless of the Equal Protection Clause, state laws impinging upon a substantive right conferred by the Constitution are presumptively invalid. Justice Stewart described Justice Powell's analysis as demonstrating "thoughtfulness and understanding."

There were three dissenting opinions. Justice Byron White, a conservative Democrat appointed by President Kennedy, wrote one of these. The two predominant liberals on the Court, who had played leading roles on the Warren Court, Democrat Justice William Douglas and Republican Justice Brennan, joined Justice White's opinion. Justice White began by expressing agreement with the proposition that "local control and local decisionmaking play an important part in our democratic system of government," but noted that as applied in Texas, Alamo Heights and like school districts could meaningfully do so, while Edgewood and similar districts with a low per-pupil real estate tax base could not. Justice White then noted that Alamo Heights, "with a tax base approximately twice the size of Edgewood's base, realized approximately six times as many maintenance dollars as Edgewood by using a tax rate only approximately two and one-half times larger." However, since Texas, by law, placed a ceiling on the maintenance tax rate, Edgewood could not possibly attain an equal yield and was effectively precluded by law, "as well as in fact, from achieving a yield even close to that of some other districts." Justice White's view of the rational review standard required that Texas show that its system sought to achieve the valid, rational purpose of maximizing local initiative in a manner that was also rationally related to the end sought. He stated that neither Texas nor the majority followed that rule.

According to Justice White, "If the State aims at maximizing local initiative and local choice, by permitting school districts to resort to the real property tax if they choose to do so, it utterly fails in achieving its purpose in districts with property tax bases so long that there is little if any opportunity for interested parents, rich or poor, to augment school district revenues." The majority's approach of requiring Texas only to establish that unequal treatment furthered a permissible goal "makes equal protection analysis no more than an empty gesture." He and the other dissenters would have found, even applying a rational review approach, that the parents and children in Edgewood and in like districts suffered from an invidious discrimination that violated the Equal Protection Clause. The essence of his argument was the significant magnitude of disparity in revenues; and, he found "no difficulty in identifying the class that is subject to the alleged discrimination," who were as entitled to equal protection as voters in underrepresented counties in reapportionment cases.

Justice Brennan also wrote a dissenting opinion, where he stated that he not only agreed with Justice White's opinion setting forth the belief "that the Texas statutory scheme is devoid of any rational basis, and for that reason is violative of the Equal Protection Clause," but also disagreed with "the Court's rather distressing assertion that a right may be deemed 'fundamental' for the purposes of equal protection analysis only if it is 'explicitly or implicitly guaranteed' by the Constitution." Instead, Justice Brennan agreed with Justice Marshall, who to his view "convincingly demonstrate[d]" that the Court's precedents stood for the proposition that "fundamentality" is largely "a function of the right's importance in terms of the effectuation of those rights which are in fact constitutionally guaranteed." In the case of education, Justice Brennan considered it "inextricably linked to the right to participate in the electoral process and to the rights of free speech and association guaranteed by the First Amendment," thereby making "any classification affecting education" subject to strict scrutiny, and since Texas conceded that the statutory scheme now failed strict scrutiny, he, like the lower court, would have found Texas's scheme constitutionally invalid.

Justice Thurgood Marshall's dissenting opinion, joined solely by Justice Douglas, reads more like a speech than merely a dissent. Justice Marshall initially characterized the decision as allowing a state to "constitutionally vary the quality of education which it offers its children in accordance with the amount of taxable wealth located in the school districts within which they reside." Justice Marshall viewed this decision as "an abrupt departure from the mainstream of recent state and federal court decisions concerning the unconstitutionality of state educational financing schemes dependent upon taxable local wealth," and "more unfortunately," as "a retreat from our historic commitment to equality of educational opportunity and as unsupportable acquiescence in a system which deprives children in their earliest years of the chance to reach their full potential as citizens." In Justice Marshall's judgment:

> [T]he right of every American to an equal start in life, so far as the provision of a state service as important as education is concerned, is far too vital to permit state discrimination on grounds as tenuous as those presented by this record. Nor can I accept the notion that it is sufficient to remit these appellees to the vagaries of the political process which, contrary to the majority's suggestion, has proved singularly unsuited to the task of providing a remedy for this discrimination.

Justice Marshall criticized Justice Powell's opinion for focusing more on the positive steps Texas had taken to equalize educational opportunities than on whether the existing scheme itself violated the Equal Protection Clause, which he believed produced a discriminatory impact on a substantial number of Texas school-aged children. Justice Marshall noted that when a "child forced to attend an underfunded school with poorer physical facilities, less experienced teachers, larger classes, and a narrower range of courses than a school with substantially more funds—and thus with greater choice in educational planning—may nevertheless excel is to the credit of the child, not the State," comparing the situation of Texas schoolchildren to early cases challenging segregation in higher education, such as *Missouri ex rel. Gaines v. Canada* (1938) and *Sweatt v. Painter* (1950). Justice Marshall quoted the Court's opinion in *Sweatt:* "It is difficult to believe that one who had a free choice between these [Texas] law schools would consider the question close." Justice Marshall had represented Heman Sweatt in that litigation.

By analogy, Justice Marshall stated that "it is difficult to believe that if the children of Texas had a free choice, they would choose to be educated in districts with fewer resources, and hence with more antiquated plants, less experienced teachers, and a less diversified curriculum." Justice Marshall noted that if financing variations really made no difference to educational quality, then it would be "difficult to understand why a number of our country's wealthiest school districts, which have no legal obligation to argue in support of the constitutionality of the Texas legislation, have nevertheless zealously pursued its cause before this Court," citing the *amicus curiae* brief filed by school districts, including San Marino Unified School District; Beverly Hills Unified School District; Bloomfield Hills, Michigan, School District; Dearborn City, Michigan, School District; and Grosse Pointe, Michigan, Public School System. While he acknowledged that precise equality of treatment is "normally unrealistic, and thus minor differences inherent in any practical context usually will not make out a substantial equal protection claim," he found that in *Rodriguez*, the case was hardly a minimal claim of discrimination "resulting from the play necessary in any functioning system."

Justice Marshall took issue with the view that as long as a state provides everyone with some unspecified amount of education which is "enough," no constitutional violation exists. According to Justice Marshall:

Even if the Equal Protection Clause encompassed some theory of constitutional adequacy, discrimination in the provision of educational opportunity would certainly seem to be a poor candidate for its application. Neither the majority nor appellants inform us how judicially manageable standards are to be derived for determining how much education is "enough" to excuse constitutional discrimination. One would think that the majority would heed its own fervent affirmation of judicial self-restraint before undertaking the complex task of determining at large what level of education is constitutionally sufficient.

Justice Marshall viewed sufficient indisputable evidence in the record to establish that the children of property-poor districts constituted a class for equal protection purposes. He then stated that since Texas chose to provide public education for all citizens, its duty consistent with equal protection was to provide education on an equal footing, and not discriminate between schoolchildren based on the amount of taxable property in the district where they lived. Justice Marshall further criticized the majority for relying not on the evidence on the record, as traditionally done, but rather relying "instead on a recent law review note concerned solely with the State of Connecticut" and in challenges never made at the trial court level, to which Mr. Rodríguez and the others were unable to respond for the first time on appeal. Justice Marshall then noted that a number of theories of discrimination were considered in *Rodriguez,* including that "the District Court found that in Texas the poor and minority group members tend to live in property-poor districts, suggesting discrimination on the basis of both personal wealth and race." According to Justice Marshall, if the Court applied what he considered a proper analysis, taking into consideration the interest (education) and classification (poor), then "the unconstitutionality of that scheme is unmistakable." Justice Marshall then stated that since the Court "suggests that only interests guaranteed by the Constitution are fundamental for purposes of equal protection analysis, and since it rejects the contention that public education is fundamental, it follows that the Court concludes that public education is not constitutionally guaranteed." At the heart of the dissent was Justice Marshall's citing of the unanimous Court's *Brown* ruling that "where the state has undertaken to provide it, is a right which must be made available to all on equal terms."

C. The Significance of *Rodriguez* and Post-*Rodriguez* Developments to Latinos in the American Legal System

Having lost in the highest Court in the federal system, the plaintiffs who resided in the Edgewood school district and others continued the fight in state court under the Texas constitution. This paralleled a trend that as the federal courts generally (and the Supreme Court specifically) became more conservative, school civil rights litigation and other civil rights litigation moved into state courts. Claims under the constitutions of the various states also provided additional avenues for redress since unlike the short, straightforward, and limited United States Constitution, many state constitutions are longer, more detailed, and address all types of issues, including public education. Those challenging Texas' system in state court continued to claim that the disparities in wealth among the districts was too great to be constitutionally permissible, under the Texas Constitution. The basic claim of those opposing the plaintiffs was that *Rodriguez* had decided the issue, that school funding was a political question not to be considered by courts, and that judicial interference would conflict with the value of control over local schools.[11] In 1984, a new suit was filed by seven districts, including Edgewood. The situation in Texas by 1989 (sixteen years after the Supreme Court decided *Rodriguez*) was such that the Texas supreme court noted:

> There are glaring disparities in the ability of various school districts to raise revenues from property taxes because taxable property varies greatly from district to district. The wealthiest district has over $14,000,000 of property wealth per student, while the poorest has approximately $20,000; this disparity reflects a 700 to 1 ratio.[12]

On October 2, 1989, the Texas Supreme Court found the school financing system violative of the Texas Constitution, based on lack of "efficiency" as that term is used in the Texas Constitution.[13] There is no corresponding "efficiency" clause in the United States Constitution. While striking down the state's funding plan, the Texas court provided no instructions and not much guidance for the Texas Legislature. The Texas Legislature, under threat of ceasing all funding to public schools pursuant to the Texas Supreme Court's injunction, made changes to the funding plan. Nevertheless, in a subsequent related case in 1992,[14] the Texas Supreme Court held that the legislative changes had failed to cure the constitutional infirmity of the school funding system. The plaintiffs in that case won a hollow victory, however, since the Texas Supreme Court subsequently struck down the "Robin Hood I" plan because it attempted to equalize education based on the collection of property taxes on a statewide level in violation of the Texas Constitution.[15] The problems of school financing in Texas are further compounded by the inability of legislators, judges, and the people of Texas to agree to a funding scheme. In May of 1993, Texan voters rejected a constitutional amendment referred to as "Robin Hood II."[16] Eventually, "Robin Hood" became the law of Texas. In 2005, the Texas Legislature again considered funding public education, which failed to produce an adequate solution.

The Supreme Court in the 1960s and early 1970s had ruled time and again that states had to meet higher standards in order to effectively guarantee constitutional rights to all their citizens, especially those traditionally excluded from spheres of power (including people of color, poor people, and women). The new members of the Burger Court believed they needed to draw the line somewhere, and in *Rodriguez* the Court drew the line at wealth. Justice Marshall's dissent was particularly spirited in part because a crucial aspect of the *Brown* case, which he had argued and won, had effectively been overruled—that education was a fundamental right. Interestingly, in *Milliken v. Bradley (Milliken II)* (1977),[17] a racial desegregation case from Detroit and nearby districts, the Supreme Court allowed a desegregation plan mandated by a lower federal court requiring monetary compensation of the additional costs of educating the plaintiff-children in Detroit to stand, even though it held in *Milliken v. Bradley (Milliken I)* (1974) that the prior proposed interdistrict desegregation remedy was unconstitutional because it went beyond the districts' borders. *Milliken II* was at least theoretically contrary to *Rodriguez,* as Justice Powell tacitly acknowledged by stating that he wrote his concurring opinion "to emphasize its uniqueness" and distinguishing *Milliken II* from *Rodriguez* on the basis that the "State has been adjudged a participant in the constitutional violations" and therefore could be ordered to participate in the remedy by redistributing funds.

Rodriguez is also significant for Latinos in the American legal system because of its role as part of a secondary wave of efforts to secure equal educational opportunities for Latino and other children in public schools, after the first wave of relatively simple, straightforward, desegregation cases. Since school segregation sometimes corresponds to residential segregation, mere desegregation of schools did not resolve the problem of unequal educational opportunities or *de facto* segregation. Additionally, *Rodriguez* is representative of the shift away from federal courts generally, and the Supreme Court specifically, as being helpful to improving opportunities for Latinos. Finally, *Rodriguez* is significant for placing issues of Latinos and public education in the political forefront.

Espinoza v. Farah Mfg. Co. (1973)
and "National Origin"
Discrimination in Employment

A. Background

On July 19, 1969, Cecilia Espinoza, a lawfully admitted resident alien born in Mexico who resided in San Antonio, Texas, with her husband, Rudolfo Espinoza, a United States citizen, sought employment as a seamstress at the San Antonio division of Farah Manufacturing Co., headquartered in El Paso, Texas, known for manufacturing pants and other clothes. At the time she applied for the job at Farah, she was a Mexican citizen, although she lived in Texas in full compliance with immigration laws. Farah rejected Ms. Espinoza's employment application on the basis of a longstanding company policy against employing aliens. She decided to challenge this policy in 1969. Four years later, the Supreme Court considered her case.

For many Latinos, as for many other Americans, employment issues have historically been directly linked to immigration issues. Stated differently, the vast majority of Latinos have immigrated to the United States seeking better economic alternatives and better means by which to "make a living" and take care of family members and themselves. The historical manifestations of employment discrimination issues are tied to the different migratory histories of various Latino groups. Employment discrimination against Latinos has varied from the open, obvious, and blatant to the subtle and not so easy to detect.[1] In 1947, the President's Committee on Civil Rights noted that employers made statements to prospective employees such as, "You know we never hire Mexicans."[2] Although overt discrimination is now less prevalent, even in recent times cases filed have presented evidence of supervisors referring to employees as "wetbacks," "spics," "taco tico," or "bandito."[3]

In the case of people of Mexican descent, Mexican labor, particularly unskilled labor, was for most of the twentieth century integral to various aspects of the American economy, particularly in the Southwest in sectors such as agriculture, construction, packing, industry, and custodial work. Mexican migration provided significant labor in the early twentieth century after Congress enacted quotas limiting or barring immigration by Asians and others. During the Great Depression, in the 1930s, the United States government began a campaign across the country to "repatriate" Mexicans, regardless of whether they were U.S. citizens, meaning that people living in the United States were forcibly shipped back to Mexico en masse. After World War II, in the context of the booming postwar economy, the U.S. government created the *bracero* program, which lasted into the mid-1960s, to lure unskilled Mexican labor to work in the United States. In part in an attempt to stem immigration from Mexico, and in part to stimulate the Mexican economy, the United States and Mexico partnered to create the *maquiladora* system. Initially the *maquiladoras* were a "twin plant" concept where raw materials were shipped to Mexico, assembled by Mexican labor in Mexico, and then shipped back to the United States, all under favorable tariff arrangements.

During this time, large portions of the Mexican population in the United States, particularly first-generation Mexican-Americans, were not citizens. When Congress passed the National Labor Relations Act in the 1930s, the primary federal law pertaining to collective bargaining and unionization, farmworkers were excluded. Similarly, protections under the Fair Labor Standards Act and other federal labor laws pertaining to minimum standards of working conditions did not apply to farmworkers until the 1980s in substantial part due to the struggles of migrant Mexican farmworkers and union leaders like César Chávez.

In contrast with the Mexican experience, since 1917, Puerto Ricans have been U.S. citizens by birth. Thus the labor issues involving the Puerto Rican communities and people of Puerto Rican descent involved race, gender, or aspects of ethnicity or national origin discrimination unrelated to alienage. As one source described the situation: "for some Puerto Ricans skin color remains a key basis of discrimination."[4] In the case of the third largest group, Cubans, the United States government considered them in the post-1959 era as refugees, and thus allowed them to work without regard to citizenship issues.

The Civil Rights Act of 1964, enacted shortly after the assassination of President John Kennedy, was the most important law Congress enacted in response to the Civil Rights movement, a social movement that attempted to dismantle segregation and otherwise change discriminatory practices against African-Americans and others in areas of public schools, social services, public accommodations, employment, voting rights, and other aspects of social, political, and civic life in the United States. Almost forgotten in contemporary debate is the vehement opposition to the passage of the Civil Rights Act, which created one of the longest debates in Congress in American history.[5] The portion of the Civil Rights Act of 1964 pertaining to employment discrimination is known as Title VII. According to the Supreme Court, Congress' purposes in enacting Title VII were "to achieve equality of employment opportunities and [to] remove barriers that have operated in the past to favor an identifiable group of white employees over other employees."[6] Title VII strives to correct long-standing practices of employment discrimination, including racial discrimination against blacks; ethnic or "national origin" discrimination against minorities such as Mexican-Americans, Asian-Americans, and Puerto Ricans; and gender discrimination against women. While there are other federal laws (such as 42 U.S.C. section 1981) as well as state laws that address discrimination in employment, Title VII is the preeminent law forbidding employment discrimination based on national origin.[7] Discrimination in employment can occur during the search for employment, in the interview process, during the hiring decision process, while on the job, in promotions and "glass ceilings," and in free association and reasonable rights to unionize. Latinas have experienced a "double minority" status, being subjected to discrimination not only as Latinos, but also as women.[8]

In *Espinoza*, the Supreme Court considered the meaning of "national origin" in Title VII's anti-discriminatory laws covering employment as well as Title VII's application to non-citizens. The Burger Court considering *Espinoza* was in transition between the liberal Warren Court and the conservative Rehnquist Court. The 1960s, the Civil Rights movement, the protests against the Vietnam War, and the general anti-establishment upheaval created an atmosphere of turmoil and change. A nation of people watched on television how the inclusion of African-Americans into integrated public schools and other public facilities was accomplished by orders from the Supreme Court and other courts, at times enforced at gunpoint. In 1973, when *Espinoza* was heard, the Watergate scandal was in full swing. The Court that considered *Espinoza* was split, including several justices carried over from the Warren Court: Brennan, Marshall, and Douglas, as well as Nixon appointees Lewis Powell, Chief Justice Burger, and Harry Blackmun. By 1973, fewer than ten years had passed since Title VII was enacted. Up to that time, the Court's interpretation of Title VII had been generally favorable to plaintiffs—employees suing under Title VII. And in 1973 the Court also decided the landmark Title VII case *McDonnell Douglas Corp. v. Green* (1973), which created a framework for the order and nature of proof required in a Title VII action for employment discrimination. Such a claim requires initially the proof of a minimal *prima facie* case of discrimination. Then, the burden shifts to the employer, who must provide some evidence of a neutral, nondiscriminatory purpose for the employment action. The burden then shifts back to the employee, who must show that the employer's reasons were pretextual and that discrimination was the motive for the employment action. Since 1973, the Court has adopted the *McDonnell Douglas* test for other types of discrimination besides Title VII. In this context, the Supreme Court considered Ms. Espinoza's case.

B. *Espinoza v. Farah Mfg. Co.* (1973): The Opinions

As required of anyone making a claim under Title VII, Ms. Espinoza filed a timely complaint of discrimination with the Equal Employment Opportunity Commission (EEOC) claiming that Farah had discriminated against her based on her national origin, being Mexican. The EEOC is the administrative agency charged with, among other things, processing complaints of employment discrimination under Title VII, and if the EEOC so deems, the EEOC may proceed with the complaint of employment discrimination as the party who files suit in a federal court. The EEOC also creates regulations and other guidelines for employers as to whether particular practices may or may not constitute employment discrimination. The EEOC issued Ms. Espinoza a "right to sue" letter, allowing her to file a suit if she so chose. In 1970, Ms. Espinoza sued Farah in a federal district court in San Antonio, again alleging national origin discrimination. The district judge on September 21, 1971, granted her a summary judgment, deciding that she was entitled to a judgment as a matter of law, based largely on an EEOC guideline stating that discrimination based on alienage constituted national origin discrimination. The EEOC's guideline, quoted by Justice Thurgood Marshall in his opinion for the Court, stated:

> Because discrimination on the basis of citizenship has the effect of discriminating on the basis of national origin, a lawfully immigrated alien who is domiciled or residing in this country may not be discriminated against on the basis of his citizenship.[9]

The district court's opinion declared that Farah's "refusal to hire [Ms. Espinoza] was an unlawful employment practice" and enjoined Farah from continuing to follow its discriminatory policy against non-citizens. Farah appealed the district court's ruling to the Fifth Circuit Court of Appeals, who on May 31, 1972, reversed the judgment and concluded that Farah was correct, and that the discrimination based on "national origin" prohibited by Title VII did not include discrimination based on citizenship. The Fifth Circuit wrote that she was "not denied a job because of her Spanish surname, her Mexican heritage, her foreign ancestry, her own or her parents' birthplace—all of which characteristics she shared with the vast majority of Farah's employees." Ms. Espinoza appealed that decision to the United States Supreme Court, which heard argument on October 10, 1973. Justice Thurgood Marshall wrote the opinion on behalf of himself and seven other justices affirming the Fifth Circuit's opinion and holding that discrimination on the basis of alienage is not discrimination on the basis of national origin. Only one of the nine, Justice Douglas, dissented. Generally, Justice Marshall's reputation was that of being a champion of claimants of discriminatory treatment. He was the first black American to serve as a Supreme Court Justice, and prior to having been appointed to the bench by President Johnson in 1967, Justice Marshall had served as solicitor general for the United States in the Johnson administration. Justice Marshall was perhaps best known for representing the winning plaintiffs in *Brown*.

As is commonly done in analyzing the meaning of terms or in construing statutes like Title VII, Justice Marshall began his opinion by stating that the "plain language" of the term "national origin" refers "to the country where a person was born, or, more broadly, the country from which his or her ancestors came." Justice Marshall then examined the legislative history, which he described as "quite meager," and found generally that the legislative history supported the position that national origin did not include alienage. Justice Marshall found that the "only direct definition given the phrase 'national origin' is the following remark made on the floor of the House of Representatives by Congressman Roosevelt, Chairman of the House Subcommittee which reported the bill: 'It means the country from which you or your forebears came. . . . You may come from Poland, Czechoslovakia, England, France, or any other country.'" [10] The Court also noted that an earlier version of the statute had included the term "ancestry," but that word was later excluded, suggesting to the Court that Congress considered the terms "national origin" and "ancestry" synonymous.

The next reason provided by Justice Marshall for concluding that the term "national origin" in the anti-discrimination provisions of Title VII does not include alienage was that since 1914, the federal government itself, through Civil Service Commission regulations, had discriminated against aliens by denying them the right to enter competitive examination for federal employment, and since the federal government had a policy and a law (Title VII) forbidding national origin discrimination, the government's acts could not constitute discrimination based on national origin. [11] In Justice Marshall's words, interpreting the term "national origin" to embrace a citizenship requirement "would require us to conclude that Congress itself has repeatedly flouted its own declaration of policy," which the Court found was contrary to Congress's intent.

Ms. Espinoza's attorney claimed that the statutes and regulations discriminating against non-citizens in federal employment are unconstitutional under the Due Process Clause of the Fifth Amendment, but the Court refused to consider that claim in *Espinoza* because it considered the issue presented in this case as not whether Congress has the power to discriminate against aliens in federal employment, but rather, whether Congress intended to prohibit alienage discrimination in private employment. The Court could not conclude that Congress would at once continue the practice of requiring citizenship as a condition of federal employment and, at the same time, prevent private employers from doing likewise. If Ms. Espinoza's argument prevailed, the Court stated that a "rather bizarre result" would occur whereby Farah could not insist on United States citizenship as a condition of employment while the very agency charged with enforcing Title VII would itself be required by Congress to place that condition on its own personnel.

Frequently, courts defer to the regulations or guidelines issued by the administrative agencies charged with interpreting and enforcing laws, such as the EEOC in the case of Title VII, and Justice Marshall's opinion recognizes that an EEOC guideline, quoted above, at the time was one of the primary grounds for the district court ruling in favor of Ms. Espinoza. The Supreme Court chose not to "question the general validity of this guideline" but stated that it did not find it applicable or controlling in the case. Justice Marshall interpreted the guideline to refer to situations where "a citizenship requirement might be but one part of a wider scheme of unlawful national-origin discrimination" or where "a citizenship test [is used] as a pretext to disguise what is in fact national-origin discrimination." The opinion, following the holding of *Griggs v. Duke Power Co.* (1971), stated that Title VII "prohibits discrimination on the basis of citizenship whenever it has the purpose or effect of discriminating on the basis of national origin," including "not only overt discrimination but also practices that are fair in form, but discriminatory in operation." However, the Court found "no indication in the record that Farah's policy against employment of aliens had the purpose or effect of discriminating against persons of Mexican national origin." In fact (unsurprisingly in light of the demographics of the population in the San Antonio area), Farah had other employees of Mexican origin, all of whom were citizens. The record showed that persons of Mexican ancestry made up "more than 96% of the employees at the company's San Antonio division, and 97% of those doing the work for which Mrs. Espinoza applied." The Court found that while statistics like those

> do not automatically shield an employer from a charge of unlawful discrimination, the plain fact of the matter is that Farah does not discriminate against persons of Mexican national origin with respect to employment in the job Mrs. Espinoza sought. She was denied employment, not because of

the country of her origin, but because she had not yet achieved United States citizenship.

The Court also noted that the worker hired in place of Mrs. Espinoza had a Spanish surname. The opinion notes that the EEOC had previously taken the opposite interpretation of citizenship and national origin.

Finally, Justice Marshall rejected Ms. Espinoza's contention that she should have prevailed because Title VII protects all individuals from unlawful discrimination, regardless of whether they are citizens; the Court found that the question in that case was not whether aliens are protected from illegal discrimination, but what kinds of discrimination are illegal under Title VII. Justice Marshall explained:

> Certainly it would be unlawful for an employer to discriminate against aliens because of race, color, religion, sex, or national origin—for example, by hiring aliens of Anglo-Saxon background but refusing to hire those of Mexican or Spanish ancestry. Aliens are protected from illegal discrimination under the Act, but nothing in the Act makes it illegal to discriminate on the basis of citizenship or alienage.

Therefore, the Supreme Court ruled in favor of Farah and against Ms. Espinoza, and held that employers can discriminate based on alienage without violating Title VII's prohibition against national origin discrimination.

Justice Douglas wrote a stinging dissent, beginning with this observation: "It is odd that the Court which holds that a State may not bar an alien from the practice of law or deny employment to aliens can read a federal statute that prohibits discrimination in employment on account of 'national origin' so as to permit discrimination against aliens." According to Justice Douglas, alienage results from only one condition: being born outside the United States. Therefore, to Justice Douglas, Farah's policy *de facto* prefers those born in the United States. Justice Douglas also criticized the majority's construction of "national origin" as being more restrictive than race or sex.

Justice Douglas noted that in *Griggs*, a racial discrimination case, the Court said that Title VII prohibits practices, procedures, or tests neutral on their face, and even neutral in terms of intent, if they create artificial, arbitrary, and unnecessary barriers to employment when the barriers operate invidiously to discriminate on the basis of racial or other impermissible classification. In *Griggs*, the Court found the superficially neutral requirements of a test or diploma as being in fact discriminatory and unrelated to job performance. Justice Douglas likewise believed that Farah's policy imposing a citizenship requirement had no relation to job performance. Describing the targets of the discrimination as Chicanos, Justice Douglas stated that "Griggs, as I understood it until today, extends its protective principles to all, not to blacks alone." Justice Douglas then criticized the majority's interpretation of "national origin" as an "extraordinary departure from prior cases" and being contrary to the guidelines established by the EEOC, the agency provided by law with the responsibility of enforcing Title VII, to whose interpretation of the statute he would have given great weight. Justice Douglas wrote that no legislative history supported the majority's ruling, and that its "construction flies in the face of the underlying congressional policy of removing artificial, arbitrary, and unnecessary barrier(s) to employment." Finally, Justice Douglas made the following observations:

> Mrs. Espinoza is a permanent resident alien, married to an American citizen, and her children will be native-born American citizens. But that first generation has the greatest adjustments to make to their new country. Their unfamiliarity with America makes them the most vulnerable to exploitation and discriminatory treatment. They, of course, have the same obligation as American citizens to pay taxes, and they are subject to the draft on the same basis. But they have never received equal treatment in the job market. Writing of the immigrants of the late 1800's, Oscar Handlin has said: "For want of alternative, the immigrants took the lowest places in the ranks of industry. They suffered in consequence from the poor pay and miserable working conditions characteristic of the sweat-shops and the homework in the garment trades and in cigar making. But they were undoubtedly better off than the Irish and Germans of the 1840's for whom there had been no place at all." The Newcomers 24 (1959).
>
> The majority decides today that in passing sweeping legislation guaranteeing equal job opportunities, the Congress intended to help only the immigrant's children, excluding those "for whom there [is] no place at all." I cannot impute that niggardly an intent to Congress.

Justice Douglas' dissent in *Espinoza* was one of the last he wrote on the Court. Justice Douglas tended to side with the poor, indigent, and minorities in constitutional, criminal, and anti-discrimination type cases. He also authored an interesting and sole dissent in *Tijerina v. Henry* (1970) involving a class action claim brought by Reies López Tijerina challenging various types of discriminatory practices toward a group then described as "Indo-Hispano, also called Mexican, Mexican-American, and Spanish-American." In his *Tijerina* dissent, Justice Douglas responded to the contention that this prospective class was too vague to be meaningful: "One thing is not vague or uncertain, however, and that is that those who discriminate against members of this and other minority groups have little difficulty in isolating the objects of their discrimination."[12]

C. Latinos and Post-*Espinoza* Developments Involving National Origin Discrimination and Employment of Aliens

The Supreme Court in *Espinoza* held that employers could discriminate on the basis of alienage without violating Title VII. Section 703(e) of Title VII provides that notwithstanding other provisions, employer-defendants are entitled to a defense based on "a bona fide occupational qualification reasonably necessary to the normal operation of that particular business or enterprise" (BFOQ). Therefore, Espinoza stands for the proposition that for Title VII purposes, citizenship could be a BFOQ. Title VII explicitly forbids discrimination on the basis of national origin. The significance of *Espinoza* for Latinos in the American legal system is well summarized by Juan Perea's observation that *Espinoza* is the "single Supreme Court decision interpreting 'national origin' under Title VII."[13]

For Latinos, accent, language, and citizenship may in some instances be proxies for discrimination on the basis of "national origin." Courts and the EEOC have also recognized that other traits such as "short height" can be surrogates for "national origin" discrimination. In 2004, the EEOC "Guidelines on Discrimination Based on National Origin" included section 29 CFR sec. 1606.5, which interprets *Espinoza* as standing for the proposition that alienage discrimination is prohibited under Title VII if "the citizenship requirement has the purpose or effect of discriminating" on the basis of national origin. The EEOC's guidelines also included sections on "Speak English Only" rules and "Harassment."[14] The Supreme Court has yet to consider those issues, and lower courts have not always agreed. For this reason, a leading scholar in this area, Juan Perea, has advocated that Congress amend Title VII to explicitly cover discrimination based on "ethnicity" and/or ethnic traits.[15]

Accent discrimination, for instance, may manifest itself in several forms, and most notably in "the refusal to hire or promote an employee or applicant because of his or her accent or manner of speaking . . . [and] the harassment of an employee (either by supervisor, co-employee, or non-employee) because of his or her accent or manner of speaking."[16] In a leading case, a bilingual radio announcer whose show was in English (with Spanish words and phrases occasionally added) was fired because a consultant hired by the station determined that speaking Spanish hurt the station's ratings, and when the program director asked him to stop using Spanish in his broadcasts, and he refused, the radio station fired him. The Ninth Circuit Court of Appeals found that the radio station's limited English-only rule "was a programming decision motivated by marketing, ratings, and demographic concerns" and was a legitimate BFOQ.[17] Since language may be a BFOQ, courts uphold terminations and other actions by employers.[18]

Recently, and related to the English-only movement, English-only rules in the workplace have been implemented and challenged. Perhaps the most eloquent statement of the general position against English-only rules is from the oft-cited dissent of Judge Reinhardt in the Ninth Circuit *Spun Steak* case, where he wrote that

> the imposition of an English-only rule may mask intentional discrimination on the basis of national origin. Even those who support the majority's view acknowledge that "language can be a potent source of racial and ethnic discrimination." History is replete with language conflicts that attest, not only to the crucial importance of language to its speakers, but also to the widespread tactic of using language as a surrogate for attacks on ethnic identity.[19]

While some courts have found English-only rules to be permissible, for a variety of reasons,[20] more recent cases have resulted in favorable results to those challenging the English-only rules in the workplace either generally or in the manner they were applied together with other activity. The EEOC has set forth guidelines allowing an employee to establish a *prima facie* case in a disparate impact claim by proving the existence of an English-only policy, thereby shifting the burden to the employer to show a business necessity for the rule.[21]

Unlike most of the other chapters, this chapter deals with *statutory*, not *constitutional*, interpretation, and these are significantly different. One of the most significant differences is that if Congress disagrees with the Supreme Court's interpretation of a congressional statute (or a regulation, for that matter), Congress can amend the law to "correct" or supersede the Court's ruling. By contrast, ever since *Marbury v. Madison* (1803), the Supreme Court has generally been considered the final arbiter of conflicting interpretations of the Constitution. Among the notable instances where Congress has passed a law to correct the Supreme Court's interpretation of Title VII are the Pregnancy Discrimination Act (PDA) of 1978 and the Civil Rights Act of 1991. Congress passed the PDA to correct and overrule the Supreme Court's ruling in *General Electric Co. v. Gilbert* (1976), where the Court held that pregnancy discrimination was not discrimination on the basis of "sex," but rather, discrimination against "pregnant people." Congress passed the Civil Rights Act of 1991 to overrule several opinions of the Rehnquist Court. Throughout the 1980s, a series of Rehnquist Court opinions made Title VII actions more and more difficult for plaintiffs. Perhaps the high point of this trend was *Wards Cove Packing v. Atonio* (1989).[22]

Atonio did not involve Latinos, but the facts resemble those confronting Latinos in parts of the United States. *Atonio* involved claims of employment discrimination by a class of Filipinos, Native Alaskan, and other nonwhite cannery workers. As the dissenters wrote, the facts in this case have characteristics "in particular, the segregation of housing and dining facilities and the stratification of jobs along racial and ethnic lines—[which] bear an unsettling resemblance to aspects of a plantation economy."[23]

Nevertheless, the Supreme Court found that the plaintiffs had failed to establish a *prima facie* case of discrimination. In so doing, the Court effectively overruled (or at least undermined) *Griggs*, reversed notions of over- and underrepresentation,[24] and established new and onerous burdens for plaintiffs in Title VII disparate impact cases.[25] Congress passed the Civil Rights Act of 1991 over the protests of President George Herbert Walker Bush and others who dubbed it a "quota bill."[26] The Civil Rights Act of 1991 effectively breathed new life into Title VII.

As far as alienage discrimination, notwithstanding Farah's practices, many other employers in the United States have hired aliens, whether documented ("legal") or undocumented ("illegal"). In 1886, the Supreme Court ruled in the landmark *Yick Wo v. Hopkins*[27] case that aliens were entitled to the equal protection of laws pursuant to the Fourteenth Amendment because that clause refers to "people" and not citizens. That case involved a local ordinance in San Francisco that sought to discriminate against Chinese laundry operators based on the fact that they were not United States citizens. Notably, the Fourteenth Amendment refers to governmental activity, not private activity. In other words, there must be *state action* for a person to establish an equal protection violation. The Supreme Court more recently struck down as unconstitutional a statute in Puerto Rico that prevented non-citizens from obtaining professional engineering licenses in *Examining Bd. of Engineers, Architects and Surveyors v. Flores de Otero* (1976), brought by a Mexican national, María Flores de Otero, and a Spaniard, Sergio Pérez Nogueiro, both of whom resided in Puerto Rico and were qualified except for the citizenship requirement.

While Title VII has not been amended with respect to the Court's ruling in *Espinoza*, and the Supreme Court has never overruled *Espinoza*, a different congressional law has altered, in part, the practical effect of *Espinoza*'s holding. In 1986, Congress passed the Immigration Reform and Control Act (IRCA),[28] whose main purpose was to curtail the hiring of illegal aliens. IRCA contains criminal provisions against employers who knowingly hire illegal aliens and mandates that prospective employers obtain certain proof of citizenship or legal residence before hiring anyone, including a form called I-9. Part of IRCA prohibits discrimination based on alienage, precisely the position Ms. Espinoza had taken as being the law under Title VII. Almost ten years after *Espinoza*, President Ronald Reagan and Congress, through IRCA, granted amnesty to millions of people who had been living in the United States without proper immigration papers. As part of the negotiation leading to the passage of IRCA, Congress included a provision making it unlawful for an employer to refuse to hire legal resident aliens (people in the same immigration status as Ms. Espinoza). While not overruling *Espinoza*, IRCA has created new potential liability for employers who have policies like Farah's. Ironically, since Title VII applies only to employers with more than fifteen employees, whereas IRCA applies to employers with four or more employees, IRCA's scope is in reality broader than what would have been covered had the Supreme Court ruled in favor of Ms. Espinoza.

As for Farah, Ms. Espinoza's lawsuit was but one of its problems with the workforce at the time. In June of 1971, Farah acquired Texas Manufacturing Company, thereby absorbing about three hundred non-citizen employees whom it declared it would not discharge. As the *Espinoza* case was making its way through the court system, on July 1972, Farah's workers' union called a strike and for a nationwide boycott. According to one source, "Recession, bad publicity from the boycott, and poor management all hurt Farah. By 1976, [Farah] began to move his operations across the border . . . [and shut down the] San Antonio factory."[29]

United States v. Brignoni-Ponce (1975), Law and Order on the Border

A. Background

"Racial profiling" became a popular phrase and politically charged issue in the late 1990s throughout the United States. For Mexican-Americans living in border areas, as well as other Latinos and Americans, "racial profiling," or the notion that law enforcement personnel use a person's physical appearance as it relates to stereotypical perceptions of an ethnic or racial group as a basis for deciding likelihood of illegal activity, had been in practice long before the 1990s. Prior to 1924, immigration laws in the United States were limited, as were enforcement and exclusion. In fact, large numbers of people living in the United States today are descendants of immigrants who came to the United States in the nineteenth and twentieth century. Discrimination and some hostility toward immigrants is nothing new in the United States, nor is it a phenomenon unique to Latinos. For instance, discrimination against Asians, Southern and Eastern Europeans, Germans, and Irish, to name a few, has been written about elsewhere. The first significant piece of immigration legislation in the twentieth century was the Immigration and Nationality Act of 1924 ("the 1924 Act"). The 1924 Act created quotas for legal immigration based on country of origin, giving priority to immigrants from Western Europe.

The 1924 Act also created the Border Patrol, which since 1924 has been the federal agency primarily responsible for preventing the illegal entry of persons, things, and contraband into the United States. The Border Patrol has had many changes and the number of personnel increased in the late 1960s, shortly before the Court considered the Border Patrol's actions in stopping a vehicle its agents suspected of transporting aliens illegally into the United States in *Brignoni-Ponce* on a highway in Southern California. The intensity of immigration law enforcement waxed and waned depending on the relative strength of the economy of the United States, the corresponding desire for cheap, plentiful Mexican labor, and other factors. In other words, in times of economic growth and prosperity and when there was a high demand for Mexican labor in agriculture, low wage services, and light manufacturing industries, immigration laws were enforced less rigorously. By contrast, at times of economic downturn, recessions, and particularly during the Great Depression, the Border Patrol and other federal immigration law enforcement agencies aggressively pursued Mexicans for deportation. The massive deportation and repatriation of people of Mexican origin in the 1930s has been the subject of scholarly publications and has been portrayed in movies.

In 1954, the United States government launched "Operation Wetback," which had the stated goal of cracking down on illegal immigration and on bringing a military approach to the problem of undocumented immigrants crossing the Rio Grande and other border regions from Mexico. The 1964 Bracero program, which involved Mexican "guest workers," the initiation of maquiladoras, or in-bond "twin plants," and the 1965 Immigration Act changed the tone of immigration policy. However, in the late 1960s and early 1970s, with increasing numbers of migrants from Mexico, easier access to transportation, and Mexico's many problems, concerns increased in the United States about uncontrolled or excessive immigration from Mexico.

The Burger Court, as described in prior chapters, had begun to reverse the course of many liberal decisions of the Warren Court. In the context of criminal procedure, this meant that Burger Court decisions began a trend (which accelerated during the Rehnquist Court) of producing results reversing, limiting, or undercutting decisions of the Warren Court, which were perceived by conservatives as undermining law enforcement, laws, order, and as benefiting criminals. In issues of constitutional criminal procedure, one of the most significant and heavily litigated areas has been the Fourth Amendment, which includes searches and seizures. Every time law enforcement commits an arrest, a search of a person, house, car, or other place, the Fourth Amendment is implicated. In the 1960s, the Warren Court expanded the Exclusionary Rule, which requires that any evidence obtained as a result of an unconstitutional search or seizure be excluded from any future criminal prosecution. In *Mapp v. Ohio* (1960), the Court ruled that the Exclusionary Rule had been "incorporated" by the Fourteenth Amendment to apply not only against the federal government but also against state governments and law enforcement agencies.

The Fourth Amendment has two basic principles: (1) searches and seizures with warrants issued by magistrates must be supported by probable cause; and (2) all searches and seizures must be "reasonable." Recognizing that in many circumstances law enforcement cannot practically do their job and obtain a warrant from a magistrate before taking each and every action, the Court has recognized numerous exceptions that do not require a warrant before police action. Some of these exceptions include the "open fields" exception, the "hot pursuit" exception, and the "plain view" exception. In *Brignoni-Ponce,* two other exceptions were implicated: the "*Terry* stop" exception and the "border" exception. In the Court's landmark *Terry v. Ohio* (1968) decision, the Court approved a limited search—a pat-down for weapons—for the protection of investigating officers. The facts of *Terry* were that an officer thought two men were "casing" a shop before committing a robbery, and that the police officer, fearing for his safety and that of members of the public, patted down the suspects and uncovered illegal guns that they were carrying. Because of the limited nature of the intrusion, the Court found that these "*Terry* stops" were justified even though the facts did not amount to the probable cause required for an arrest. Subsequent cases expanded the scope of the *Terry* stops. The "border" exception refers to the fact that the government has a right to check people and vehicles entering the United States even without warrants or probable cause. Prior to *Brignoni-Ponce,* the Supreme Court had considered some cases involving border searches. Most relevant was the Court's decision in *Almeida-Sanchez v. United States* (1973), decided just two years before *Brignoni-Ponce,* where the Court ruled that "roving patrols" of the Border Patrol could not conduct warrantless searches of vehicles approximately twenty miles north of the border without violating the Fourth Amendment.

B. *United States v. Brignoni-Ponce* (1975): The Opinions

As a part of the Border Patrol's regular traffic-checking operations in Southern California, the Border Patrol operated a fixed checkpoint on Interstate Highway 5 south of San Clemente. On the evening of March 11, 1973, the checkpoint was closed because of bad weather, but two officers were observing northbound traffic from a patrol car parked at the side of the highway. The road was dark, and they were using the patrol car's headlights to illuminate passing cars. The Border Patrol agents pursued the car Mr. Brignoni-Ponce rode in, and stopped it. When questioned later, the Border Patrol agents testified that the only reason they had stopped the car was that the three people in the car "appeared to be of Mexican descent." During the stop, the Border Patrol officers questioned the men about their citizenship and learned that the passengers were aliens who had entered the country illegally. All three were arrested, and Mr. Brignoni-Ponce was charged with two counts of knowingly transporting illegal immigrants.

At the criminal trial, Mr. Brignoni-Ponce's attorney moved to suppress the testimony about the two passengers, claiming that this evidence was the "fruit of an illegal seizure." The trial court denied the motion, the aliens testified at trial as to their status, and Mr. Brignoni-Ponce was convicted. Mr. Brignoni-Ponce then appealed the conviction to the Ninth Circuit Court of Appeals, which issued its opinion on June 14, 1974. The Ninth Circuit concluded that looking Mexican alone did not constitute a reasonable basis to suspect illegal activity that would warrant the Border Patrol stopping Mr. Brignoni-Ponce's car. Accordingly, any evidence gathered from the illegal seizure should have been excluded under the Exclusionary Rule. The United States appealed to the Supreme Court, which accepted *certiorari* review on October 15, 1974, heard argument on February 18, 1975, and issued its opinion on June 30, 1975. Andrew Frey argued for the United States to the Supreme Court and John J. Clearly argued for Mr. Brignoni-Ponce.

Justice Powell wrote the opinion of the Court, which was joined in full by six other justices. Two other justices joined solely in the result and wrote concurring opinions. Justice Powell succinctly described the only issue for the Court to decide as follows: "whether a roving patrol may stop a vehicle in an area near the border and question its occupants *when the only ground for suspicion is that the occupants appear to be of Mexican ancestry*" (emphasis added). All nine justices agreed that looking like a person of Mexican origin or ancestry, *alone,* did not provide adequate basis for the Border Patrol to pull a car over in ordinary traffic away from border checkpoints. The officers that stopped the car Mr. Brignoni-Ponce was riding in were in a roving patrol, not a fixed checkpoint.

In *Brignoni-Ponce,* the government took the position that, at least in Mexican border areas, a person's "apparent Mexican ancestry alone justifies belief that he or she is an alien" and satisfies the requirement of the Immigration and Nationality Act (INA). The government claimed that two statutes allowed Border Patrol agents to stop cars without warrants in the border areas. Section 287(a)(1) of the INA, which authorizes any INS employee to interrogate any alien or person believed to be an alien as to his right to be in the United States, without a warrant, anywhere. The government also relied on section 287(a)(3) of the INA, which authorizes warrantless searches "within a reasonable distance from any external boundary," which then existing regulations defined as one hundred miles, "to board and search for aliens any vessel within the territorial waters of the United States and any railway car, aircraft, conveyance, or vehicle." The Border Patrol interpreted these statutes as granting it authority to stop moving vehicles and question occupants about their citizenship, even when officers had no reason to believe that the occupants were aliens or that other aliens might be concealed. Justice Powell noted that no law of Congress can violate the Constitution, so the Court had to decide whether the Fourth Amendment allows those kinds of random vehicle stops in the Mexican border areas. Mr. Brignoni-Ponce's attorney contended that these searches generally, and the search of Mr. Brignoni-Ponce's car specifically, violated the Fourth Amendment.

The Fourth Amendment applies to all seizures of the person, including seizures that involve only a brief detention short of traditional arrest. Whenever a law enforcement officer "accosts an individual and restrains his freedom to walk away," the person has been seized. The Fourth Amendment requires seizures to be "reasonable." Determining the reasonableness of searches, according to Justice Powell, involves balancing "between the public interest and the individual's right to personal security free from arbitrary interference by law officers."

On the one hand, Justice Powell stated that the government made a "convincing" showing that the public interest "demands effective measures to prevent the illegal entry of aliens at the Mexican border." Justice Powell then discussed various estimates of the number of illegal immigrants in the United States, which varied widely from 1 to 12 million, and in footnote 1 he cited testimony of the commissioner of the INS for the Immigration and Nationality Subcommittee of the House Judiciary Committee in 1972 and the INS' annual reports in 1974. Justice Powell then noted that regardless of the number, "these aliens create significant economic and social problems, competing with citizens and legal resident aliens for jobs, and generating extra demand for social services. The aliens themselves are vulnerable to exploitation because they cannot complain of substandard working conditions without risking deportation." Over the decades following *Brignoni-Ponce,* as a result of intensified immigration and the expansion of government entitlement benefits, these concerns became voiced with increasing frequency.

The government estimated that 85% of the aliens illegally in the country were from Mexico, an estimate which the Court found confirmed by "the consistently high proportion of Mexican nationals in the number of deportable aliens arrested each year. In 1970, for example, 80% of the deportable aliens arrested were from Mexico [whereas in 1974] the figure was 92%." Justice Powell further described some of the problems faced by the Border Patrol:

The Mexican border is almost 2,000 miles long, and even a vastly reinforced Border Patrol would find it impossible to prevent illegal border crossings. Many aliens cross the Mexican border on foot, miles away from patrolled areas, and then purchase transportation from the border area to inland cities, where they find jobs and elude the immigration authorities. Others gain entry on valid temporary border-crossing permits, but then violate the conditions of their entry. Most of these aliens leave the border area in private vehicles, often assisted by professional "alien smugglers." The Border Patrol's traffic-checking operations are designed to prevent this inland movement. They succeed in apprehending some illegal entrants and smugglers, and they deter the movement of others by threatening apprehension and increasing the cost of illegal transportation.

The Court then balanced the valid public interest with the interferences with individual liberty that result when officers stop cars and question their occupants. Justice Powell, based on the government's briefs submitted to the Court, concluded that the "intrusion is modest," taking less than a minute, and involving only a few questions about citizenship absent other reasonable suspicion. Therefore, because of the limited nature of the intrusion, the Court found these stops justified on facts that do not amount to the probable cause required for an arrest, following *Terry*, where the Court approved limited pat-down searches.

In the case of border searches and seizures, Justice Powell and six other justices concluded that because of the importance of the governmental interest, the minimal intrusion of a brief stop, and the absence of practical alternatives for policing the border, "when an officer's observations lead him reasonably to suspect that a particular vehicle may contain aliens who are illegally in the country, he may stop the car briefly and investigate the circumstances that provoke suspicion." The officer may question the driver and passengers about their citizenship and immigration status, and to explain suspicious circumstances, but any further detention or search must be based on consent or probable cause.

Justice Powell stated that the Court was unwilling to let the Border Patrol dispense entirely with the reasonable suspicion requirement to justify roving-patrol stops. In the context of border area stops, the reasonableness requirement of the Fourth Amendment demands something more than "the broad and unlimited discretion sought by the Government." Justice Powell noted that "[r]oads near the border carry not only aliens seeking to enter the country illegally, but a large volume of legitimate traffic as well." The Court then referred to three large border metropolitan areas and their population in the 1970s (San Diego, California, 1.4 million; El Paso, Texas, 360,000; and the Brownsville-McAllen, Texas, area, 320,000). The Court reaffirmed a legal presumption that border residents are law-abiding:

> We are confident that substantially all of the traffic in these cities is lawful and that relatively few of their residents have any connection with the illegal entry and transportation of aliens. To approve roving-patrol stops of all vehicles in the border area, without any suspicion that a particular vehicle is carrying

illegal immigrants, would subject the residents of these and other areas to potentially unlimited interference with their use of the highways, solely at the discretion of Border Patrol officers. The only formal limitation on that discretion appears to be [the 100 air miles from the border]. Thus, if we approved the Government's position in this case, Border Patrol officers could stop motorists at random for questioning, day or night, anywhere within 100 air miles of the 2,000-mile border, on a city street, a busy highway, or a desert road, without any reason to suspect that they have violated any law.

Having balanced the competing interests, Justice Powell found that the legitimate needs of law enforcement did not require this degree of interference with lawful traffic. The Court would require that the Border Patrol articulate a "reasonable suspicion for stops" under the Fourth Amendment.

The Court likewise rejected the Government's argument that Congress' broad plenary power on enforcing legal alien entry justified stopping persons who might be aliens for questioning about their citizenship and immigration status; the Court found this use of the power too broad in light of the Fourth Amendment rights of citizens who might be mistaken for aliens. According to the Court, "Except at the border and its functional equivalents, officers on roving patrol may stop vehicles only if they are aware of specific articulable facts, together with rational inferences from those facts, that reasonably warrant suspicion that the vehicles contain aliens who may be illegally in the country."

While the Court could not list all the facts and circumstances, Justice Powell did discuss some factors that might apply to determining whether law enforcement had reasonable suspicion to stop a car in the border area. The Court cited factors in prior cases, such as proximity to the border, patterns of road traffic, the driver's behavior (erratic driving or evading officers), driving certain cars (e.g., station wagons, which may have large compartments for fold-down seats used to conceal aliens), and heavily loaded vehicles. The Court seemed to approve the argument in a reply brief by the government that "trained officers can recognize the characteristic appearance of persons who live in Mexico, relying on such factors as the mode of dress and haircut."

Then Justice Powell's opinion repeats the gist of the argument: the Government's candid, single factor to justify stopping the car—"the apparent Mexican ancestry of the occupants"—would justify neither a reasonable belief that they were aliens nor a reasonable belief that the car concealed other aliens who were illegally in the country. However, the Court said that with other factors, looking Mexican might justify a search as being reasonable. In the *Brignoni-Ponce* case, the "likelihood that any given person of Mexican ancestry is an alien is high enough to make Mexican appearance a relevant factor, but standing alone it does not justify stopping all Mexican-Americans to ask if they are aliens." The Court also rejected, in footnote 11, the government's argument that the location of this particular stop should be considered in deciding whether the officers had adequate reason to stop the car, because the Court considered it "an after-the-fact justification" which had not been presented at the trial court or the Ninth Circuit.

Justice William Rehnquist, a Nixon appointee and Arizona Republican, concurred with the result, but noted that the opinion was "joined by a somewhat different majority than that which comprised the *Almeida Sanchez* Court . . . [and that by] its terms and by its reasoning [was] concerned only with the type of stop involved in this case." According to Justice Rehnquist, just as travelers entering the country may be stopped and searched without probable cause and without founded suspicion, national security concerns allow cars to be searched. Finally, he noted that "these and similar situations, such as agricultural inspections and highway roadblocks to apprehend known fugitives, [would not be] . . . in any way constitutionally suspect by reason of today's decision."

Justice Douglas also wrote a concurring opinion, but the gist of his opinion was totally different. Justice Douglas was primarily concerned about the trend of the Court to expand the scope of the *Terry* stop and its "suspicion test," which he found to be (both at the time of *Terry* in 1968, and at the time of *Brignoni-Ponce* in 1975) "an unjustified weakening of the Fourth Amendment's protection of citizens from arbitrary interference by the police." As to why the Court's ruling was correct, Justice Douglas succinctly stated the holding that "the stopping of [Mr. Brignoni-Ponce's] automobile solely because its occupants appeared to be of Mexican ancestry was a patent violation of the Fourth Amendment." Regarding the expansion of *Terry,* Justice Douglas noted that the fears he had voiced in *Terry* about the "weakening of the Fourth Amendment have regrettably been borne out by subsequent events." Justice Douglas noted that the suspicion test had been expanded beyond the pursuit of violent crimes, to drug investigations, apprehension of illegal aliens, and "has come to be viewed as a legal construct for the regulation of a general investigatory police power." Justice Douglas cited examples of border stops that would be potentially dangerous and violative of the Fourth Amendment in his view, including a "station wagon near the border because there was a spare tire in the back seat," low-riders, and others which led Justice Douglas to conclude that the "suspicion test has indeed brought a state of affairs where the police may stop citizens on the highway on the flimsiest of justifications." Justice Douglas noted that this was the first case in seven years where the Court had invalidated a stop on the basis of the suspicion standard, but he wrote that that standard would not significantly protect "the comprehensive right of personal liberty in the face of governmental intrusion, that is embodied in the Fourth Amendment."

C. The Significance of *Brignoni* and Post-*Brignoni* Developments to Latinos in the American Legal System

Brignoni-Ponce stands for the proposition that looking Mexican, even in a border area, does not *itself* create a "reasonable suspicion" that the "Mexican-looking" driver or passenger is violating some law, such as immigration laws or laws prohibiting contraband or drugs. The same day the Court issued its decision in *Brignoni-Ponce,* it ruled in *United States v. Ortiz* (1975), another case involving border searches, that the Border Patrol could not set up fixed checkpoints too far away from the border because the Fourth Amendment requires probable cause of searches in such cases. In other words, fixed checkpoints are permissible at the border and near the border, but as the traffic moves toward the interior of the United States, fixed points to check for aliens illegally in the United States was not allowed without probable cause. Just one year after *Brignoni-Ponce,* the Court limited *Brignoni-Ponce's* holding in another border car search case, *United States v. Martinez-Fuerte* (1976), where the Court found the Border Patrol's brief stop of vehicles at permanent checkpoints north of the Mexican border, where cars would be sent off for an additional inspection, was permissible even where the basis of the suspicion was that the occupants "looked Mexican."

Brignoni-Ponce is particularly significant for Latinos in the American legal system because all nine justices of the Supreme Court agreed that being "Mexican-looking" alone does not justify a warrantless search, stop, seizure, or arrest as being "reasonable," even at the border. However, the Court in *Brignoni-Ponce* also made clear that being "Mexican-looking" can be one of several factors that would make a warrantless search "reasonable" and therefore constitutionally consistent with the Fourth Amendment in border areas. Since *Brignoni-Ponce,* lower courts have subsequently created various guidelines or criteria for what factors can be considered in addition to being "Mexican-looking." The two largest federal lower circuit courts covering the border, the Ninth (which includes California and Arizona) and the Fifth (which includes Texas) have included the following as some factors that may justify a warrantless search or seizure as being "reasonable." A Fifth Circuit case from 2003 indicated that the reasonable suspicion factors in roving-patrol searches include proximity to the border, characteristics of the area, usual traffic patterns, agent's previous experience in detecting illegal activity, behavior of the driver, particular aspects or characteristics of the vehicle, information about recent illegal trafficking of aliens or narcotics in the area, and the "number, appearance, and behavior of the passengers." [1]

Notwithstanding *Brignoni-Ponce*'s holding, Alfredo Mirandé has made a credible case for what he terms a "Mexican exception" to the Fourth Amendment, citing a series of decisions which reflect that Hispanic appearance is a factor that, together with other factors like "driving a late model sedan," "wearing a cap," "driving a car that appears to be weighed down," have been used to stop drivers.[2] Cheech Marín's comic movie *Born in East L.A.* chronicles the plight of a United States citizen of Mexican descent who is wrongly deported to Mexico and who tries to return to his birth country.

In considering checkpoints outside the Mexican border area, the Rehnquist Court found them unconstitutional in *City of Indianapolis v. Edmond* (2000), where the Court concluded that drug interdiction checkpoints at roadblocks on cities in Indiana violated the Fourth Amendment. The Court distinguished *United States v. Martinez-Fuerte* (1976) because the border region is different due to the "formidable law enforcement problems posed by the northbound tide of illegal entrants"; the Court noted that checkpoints away from the border itself, but near the border, were "made necessary by the difficulty of guarding the border's entire length." [3]

Throughout the 1980s interdiction of illegal drug smuggling became an increasingly more important function of the Border Patrol and other officials securing the United States border and its points of entry. Interdicting the smuggling of aliens and drugs became increasingly difficult as smugglers became more sophisticated. For instance, agents have uncovered long, elaborate tunnels that smugglers created to subvert Border Patrol checkpoints. As law enforcement became more adept at intercepting drug smuggling, drug smugglers and traffickers developed additional, inhumane methods of transporting drugs into the United States. Consistent with the Rehnquist Court's inclination to provide greater latitude to law enforcement and to construe narrowly constitutional protections, the Court found no violation of the Fourth Amendment in *United States v. Montoya de Hernandez* (1985), where a Colombian woman, after an extended warrantless detention at Los Angeles International Airport because she was profiled as an "alimentary canal smuggler," finally passed eighty-eight balloons that she had ingested containing large quantities of cocaine. In dissent, Justice Brennan (joined by Justice Marshall) referred to the incident as a "disgusting and saddening episode at our Nation's border"[4] and added that no warrant was sought until almost twenty-four hours had passed after her detainment, and she was not arrested until almost twenty-seven hours from the time her detainment began. Justice Brennan noted that "indefinite involuntary incommunicado detentions 'for investigation' are the hallmark of a police state, not a free society."

The military presence at the Mexican border goes back to the middle of the nineteenth century, but after *Brignoni-Ponce*, militarization increased significantly. The Border Patrol, a highly trained, specialized, and professional unit, has increased not only in numbers, but also in technological capacities for tracking smuggling. Abuses by Border Patrol agents have been reported in the media and in law cases from time to time. The Border Patrol is hardly primarily responsible for the increase in border violence. Drug cartels, smugglers, coyotes, and others have become more heavily armed, institutional, and ruthless, and are responsible for many of the atrocities to people in border areas. Similarly, Mexican police officers have been less than completely blame-free in some episodes of violence to people along the border. While many immigrants that cross from Mexico do so seeking a better life through hard work for themselves and their families, there are also criminals who cross through the border. In the late 1990s, perceptions that the border and immigration were "out of control" or that the Border Patrol was doing an inadequate job of excluding aliens from Mexico led to a rise in vigilantism. Apart from individual acts of vigilantism, groups also organized with the stated and avowed purpose of stopping immigrants from coming to the United States.

Plyler v. Doe (1982)

and Educating Children of Illegal Aliens

A. Background

The controversial *Plyler v. Doe* (1982) case resulted from a convergence of factors during the 1970s and early 1980s. At its core, *Plyler* raised the question of who should pay to educate children whose parents migrated to the United States "illegally," without proper immigration documents or compliance with federal immigration laws. First, beginning with FDR's New Deal, and accelerating in the post–World War II era, particularly after LBJ's "Great Society," benefits or "entitlements" that the federal government and state governments became obligated to provide to citizens and those legally residing in the United States increased dramatically. Foremost among those was public education. Additionally, due to a variety of factors, immigration to the United States, including illegal immigration from Mexico, increased tremendously through the 1960s and 1970s. The specter of a border out of control, a "flood of illegal aliens," and other images made their way onto the national scene in the United States. Because the Constitution mandates that people become U.S. citizens as a result of being born in the United States, as opposed to basing citizenship on other limited criteria such as blood lines (as in some European countries), there were also fears that pregnant Mexican women would "run across the border" in droves to deliver their babies in the United States, thereby apparently vesting them with citizenship and its "entitlements." [1]

Also at the forefront in the United States during this time period, when public expenditures and commitments greatly expanded, were the worst economic circumstances in decades, including "stagflation," recession, and other economic problems partially blamed on the gas crisis in the 1970s. Blockbuster movies during the 1970s such as *Jaws, Towering Inferno,* and others expressed increasing sensations of losing control.

The Court's rulings on constitutional matters had also expanded the scope of constitutional protections, rights, and interests in many areas, including employment and alienage. The Court ruled in a series of cases that states could not impinge on the fundamental right to travel by denying newly arrived citizens in the new state welfare or other benefits that other residents were entitled to. In *Matthews v. Diaz* (1976), a case where a Cuban-American man who was a resident alien filed a class action against the federal government through the Secretary of Health, Education, and Welfare, the Supreme Court distinguished between discrimination based on alienage that states could engage in (which was limited) and discrimination based on alienage by the federal government. Specifically, the Court upheld the constitutionality of a five-year continuous residency requirement for non-citizens to qualify for Medicare benefits. In ruling against Mr. Diaz, the Court found that due to the federal government's exclusive jurisdiction over immigration affairs, it could discriminate against aliens in a manner that states could not, consistent with equal protection.

Plyler involved a constitutional challenge under the Equal Protection Clause based on a deprivation of educational opportunities in public schools in Texas. One issue was whether the Equal Protection Clause applied to aliens illegally in the United States as opposed to legal resident aliens, who were clearly covered. Additionally, *Plyler* seemed to raise questions similar to *San Antonio ISD v Rodriguez* (1973) (Chapter 6) about the importance of public education. Would the Court, just nine years after issuing its 5–4 decision in *Rodriguez* that education was not a fundamental right entitled to strict scrutiny review, reverse itself? If only a "rational review" standard applied, would the Court find the pressures placed on Texas' fiscal health in providing free or discounted services to children of illegal aliens a rational reason to treat them differently from other children living in Texas and showing up at a public school? The Burger Court that considered *Plyler* was virtually identical to the Burger Court that had considered *Rodriguez,* the sole change being that President Ford had appointed Justice John Paul Stevens, a moderate Republican from Illinois, to the Court when Justice William Douglas resigned in 1975.

As the Fifth Circuit's opinion in *Plyler* states, "Texas commands the free public education of its children. The State, however, extends that command only to those children legally within its borders." In 1975, Texas amended its education code to allow school districts to charge tuition to undocumented children. The Tyler Independent School District in East Texas implemented a policy of charging tuition of $1,000 per year for each undocumented child as a prerequisite for enrolling in one of its public schools. In September of 1977, a person known in the court papers in the litigation as J and R Doe, together with other parents of undocumented children, sued the Tyler ISD in federal court in Tyler, Texas, seeking to enjoin them from enforcing that policy and to have the policy declared unconstitutional. At the time the Does filed suit, James Plyler was Tyler ISD's superintendent. The presiding federal district judge was the infamous Judge William Wayne Justice, a liberal who presided over many famous civil rights cases during his tenure on the bench, including a case declaring Texas' prison system unconstitutional.

At the trial court, an expert testified that "the exclusion of a child from education locks the child into a life of poverty" and on examination by the trial judge, one of the defendants' witnesses "conceded that the plight of an uneducated illegal alien approaches a state of serfdom." On September 14, 1978, Judge Justice issued an injunction and declared that the state law, Texas Education Code section 21.031, and Tyler ISD's tuition policy, violated equal protection. The Fifth Circuit Court of Appeals issued its opinion on October 20, 1980, affirming the district court as to the injunction and the finding of an equal protection violation. The Fifth Circuit wrote that in Texas and other border states, "the illegal immigration of aliens is a hotly debated, many-faceted political and economic issue" and that the basis of much of the resentment sprang from the federal government not enforcing the immigration laws "and the fears that the aliens illegally in the United States will depress local labor markets or drain states' social programs." The Fifth Circuit further wrote that these fears served as the basis for statutes like the Texas law and Tyler ISD's tuition policy.

B. *Plyler v. Doe* (1982): The Opinions

The Court heard argument on December 1, 1981, and issued its decision on June 15, 1982. Justice Brennan delivered the 5–4 opinion of the Court, joined by Justices Marshall, Blackmun, Powell, and Stevens. Justice Brennan began by phrasing the issues as whether, "consistent with the Equal Protection Clause of the Fourteenth Amendment, Texas may deny to undocumented school-age children the free public education that it provides to children who are citizens of the United States or legally admitted aliens." Before answering the question, Justice Brennan's opinion discusses the history of immigration laws in the United States, noting that since the late nineteenth century, the United States has restricted immigration and made unsanctioned entry a crime. The Court then recognized that despite "these legal restrictions, a substantial number of persons have succeeded in unlawfully entering the United States, and now live within various States" including Texas.

The Court then discussed changes in Texas' education laws, particularly that in May of 1975, the Texas Legislature revised the laws "to withhold from local school districts any state funds for the education of children who were not 'legally admitted' into the United States" and authorized local school districts to deny enrollment in public schools to children not "legally admitted." *Plyler* was consolidated for briefing and argument with *In re Alien Children Education Litigation* (1982), which had also challenged the constitutionality of Texas' changes to the education laws to exclude children whose parents migrated to the United States without legal papers.

Justice Brennan rejected arguments from the State of Texas and others that the Fourteenth Amendment does not apply to undocumented aliens because of their immigration status, in other words, that they were not "persons within the jurisdiction" of Texas, and therefore had no right to the equal protection of Texas' laws. Justice Brennan quoted the portions of the Fourteenth Amendment providing that "[n]o State shall . . . deprive any person of life, liberty, or property, without due process of law; nor deny to any person within its jurisdiction the equal protection of the laws." According to the Court, regardless of immigration status, "an alien is surely a 'person' in any ordinary sense of that term." In support, the Court cited precedent of prior Supreme Court cases going back to the nineteenth century, including the landmark *Yick Wo v. Hopkins* (1886) case, which involved a successful challenge to a San Francisco ordinance discriminating against owners of laundromats of Chinese descent. The Court cited *Matthews v. Diaz* (1976) for the proposition that like the Fourteenth Amendment's Equal Protection Clause, the Fifth Amendment (which does not explicitly mention equal protection) has an "equal protection component" that protects illegal aliens from invidious discrimination by the federal government.

The State of Texas argued that those cases were different and that the Equal Protection Clause directs a state to afford its protection only to persons *within* its jurisdiction, while the due process clauses of the Fifth and Fourteenth Amendments contain no limiting phrase. According to Texas, persons who have entered illegally are not "within the jurisdiction" of a state even if physically present in the state. Justice Brennan stated, "Neither our cases nor the logic of the Fourteenth Amendment supports that constricting construction" of the phrase "within its jurisdiction." According to Justice Brennan's opinion, the due process and equal protection guarantees in the Fourteenth Amendment are "universal in their application, to all persons within the territorial jurisdiction, without regard to any differences of race, of color, or of nationality," citing *Yick Wo*. Limiting the construction of the term "within the jurisdiction" would, according to the Court, undermine the "principal purpose for which the Equal Protection Clause was incorporated in the Fourteenth Amendment." In support, Justice Brennan cited speeches and legislative history from Representative John Bingham and Senator Jacob Howard in the 1860s. According to the Court, the "Fourteenth Amendment extends to anyone, citizen or stranger, who is subject to the laws of a State, and reaches into every corner of a State's territory." Since a person in the state is subject to the civil and criminal laws of the state, while that person is in the state, he or she is entitled to equal protection. However, the Court's "conclusion that the illegal aliens who are plaintiffs in these cases may claim the benefit of the Fourteenth Amendment's guarantee of equal protection" only began the Court's inquiry. The "more difficult question" was whether Texas' refusal to reimburse local school boards for the education of children who could not document legal residence or the imposition by school boards of tuition on those children violated the constitutional equal protection guarantee.

To this inquiry, Justice Brennan cited precedent of the Court for the proposition that the Equal Protection Clause directs that "all persons similarly circumstanced shall be treated alike" but that the Constitution "does not require things which are different in fact or opinion to be treated in law as though they were the same." Each state legislature initially determines what is "different" and what is "the same." In applying the Equal Protection Clause to most forms of state action, the Court generally only seeks assurance that "the classification at issue bears some fair relationship to a legitimate public purpose." However, that deferential standard does not apply to classifications that disadvantage a "suspect class" or that impinge upon the exercise of a "fundamental right." In those circumstances, a higher standard applies, and according to Justice Brennan, "in these limited circumstances we have sought the assurance that the classification reflects a reasoned judgment consistent with the ideal of equal protection by inquiring whether it may fairly be viewed as furthering a substantial interest of the State."

Turning to the particular challenge in *Plyler,* Justice Brennan noted the existence of a "shadow population" of illegal migrants—numbering in the millions—in the United States which the Court attributed to "[s]heer incapability or lax enforcement of the laws barring entry into this country, coupled with the failure to establish an effective bar to the employment of undocumented aliens." Justice Brennan raised "the specter of a permanent caste of undocumented resident aliens, encouraged by some to remain here as a source of cheap labor, but nevertheless denied the benefits that our society makes available to citizens and lawful residents," which "presents most difficult problems for a Nation that prides itself on adherence to principles of equality under law." Justice Brennan then turned to the children who were the real interested plaintiffs and who the Court considered "special members of this underclass." Even though "[p]ersuasive arguments support the view that a State may withhold its beneficence from those whose very presence within the United States is the product of their own unlawful conduct," the Court found that those arguments did not apply equally to children, who cannot affect their own immigration status. The Court found that "legislation directing the onus of a parent's misconduct against his children does not comport with fundamental conceptions of justice." Citing a case involving different treatment of children born to unmarried parents, the Court noted that "[o]bviously, no child is responsible for his birth and penalizing the . . . child is an ineffectual—as well as unjust—way of deterring the parent." Accordingly, the Court found no rational justification for penalizing these children for their presence within the United States, as the Texas statutes did.

The Court then noted that public education is not a fundamental right granted to individuals by the Constitution, citing *San Antonio ISD v. Rodriguez* (1973) (Chapter 6). However, the Court noted that public education is not merely some governmental "benefit" indistinguishable from other forms of social welfare legislation; education is the "most vital civic institution for the preservation of a democratic system of government," the primary vehicle for transmitting "the values on which our society rests," and provides "the basic tools by which individuals might lead economically productive lives to the benefit of us all." Therefore, because of education's "fundamental role in maintaining the fabric of our society," the Court could not simply ignore the "significant social costs borne by our Nation when select groups are denied the means to absorb the values and skills upon which our social order rests." Additionally, the Court reasoned that by depriving these children an education, the means by which that group might raise the level of esteem held by the majority might be deprived. Stated differently, or using the Court's phrase more directly, the Court considered education the basis for preparing individuals to be self sufficient participants in society, as contrasted with the "enduring disability" of illiteracy. The Court then quoted the language from *Brown v. Board of Education* (1954), which still held true in 1982, that among other things, "education is perhaps the most important function of state and local governments." Accordingly, the Court's analysis turned to the level of scrutiny that should apply. The Court rejected strict scrutiny because the presence of undocumented aliens in violation of federal law was not a "constitutional irrelevancy" and because education was not a fundamental right, again citing *Rodriguez*. However, because of the countervailing concerns expressed in the opinion, Justice Brennan contended that the rationality of Texas' statute could "hardly be considered rational unless it furthers some substantial goal of the State." The Court applied an intermediate scrutiny, higher than rational review, but less than strict scrutiny.

The Court also contrasted what the federal government could do in classifying aliens with what states could do, since traditionally states "enjoy no power with respect to the classification of aliens." The Court acknowledged that the states can act with respect to illegal aliens where their actions mirror federal objectives and further a legitimate state goal, such as barring all aliens except those possessing work permits from lawfully working. However, the Court found no corresponding congressional policy in the context of public education. While acknowledging that like their parents, these children could be deported, the Court noted that they might also be granted permission by the federal government to remain legally in the country, or even become citizens. The Court was therefore "reluctant to impute to Congress the intention to withhold from these children, for so long as they are present in this country through no fault of their own, access to a basic education." Justice Brennan then noted that the Court might very well rule differently in other contexts where "undocumented status, coupled with some articulable federal policy, might enhance state authority with respect to the treatment of undocumented aliens."

Justice Brennan then turned to Texas' stated objectives and the justifications to determine if they satisfied the burden of being "substantial" enough under the intermediate scrutiny test the opinion had articulated. Texas argued in its brief to the Court that the classification at issue furthered an interest in the "preservation of the state's limited resources for the education of its lawful residents," which the Court dismissed because "a concern for the preservation of resources standing alone can hardly justify the classification used in allocating those resources." Justice Brennan stated that the "State must do more than justify its classification with a concise expression of an intention to discriminate." In support, Justice Brennan cited *Examining Bd. of Engineers, Architects and Surveyors v. Flores de Otero* (1976), a case involving a statute from Puerto Rico that had discriminated against resident aliens in licensing engineers, architects, and surveyors.

Apart from the asserted state prerogative, the Court mentioned "three colorable state interests that might support 21.031." First, the statute charging tuition to children of illegal aliens was part of Texas' attempt "to protect itself from an influx of illegal immigrants." Justice Brennan dismissed this claim because while a state "might have an interest in mitigating the potentially harsh economic effects of sudden shifts in population, 21.031 hardly offers an effective method of dealing with an urgent demographic or economic problem." The Court noted the record contained no evidence suggesting that illegal entrants imposed any significant burden on Texas' economy. The Court cited the lower courts' opinions in stating that "[t]o the contrary, the available evidence suggests that illegal aliens underutilized public services, while contributing their labor to the local economy and tax money to the state fisc." The Court stated that the "dominant incentive for illegal entry into the State of Texas is the availability of employment; few if any illegal immigrants come to this country, or presumably to the State of Texas, in order to avail themselves of a free education." Thus, the Court found that charging tuition to "undocumented children constitutes a ludicrously ineffectual attempt to stem the tide of illegal immigration, at least when compared with the alternative of prohibiting the employment of illegal aliens." Justice Brennan began the discussion of the second rationale by stating that a state could not reduce its expenditures for education by arbitrarily excluding a chosen class of children from its schools. The Court rejected Texas' contention that the scheme was rational because of the "special burden" these children imposed on Texas' ability to provide high-quality education. The Court further noted that Texas had no basis to single out these kids, who were, according to the lower court's opinions, "basically indistinguishable" from legally resident alien children. The third and final rationale the Court considered was Texas' claim that these children were less likely to remain in Texas and contribute to Texas by having productive or social use within Texas. The Court rejected that claim because apart from the fact that no state can be sure that any child, regardless of citizenship status, will remain confined to the state's borders, the record in the case clearly established "that many of the undocumented children disabled by this classification will remain in this country indefinitely, and that some will become lawful residents or citizens of the United States." The Court noted that it could not understand what Texas hoped "to achieve by promoting the creation and perpetuation of a subclass of illiterates within our boundaries, surely adding to the problems and costs of unemployment, welfare, and crime." On balance, the Court considered the costs to the children and the United States to outweigh any savings to Texas. Justice Brennan concluded that Texas had failed to show that denying the "discrete group of innocent children the free public education that it offers to other children residing within its borders" furthered a substantial state interest and therefore affirmed the lower courts' rulings.

Justice Marshall wrote a concurring opinion, reiterating the belief he had expressed in his dissent in *Rodriguez,* and in other cases, that the Court should adopt a "sliding scale" scrutiny approach depending on the relative importance of the interest. He also reiterated his belief that "an individual's interest in education is fundamental," and that this view is amply supported "by the unique status accorded public education by our society, and by the close relationship between education and some of our most basic constitutional values."

Justice Blackmun and Justice Powell also wrote concurring opinions, both agreeing that the children involved in the litigation "should not be left on the streets uneducated." Justice Blackmun focused on the nature of the interest at stake and explained his reaffirmance of *Rodriguez* and his continuing belief that only explicitly guaranteed rights are "fundamental." However, Justice Blackmun wrote that he believed the Court's experience from 1973 to 1982 had demonstrated that the *Rodriguez* formulation did not settle every issue of "fundamental rights" arising under the Equal Protection Clause: "Only a pedant would insist that there are *no* meaningful distinctions among the multitude of social and political interests regulated by the States, and *Rodriguez* does not stand for quite so absolute a proposition." According to Justice Blackmun, "when the State provides an education to some and denies it to others, it immediately and inevitably creates class distinctions of a type fundamentally inconsistent with those purposes, mentioned above, of the Equal Protection Clause. Children denied an education are placed at a permanent and insurmountable competitive disadvantage," and when those children are part of an identifiable group, the State has created a "discrete underclass." The public education at issue was different, according to Justice Blackmun, from other important benefits provided by the State, such as housing and public assistance, because "the complete denial of education [is] in a sense unique, for [it strikes] at the heart of equal protection values by involving the State in the creation of permanent class distinctions." He cited Justice Marshall's dissent in *Rodriguez,* arguing that the right to education was analogous to the right to vote. Justice Blackmun then attempted to reconcile the Court's holding in *Plyler* with *Rodriguez,* claiming that the result was "fully consistent." The basis for that rationale was that *Plyler* involved, according to Justice Blackmun, a complete deprivation to a portion of the population, requiring more than a rational basis for the classification. He also claimed that, unlike in *Rodriguez,* "it does not take an advanced degree to predict the effects of a complete denial of education upon those children targeted by the State's classification." Justice Blackmun noted that he joined the opinion because of the "extraordinary nature of the interest involved" and agreed that "the Court's carefully worded analysis recognizes the importance of the equal protection and pre-emption interests" he considered crucial.

By contrast, Justice Powell's concurring opinion focused on emphasizing what he termed as "the unique character of the cases before us." According to Justice Powell, the classification involved "severely disadvantage[d] children who are the victims of a combination of circumstances." He then discussed the "readily available and virtually uncontrollable" access from Mexico into the United States because of the two-thousand-mile border and the employment opportunities and other benefits of living in the United States. Justice Powell had made similar observations just seven years earlier in *United States v. Brignoni-Ponce* (1975) (Chapter 8). Justice Powell characterized the matter as a "problem of serious national proportions." He called the continuous flow of illegal aliens a certainty, but with "an unknown percentage of them" that will remain in the United States. He then made an admittedly imperfect analogy to the context of illegitimate children, as cited in the majority's opinion, where the Court said that a child should not be condemned because of the parents' conduct. In *Plyler,* the children were denied the benefit of public education solely based on the conduct of their parents or guardians in violating immigration laws and their unlawful presence in the United States, which the children could not affect. Justice Powell distinguished *Plyler* from *Rodriguez;* he viewed *Plyler* as involving a total deprivation of a right to education to a specific group of children, whereas in *Rodriguez,* no group of children had been singled out. Accordingly, Justice Powell considered the circumstances as warranting the heightened review of classifications, citing a landmark gender case. Cases challenging gender discrimination based on the Constitution's equal protection guarantee are generally reviewed under an intermediate level of scrutiny. Because Justice Powell found that Texas' denial of education to the children bore no rational, much less substantial, relation to any substantial state interest, he concluded that the law violated equal protection. Finally, Justice Powell articulated a degree of empathy with Texas, Texans, and others residing in border states:

> In reaching this conclusion, I am not unmindful of what must be the exasperation of responsible citizens and government authorities in Texas and other States similarly situated. Their responsibility, if any, for the influx of aliens is slight compared to that imposed by the Constitution on the Federal Government. So long as the ease of entry remains inviting, and the power to deport is exercised infrequently by the Federal Government, the additional expense of admitting these children to public schools might fairly be shared by the Federal and State Governments.

According to Justice Powell, no rational argument supports the notion that anyone "benefits from the creation within our borders of a subclass of illiterate persons many of whom will remain" in Texas or the United States, and which might add to social problems like unemployment, welfare, and crime.

Chief Justice Burger wrote a passionate dissenting opinion, joined by three other justices: Justice White, Justice Rehnquist, and Justice Sandra Day O'Connor. Both Justice Rehnquist and Justice O'Connor were Arizona Republicans. President Reagan appointed Justice O'Connor in 1981 to succeed Potter Stewart, and she became the first woman to serve as a United States Supreme

Court Justice. The tone of the dissent and the stern rebuke of the majority's opinion resembles the tone of Justice Marshall's passionate dissent in *Rodriguez*, albeit in the opposite direction. The essence of the dissenting opinion was the recurrent theme of the Burger Court of judicial restraint, rejecting the view that the Constitution makes Supreme Court justices "Platonic Guardians" vested with the authority to strike down legislation because it fails to meet their standards of a "desirable social policy," wisdom, or common sense. Chief Justice Burger's dissent professed to "agree without hesitation that it is senseless for an enlightened society to deprive any children—including illegal aliens—of an elementary education"; however, if the Court's business were to set the nation's social policy, the Court would be trespassing on the role of the political branches, violating the notion of separation of powers in the Constitution. Additionally, Chief Justice Burger charged the majority with attempting to give the Court the role of "omnipotent and omniscient problem solver." Regardless of noble or compassionate motives, the Court's opinion went too far, according to the dissent. Chief Justice Burger claimed to find solace in the view that because of the "unique confluence of theories and rationales [the majority's opinion] will likely stand for little beyond the results in these particular cases. Yet the extent to which the Court departs from principled constitutional adjudication is nonetheless disturbing."

Chief Justice Burger's dissent then turned to its specific constitutional analysis. He agreed with the majority that illegal aliens are entitled to protection under the Equal Protection Clause, that education is not a fundamental right, and that illegal aliens are not a constitutionally protected suspect class. Flowing from that, since strict scrutiny could not apply to the challenge, the "dispositive issue in these cases, simply put, is whether, for purposes of allocating its finite resources, a state has a legitimate reason to differentiate between persons who are lawfully within the state and those who are unlawfully there." The dissenters would have upheld Texas' statute as rational and constitutional, based not only on Texas' own classifications, but on federal immigration laws and policies.

The dissenters stated that the majority, having conceded that strict scrutiny did not apply, patched "together bits and pieces of what might be termed quasi-suspect-class and quasi-fundamental-rights analysis," thereby spinning out "a theory custom-tailored to the facts of these cases." According to the dissenters, "If ever a court was guilty of an unabashedly result-oriented approach, this case is a prime example." The dissenting opinion then dissected Justice Brennan's opinion. First, Chief Justice Burger's dissent rejected the argument that the children were uniquely situated because they lacked control over their entry into the United States and their immigration status. Chief Justice Burger noted that other people are classified, consistent with equal protection, on criteria over which they lack control, citing the examples of the "differences between the mentally healthy and the mentally ill, or between the residents of different counties," which might be unrelated to individual choice or any wrongdoing. He noted that the children could still be properly deported regardless of their innocence. He stated that the Equal Protection Clause protects against arbitrary and irrational classifications and invidious discrimination based on prejudice and hostility, but is "not an all-encompassing 'equalizer' designed to eradicate every distinction for which persons are not 'responsible.'" The dissenters characterized the Court's analogy to illegitimates as "grossly misleading" because the distinction was premised not on the status of birth, but rather their immigration status, over which the federal government has broad constitutional powers.

The dissenters stated that while the "importance" of education was "beyond dispute," it was not a fundamental right for equal protection purposes, citing *Rodriguez*. Chief Justice Burger noted that Justice Powell (who joined the *Plyler* majority) had written the Court's opinion in *Rodriguez,* and claimed that *Plyler* was at odds with *Rodriguez*. In footnote 5, Chief Justice Burger noted that the children living in property-poor districts had no "control" over their situation either. The dissenters also rhetorically asked: "Is the Court suggesting that education is more 'fundamental' than food, shelter, or medical care?" While the dissenters wrote that the Equal Protection Clause "guarantees similar treatment of similarly situated persons," to them "it does not mandate a constitutional hierarchy of governmental services."

The dissenting opinion implies that the case should have been easily decided under a rational review analysis. Specifically, the dissenters found the rationales of preventing the "undue depletion" of Texas' limited revenues available for education and preserving Texas' fiscal integrity "against an ever-increasing flood of illegal aliens—aliens over whose entry or continued presence it has no control"—made charging tuition to illegal alien children attending public schools a "rational and reasonable" means of furthering Texas' legitimate fiscal ends. According to the dissenters, "By definition, illegal aliens have no right whatever to be here, and the state may reasonably, and constitutionally, elect not to provide them with governmental services at the expense of those who are lawfully in the state." Similarly, the dissenters argued, a state could charge tuition to residents of neighboring or other states, citing Louisiana schoolchildren in the case of Texas.

The dissenters found it significant that the federal government had excluded illegal aliens from numerous social welfare programs, including food stamps, old-age assistance, aid to families with dependent children, aid to the blind, aid to the permanently and totally disabled, and supplemental security income programs, the Medicare hospital insurance benefits program, and the

Medicaid hospital insurance benefits for the aged and disabled program. The dissenters stated that these federal classifications supported Texas' use of the same classification of excluding illegal aliens from state programs "so as to preserve the state's finite revenues for the benefit of lawful residents," citing *Matthews v. Diaz* (1976).

The dissenters proclaimed that "[t]he Constitution does not provide a cure for every social ill, nor does it vest judges with a mandate to try to remedy every social problem." Chief Justice Burger then reiterated that while "[d]enying a free education to illegal alien children is not a choice I would make were I a legislator," that decision by the Texas Legislature and the Tyler ISD was nonetheless rational and constitutional. Chief Justice Burger's dissent then criticized the Court for interfering in the political process in "yet another example of unwarranted judicial action which in the long run tends to contribute to the weakening of our political processes." Congress, not the Court, bears responsibility for protecting the country's borders and dealing with aliens and "bears primary responsibility for addressing the problems occasioned by the millions of illegal aliens flooding across our southern border." While acknowledging that the "specter of a permanent caste of illegal Mexican residents of the United States is indeed a disturbing one," the dissenters believed that Congress, not the Court, should have acted. Chief Justice Burger found it "difficult to believe that Congress would long tolerate such a self-destructive result—that it would fail to deport these illegal alien families or to provide for the education of their children." As the dissent noted in footnote 1, "Surely if illegal alien children can be identified for purposes of this litigation, their parents can be identified for purposes of prompt deportation."

C. The Significance of *Plyler* and Post-*Plyler* Developments to Latinos in the American Legal System

To some extent, the dissenting opinion correctly asserted that the "unique" circumstances of *Plyler* have made it a case with limited precedential value. According to Earl Maltz, *Plyler*, particularly when compared with *Rodriguez*, "provides a classic example of the basic structure of Burger Court jurisprudence . . . marked by shifting alliances among the justices that produced an extraordinarily complex pattern of decisions."[2]

Since 1982, the problems of state financial resources and the influx of more migrants from Mexico and Latin America have increased, not decreased. Many Latinos live in border states and other states where the large number of migrants, including illegal aliens, strain not only the public schools, but also services provided by medical facilities and other social services. On November 8,

1994, Californians voted to adopt Proposition 187, which a federal district court declared unconstitutional, largely relying on *Plyler*. Governor Gray Davis and California's government chose not to appeal the ruling, and therefore the Supreme Court did not reconsider the issues raised in *Plyler* in connection with that case, contrary to the expectation of some scholars.[3]

On November 2, 2004, a majority of Arizona voters passed Proposition 200, a ballot initiative that intended to require employees of state or local governments to verify the immigration status of applicants for state or local benefits and report to federal immigration authorities any applicant for benefits who was violating federal immigration law. One day before Governor Janet Napolitano's proclamation to make Proposition 200 formally the law in Arizona, MALDEF and Arizona attorney Daniel Ortega filed suit against Governor Napolitano and others and obtained a temporary restraining order in federal district court in Arizona. After a more complete hearing on a temporary injunction which would have continued in effect pending trial on the merits, the district judge denied the injunction. MALDEF's President and General Counsel Ann Marie Tallman indicated an intent to fight and appeal Proposition 200 "all the way to the U.S. Supreme Court, if necessary."[4] On August 9, 2005, the Ninth Circuit vacated the orders based on the employee's lack of standing.[5] If that or a similar challenge were to reach the U.S. Supreme Court, the Court may very well revisit *Plyler*, and issues related to state services, undocumented newly arrived immigrants, and the constitutional mandate of equal protection. Were another case regarding the issues of social services to undocumented aliens to be presented to the Roberts Court, with its changed composition and hostility shown to undocumented aliens in recent years, as illustrated by *Hoffman Plastics Compound v. National Labor Relations Board* (2002), which prevented undocumented aliens from recovering back pay under the Fair Labor Standards Act, the Court would very likely overrule and/or try to further limit or distinguish the holding in *Plyler*.

E

THE REHNQUIST COURT (1986–2005)

10. *INS v. Cardoza-Fonseca* (1987),
Refugees, and Political Asylum

11. *U.S. v. Verdugo-Urquidez* (1990)
and Limits to the Applicability of the Bill of Rights
Geographically and as to Only "The People"

12. *Hernandez v. New York* (1991)
and the Exclusion of Bilingual Jurors

13. *Johnson v. DeGrandy* (1994),
Cuban-Americans, and Voting Rights
in the American Legal System

14. *Alexander v. Sandoval* (2001),
Title VI, and the Court's Refusal to Consider
the Validity of English-Only Laws or Rules

INS v. Cardoza-Fonseca (1987),
Refugees, and Political Asylum

A. Background

As discussed in the introductory chapter, the Latino/Hispanic classification includes a diverse group of people with diverse backgrounds and issues. The number of people considered as Latino/Hispanic has increased not just through birth rates inside the United States, but also through migration from Latin American countries. Prior to 1980, the largest ethnic groups comprising Latinos in the United States were Mexican-Americans, Puerto Ricans, and Cubans. Migration from Mexico continues and has been discussed extensively elsewhere and in sections in this book involving alien issues (legal, resident aliens and "illegal" aliens; Chapters 7–9); Mexican immigration involves complex issues, but the search for better economic opportunities is generally the motivation of most immigrants from Mexico. Since 1917, Puerto Ricans have been U.S. citizens by birth, and therefore the migration of Puerto Ricans from Puerto Rico to the United States does not involve any citizenship or immigration issues in a technical, legal sense. Since Fidel Castro took power in 1959, Cuban immigrants who fled political persecution and the conditions imposed by the Castro dictatorship were provided a favorable immigration status as a result of the Cuban Adjustment Act. This chapter focuses on INS v. Cardoza-Fonseca (1987), a landmark case involving refugees.

Political asylum is an additional reason why people come to the United States from different parts of the world, including Latin America. In other words, apart from migration for economic reasons, or for reasons such as joining family members, some Latin American migrants have come to the United States as refugees seeking protection from governments or others that persecute for political reasons.

True to its name, the area of political asylum law has always been political. "Until 1980, the Executive Branch enjoyed considerable latitude, if not complete discretion, in admitting refugees. The result was that refugee admissions were greatly influenced by the foreign policy of the day."[1] The Refugee Act of 1980 provided for two ways where an otherwise deportable person could prevent deportation: (1) obtaining political asylum under section 208(a) of the Immigration and Nationality Act (INA) or (2) by withholding of deportation under section 243(h) of the INA.[2] At issue in *Cardoza-Fonseca* was whether the standards for determining whether a person is entitled to relief under these two categories were the same or different. After the 1980 changes, a refugee was defined as any person outside either the country of their "nationality" or the last country a person "habitually resided" in, and who was unable or unwilling to return to, or avail himself or herself of the protection of, that country "because of persecution or a well-founded fear of persecution *on account of race, religion, nationality, membership in a particular social group, or political opinion*" (emphasis added).[3] Representative Peter Rodino referred to the Refugee Act of 1980 as "one of the most important pieces of humanitarian legislation ever enacted by a U.S. Congress."[4]

B. *INS v. Cardoza-Fonseca* (1987): The Opinions

Luz Marina Cardoza-Fonseca entered the United States from Nicaragua as a non-immigrant visitor on June 25, 1979, the same year the Sandinistas consolidated power and took over the government in Nicaragua after years of struggling to depose President Anastasio Somoza Jr. Ms. Cardoza-Fonseca remained in the United States longer than permitted. When the Immigration and Naturalization Service (INS) offered her voluntary departure, she refused, and the INS commenced deportation proceedings against her. While conceding that she was in the United States illegally, she requested withholding of deportation pursuant to section 243(h) and asylum as a refugee pursuant to section 208(a).

On December 14, 1981, at the hearing before the immigration judge (administrative judges, not juries, make factual decisions at immigration hearings, including determining the credibility of the witnesses), Ms. Cardoza-Fonseca testified, as did her brother, who had been tortured and imprisoned because of his political activities in Nicaragua. Both testified that the left-wing Sandinistas knew that the two of them had fled Nicaragua together. They further testified that even though she had not been active politically herself, she would be interrogated about her brother's whereabouts and activities, and that because of her brother's status, her own political opposition to the Sandinistas would be brought to that government's attention. Ms. Cardoza-Fonseca testified that she would be tortured if forced to return to Nicaragua and that her "life or freedom would be threatened." The law required her to show that she had a "well-founded fear" of persecution upon her return based on one of the criteria listed in the statute: persecution on account of "race, religion, nationality, membership in a particular social group, or political opinion." Ms. Cardoza-Fonseca based her claims on her political opposition to the Sandinistas. The immigration judge applied the same standard in evaluating Ms. Cardoza-Fonseca's claim for withholding of deportation under section 243(h) as in evaluating her application for asylum under section 208(a). The immigration judge stated:

> None of the evidence indicates that [Ms. Cardoza-Fonseca] would be persecuted for political beliefs, whatever they may be, or because she belongs to a particular social group. She has not proven that she or any other members of her family, other than her brother, has been detained, interrogated, arrested and imprisoned, tortured and convicted and sentenced by the regime presently in power in Nicaragua.

Many members of Ms. Cardoza-Fonseca's family—her parents, two sisters, her brother's wife, and her brother's two children—still lived in Nicaragua and thus presumably were subjected to the same persecution Ms. Cardoza-Fonseca feared. The immigration judge rejected Ms. Cardoza-Fonseca's claim, finding "no evidence of any substance in the record other than her brother's claim to asylum."

The immigration judge is an administrative judge under the INS, which is under the executive branch of government. At the time, appeals from a determination of granting or denying asylum or withholding of deportation would be to a three-judge panel called the Board of Immigration Appeals (BIA). Once the BIA makes a determination, either the person seeking relief or the INS may appeal to the federal court of appeals for the applicable geographic area. The last possible appeal is to the Supreme Court.

Ms. Cardoza-Fonseca appealed to the BIA. The BIA affirmed the ruling of the immigration judge, and at the time there were various potentially applicable standards to establish a "well-founded fear": the "clear probability" test, the "good reason" test, and the "realistic likelihood" test. The BIA concluded that regardless of the standard, Ms. Cardoza-Fonseca's claims failed in part because she "openly admitted that she herself has taken no actions against the Nicaraguan government. She admits that she has never been politically active. She testified that she never assisted her brother in any of his political activities. Moreover, she admits that she has never been singled out for persecution by the present government." The BIA also concluded that Ms. Cardoza-Fonseca had failed to present objective evidence that she *would* suffer persecution. Ms. Cardoza-Fonseca appealed the BIA's ruling to the Court of Appeals for the Ninth Circuit, claiming that the immigration judge should have applied a lighter standard of proof—the "well-founded fear" standard—to her asylum claim rather than the "clear probability" standard governing withholding of deportation proceedings. She did not pursue her withholding of deportation claim at the court of appeals, which heard argument on her case on June 10, 1985. The Ninth Circuit agreed with Ms. Cardoza-Fonseca, and combining her case with another case involving a woman from Nicaragua seeking asylum, Francisca Rosa Arguello-Salguera, issued its opinion on August 23, 1985, ordering the immigration judge to reconsider her claim applying the lesser standard. The INS appealed to the Supreme Court, which granted *certiorari* to decide the proper standard applicable to political asylum claims.

On October 7, 1986, the Court heard argument on the case. Deputy Solicitor General Wallace argued for the INS. Dana Marks Keener argued for Ms. Cardoza-Fonseca. The Court issued its opinions on March 9, 1987. The INS took the position that withholding of deportation and political asylum should be evaluated under the same standard. Justice John Paul Stevens delivered the opinion of the Court. His opinion begins by describing the statutory framework. As Justice Stevens noted, section 243(h) requires the attorney general to withhold deportation of an alien who demonstrates that his "life or freedom would be threatened" on account of one of the listed factors if deported. In a prior decision of the Supreme Court, *INS v. Stevic* (1984), a unanimous Court held that an alien must demonstrate a clear probability of persecution to obtain withholding of deportation, or, in other words, a clear probability that "more likely than not" the alien would be subject to persecution based on the defined criteria in the home country. In addition, section 208(a) authorized the attorney general to grant political asylum, at the attorney general's discretion, to an alien who is unable or unwilling to return to his home country because of persecution or a well-founded fear of persecution on account of race, religion, nationality, membership in a particular social group, or based on his political opinion.

In *Stevic,* the Court had rejected an alien's contention that the section 208(a) "well-founded fear" standard governed applications for withholding of deportation under section 243(h). Similarly, in *Cardoza-Fonseca,* the Court rejected the government's contention that the section 243(h) standard, which requires an alien to show that he or she is more likely than not to be subject to persecution, governs applications for asylum under section 208(a). Justice Stevens' reasons were that Congress used different, broader language to define the term "refugee" as used in section 208(a) than it used to describe the class of aliens who have a right to withholding of deportation under section 243(h), because of the plain language of the act on the "well-founded fear" standard, and because the legislative history of the Refugee Act of 1980, which according to Justice Stevens made it "perfectly clear that Congress did not intend the class of aliens who qualify" for withholding of deportation relief.

Justice Stevens then discussed some history of immigration laws: "Prior to 1968, the Attorney General had discretion whether to grant withholding of deportation to aliens under § 243(h) [the withholding of deportation statute]. In 1968, however, the United States agreed to comply with the substantive provisions of Articles 2 through 34 of the 1951 United Nations Convention Relating to the Status of Refugees." The Refugee Act of 1980 removed the attorney general's discretion in withholding of deportation proceedings. Justice Stevens then stated the central holding of the Court's opinion:

> Our analysis of the plain language of the Act, its symmetry with the United Nations Protocol, and its legislative history, lead inexorably to the conclusion that to show a "well-founded fear of persecution," an alien need not prove that it is more likely than not that he or she will be persecuted in his or her home country. We find these ordinary canons of statutory construction compelling, even without regard to the longstanding principle of construing any lingering ambiguities in deportation statutes in favor of the alien.

That the fear had to be "well-founded" did not alter the obvious focus on the individual's subjective beliefs, nor did it transform the standard into a "more likely than not" one. One could have a well-founded fear of an event happening when there is less than a 50% chance of the occurrence taking place. The Court then cited a commentator's example that a 10% chance (where each tenth adult male person is put to death or sent to a remote labor camp) could suffice. Justice Stevens found that Congress' primary purpose in enacting the Refugee Act of 1980 was to bring United States refugee law into conformance with the 1967 United Nations Protocol Relating to the Status of Refugees, including the new definition of "refugee" that Congress adopted.

The origin of the protocol's definition of "refugee" was found in the 1946 Constitution of the International Refugee Organization (IRO), which was incorporated into the United Nations Convention Relating to the Status of Refugees in 1951, which included the "well-founded fear" test, without modification. Justice Stevens also found support in the United Nations High Commissioner for Refugees' *Handbook on Procedures and Criteria for Determining Refugee Status*. Additionally, Justice Stevens rejected the INS' argument that the statute was anomalous in that section 208(a), which affords greater benefits than section 243(h), has a less stringent standard of eligibility. According to Justice Stevens, this argument failed to consider that "an alien who satisfies the applicable standard under § 208(a) does not have a right to remain in the United States; he or she is simply eligible for asylum, if the Attorney General, in his discretion, chooses to grant it. An alien satisfying § 243(h)'s stricter standard, in contrast, is *automatically* entitled to withholding of deportation" (emphasis added). Justice Stevens and the other justices in the majority did not consider it "at all anomalous" that out of the entire class of "refugees," those who can show a clear probability of persecution are entitled to mandatory suspension of deportation and are eligible for discretionary asylum, while those who can only show a well-founded fear of persecution are not entitled to anything, but are eligible for the discretionary relief of asylum. As the Court pointed out, the vesting of discretion in the attorney general is typical in immigration law.

Justice Stevens also rejected the INS' second argument, that the "well-founded fear" and "clear probability" standard are equivalent because the BIA so construed the two standards. Justice Stevens began this discussion with the proposition that whether Congress intended the two standards to be identical was a pure question of statutory construction for the courts and the Supreme Court, having used traditional tools of statutory construction (plain meaning, legislative history review, and comparison of preexisting laws), and he concluded that Congress intended two different standards. The Court concluded that although agencies charged with enforcing laws (BIA and the INS in immigration) are entitled to deference from courts in interpretation of ambiguous laws, the laws were not ambiguous.

Finally, Justice Stevens observed that "[d]eportation is always a harsh measure; it is all the more replete with danger when the alien makes a claim that he or she will be subject to death or persecution if forced to return to his or her home country." Congress' purpose in enacting the Refugee Act of 1980 was to give the United States flexibility to respond to situations involving political or religious dissidents throughout the world; the Court's decision in *Cardoza-Fonseca* would further Congress' purpose by increasing that flexibility. Justice Stevens concluded by noting that Congress intended for the attorney general to have discretion to determine whether to grant asylum to a particular refugee. By contrast, Congress did not intend to restrict political asylum eligibility to those who could prove harm "more likely than not" if deported. Therefore, the INS lost its appeal, and Ms. Cardoza-Fonseca's case was sent back to proceedings before an immigration judge, who like all other immigration judges, was ordered to apply the "well-founded fear" test, not the "clear probability" test.

Justice Blackmun concurred, but wrote separately to chastise the INS and to emphasize that the Court directed the INS to the appropriate sources from which the agency should derive the meaning of the "well-founded fear" standard. Justice Blackmun emphasized this because of the INS' previous interpretation of the statutory term, which was "so strikingly contrary to plain language and legislative history." The conflicting standards between courts, according to Justice Blackmun, "stand in stark contrast to—but, it is sad to say, alone cannot make up for—the years of seemingly purposeful blindness by the INS, which only now begins its task of developing the standard entrusted to its care."

Justice Antonin Scalia, whom President Reagan appointed in 1986, when Chief Justice Burger stepped down, also concurred but wrote a separate opinion. The gist of Justice Scalia's opinion was that because the language of a statute was so clear, under established rules of construction "that language must be given effect—at least in the absence of a patent absurdity." Justice Scalia hammered, using a Republican theme of the post–Warren Court era: "Judges interpret laws rather than reconstruct legislators' intentions. Where the language of those laws is clear, we are not free to replace it with an unenacted legislative intent." He then described the Court's explanation of the legislative history of the act as "excessive." Justice Scalia objected to it, "not only because it is gratuitous. I am concerned that it will be interpreted to suggest that similarly exhaustive analyses are generally appropriate (or, worse yet, required) in cases where the language of the enactment at issue is clear." The other argument, and the heart of his concurrence, involved his view that Justice Stevens' opinion misconstrued the circumstances under which an agency's interpretation is entitled to deference and when the Court may substitute its own view.

Justice Powell wrote a substantial dissenting opinion which Chief Justice Rehnquist and Justice White joined. Justice Powell began with the proposition that "[m]any people come to our country because they fear persecution in their homeland." Justice Powell and the other dissenters would have deferred to the INS and the BIA, contending that the BIA's interpretation—that both withholding and asylum determinations should be evaluated under a standard with "no practical distinction between the objective proofs an alien must submit to be eligible for these two forms of relief"—was reasonable. Justice Powell criticized the majority's opinion for misconstruing the BIA as having "a rigorous mathematical approach to asylum cases, requiring aliens to demonstrate an objectively quantifiable risk of persecution in their homeland that is more than 50%." Justice Powell's dissent then sets forth the standards it understood the BIA applied prior to this case. The dissent states that the "major point of contention in this case concerns that section's requirement that the fear be well-founded." Citing cases from the BIA, Justice Powell concluded that the Court misunderstood the BIA standard, and the BIA does not contend that both the "well-founded fear" standard and the "clear probability" standard require proof of a 51% chance that the alien will suffer persecution if he is returned to his homeland but instead applies "a four-part test requiring proof of facts that demonstrate a realistic likelihood of persecution actually occurring."

According to Justice Powell, the "critical question presented by this case is whether the objective basis required for a fear of persecution to be 'well-founded' differs in practice from the objective basis required for there to be a 'clear probability' of persecution." Justice Powell viewed the INS' position that both standards necessarily contemplate some objective basis as reasonable and correct. Justice Powell criticized the majority's decision because the evidence presented in asylum and withholding of deportation cases would rarely, if ever, meet one of these standards without meeting both. This is the type of expert judgment of an administrative agency (in this case the INS) that the dissenters believed the Court should have deferred to. The dissent referred to the materials interpreting the UN Protocol as "irrelevant."

Justice Powell then turned to the facts of Ms. Cardoza-Fonseca's case, citing the immigration judge's findings concerning her relatives and the absence of a direct claim apart from the persecution in Nicaragua against her brother, and states that the dissenters would have affirmed the BIA's ruling. According to Justice Powell's dissent, the Ninth Circuit, not the BIA, "misunderstood the proper relation between courts and agencies." In conclusion, the dissenters believed that the Court misconstrued the act and misread the legislative history. The dissenters would have reversed the Ninth Circuit, would have affirmed the BIA's denial of Ms. Cardoza-Fonseca's claims, and would therefore have ordered her deportation.

C. The Significance of *Cardoza* and Post-*Cardoza* Developments to Latinos in the American Legal System

Cardoza-Fonseca became the leading opinion setting forth a lesser burden for those seeking to remain in the United States as refugees, and is thereby a very significant case to Latinos and for the American legal system generally. As a result of *Cardoza-Fonseca,* if a person establishes a "well-founded fear," even if less than a 50% chance, then an immigration judge can grant asylum at the judge's discretion. Because of the increased number of people from Latin America seeking asylum during the 1980s, this opinion had a significant impact on the claims made by those people. *Cardoza-Fonseca* also illustrates some of the diversity in the group called Latinos in the United States. Ms. Cardoza-Fonseca came to the United States from Nicaragua and therefore had a national origin outside the three primary groups that primarily constitute Latinos: Mexicans, Puerto Ricans, and Cubans. Also, politically, Ms. Cardoza-Fonseca testified that her political beliefs were strongly anti-Sandinista, which was not universal among Latinos at the time.

During the 1980s the number of refugees from Latin America, particularly from Central America, increased substantially in large part due to the bloody civil wars that reigned in that region. This coincided with a resurgence of tensions during the Cold War. In the late 1970s the United States had a perception of lost prominence in the world stage, having gone through the Vietnam War, the Iran Hostage crisis, the Soviet invasion of Afghanistan, and the takeover of the Communist Sandinistas in Nicaragua. Taking office in January of 1981, President Ronald Reagan set an entirely different tone, which among other things reinvigorated struggles against Communism, including supporting anti-Communist regimes in El Salvador and the Contras seeking to overthrow the Communist regime in Nicaragua. During this time period, political asylum determinations continued to be political and reflected the political agenda of the Reagan administration, creating a presumption in favor of those fleeing the Communist regime in Nicaragua and a presumption against those fleeing the anti-Communist regime in El Salvador. According to one source, between 1983 through 1991,

> approval rates for people fleeing communist, or other countries considered "hostile" to United States foreign policy interests (such as China, U.S.S.R., and Iran), [exceeded] 50% while approval rates for those fleeing three countries the United States supported—El Salvador, Guatemala, and Haiti—were less than 3% despite extensive documentation of widespread human rights abuses and political violence in all three countries.[5]

In a settlement to a class action lawsuit challenging discriminatory asylum practices against legitimate seekers from El Salvador and Guatemala called *American Baptist Churches v. Thornburg* (N.D. Cal. 1991), those in the so-called ABC class who had been denied asylum during the 1980s were allowed to reapply for asylum. Congress also passed in 1997 the Nicaraguan Adjustment and Central American Relief Act, which created a procedure for ABC class members to apply for legal permanent residency, even if they could not meet the asylum standards in force at the time they had initially applied.[6]

Some later significant cases where the Rehnquist Court reversed lower courts' rulings granting asylum to refugees from Latin America show how difficult obtaining asylum and/or withholding it can be, particularly for those from Central America. In *INS v. Elias-Zacarias* (1992), the Court determined that a Guatemala man whom Guatemalan rebels had personally tried to coerce into performing military service in Guatemala before he fled to the United States did not constitute persecution *on account of* a "political opinion." Mr. Elias-Zacarias had testified that in late 1987, when he was eighteen, "two armed uniformed

143

guerrillas with handkerchiefs covering part of their faces came to his home . . . he did not want to join the guerrillas because the guerrillas are against the government and he was afraid that the government would retaliate against him and his family if he did join the guerrillas. [H]e left Guatemala at the end of March [1987] . . . because he was afraid that the guerrillas would return." Justice Scalia, writing for himself and five other justices, found that refusing to join the rebels did not "necessarily constitute a political opinion." *Elias-Zacarias* is also significant because the Court clarified that "persecution on account of political opinion" under the INA means "on account of the victim's political opinion, not the persecutors." According to Justice Stevens, who dissented with Justices Blackmun and O'Connor, a political opinion "can be expressed negatively as well as affirmatively. A refusal to support a cause—by staying home on election day, by refusing to take an oath of allegiance, or by refusing to step forward at an induction center—can express a political opinion as effectively as an affirmative statement or affirmative conduct." Justice Stevens' dissenting opinion suggested that an individual remaining neutral "is no less a political decision than is choosing to affiliate with a particular political faction. Just as a nation's decision to remain neutral is a political one, so is an individual's." Finally, the dissenters noted that the "narrow, grudging construction of the concept of 'political opinion'" that the Court adopted in *Elias-Zacarias* was inconsistent with the Court's approach and standard as set forth in *INS v. Cardoza-Fonseca*.

In another case, *INS v. Aguirre-Aguirre* (1999), a Guatemalan political activist was denied asylum because the Court concluded that his activities in participating in strikes that included burning buses, breaking windows, or just attacking police cars constituted a "serious nonpolitical crime," which is an exception to asylum even if the person otherwise established a right to relief. Finally, in *INS v. Orlando Ventura* (2002), the Supreme Court likewise reversed the Ninth Circuit's granting of asylum in that case.

The Supreme Court did not use its power of discretionary review in *Gonzalez v. Reno* (11th Cir. 2000) to consider the appeal of the most well known political asylum seeker from Latin America, Elian Gonzalez. The heartbreaking story of Elian Gonzalez, a six-year-old boy whose mother died on the open sea while fleeing Castro's Cuba, made national and international news in 1999. As sometimes occurs in litigation, a technical or procedural defect was dispositive of the case. Specifically, minors cannot file suits or make claims; only their parents or guardians can make claims on their behalf "as next friend" of the minor. Since Elian Gonzalez' mother had died, his father was the only surviving parent, and since he testified that he wanted his son back in Cuba, the claim was dismissed notwithstanding the efforts of his great uncle, Lazaro Gonzalez, and other relatives in Miami.[7]

U.S. v. Verdugo-Urquidez (1990)

and Limits to the

Applicability of the Bill of Rights

Geographically and as to Only "The People"

A. Background

Throughout the 1980s violent crime in the United States and drug smuggling into the country was on the rise.[1] Increasing drug prosecutions, the "war on drugs," and the proliferation of all types of guns, including semi-automatic weapons, in urban centers and in schools, altered public perceptions of crime. Congress responded by federalizing more crimes, as through the passage of the Violent Crime Control and Law Enforcement Act of 1993.[2] As one senator said:

> Americans are sick and tired of a criminal justice system that is not working. They want to know why a murderer is on the streets and not in jail. They want to be sure that the criminals who rob people at gunpoint in their driveways, actually do their time. And in fact, Americans want the criminals to serve every single day of that sentence—no parole, no leniency, and no time off because of overcrowding.[3]

Both crime and the war on that crime, particularly drug-related crime, affected Latinos in significant ways. Latinos are frequently victims of crimes, especially since many Latinos live in cities or areas with a high concentration of drugs or drug trafficking, including Miami, Los Angeles, New York, and the Mexican border regions.

The damage to Latinos caused by the drug trade is immeasurable. Many Hispanics, like other Americans, have been involved in, hurt by, or otherwise affected by the drug trade in one manner or another. Many lives have been lost, more lives damaged or destroyed. Entire towns and communities both on the border and throughout the United States became war zones even before the "war on drugs" was formally launched.

The war on drugs and other attempts to curtail the drug cancer have created other problems and victims, with a significant impact on Latinos. One well-known example is a Mexican-American named Enrique Camarena Salazar, who signed up as a soldier in the war on drugs, having joined the United States Drug Enforcement Agency (DEA). Mr. Camarena and his family emigrated from Mexico when he was in elementary school. He served as a United States Marine and eventually joined the DEA, where he worked primarily from DEA offices in California. In the mid-1980s, the DEA sent special agent Camarena undercover to Mexico to investigate powerful drug smugglers in Central Mexico. During that mission, Mr. Camarena was kidnapped, tortured, and brutally murdered in what became a very high-profile conflict between Mexico and the United States. *Time* magazine ran Mr. Camarena's face on the cover of its November 1988 issue. Mr. Camarena's tragic situation became the subject of the movie *Drug Wars: The Camarena Story*. At the time, the United States and Mexico had been courting each other to form a free trade zone (which eventually became NAFTA) as a response to the unification of Europe, which was heading toward a common market in 1992.

B. *U.S. v. Verdugo-Urquidez* (1990): The Rulings and the Opinions

U.S. v. Verdugo-Urquidez (1990) related to the tragic and inhumane killing of DEA Special Agent Enrique Camarena in Guanajuato, Mexico. The DEA and other federal agencies suspected that René Martin Verdugo-Urquidez, a citizen and resident of Mexico, was the leader of a large and violent organization in Mexico that smuggled drugs into the United States. Based on a complaint charging Mr. Verdugo-Urquidez with various drug-related offenses, the United States obtained a warrant for his arrest on August 3, 1985. On January 24, 1986, while Mr. Verdugo-Urquidez drove his car in San Felipe, Baja California, Mexico, six Mexican police officers, after discussions with United States marshals, stopped him and apprehended Mr. Verdugo-Urquidez. They then ordered him from his car, arrested, handcuffed, and placed him in the backseat of an unmarked Mexican police car in Mexico and transported him blindfolded or covered with his jacket for a two-hour ride to the border without an explanation of where he was going or why he had been arrested. When the Mexican officers arrived at the border, they removed Mr. Verdugo-Urquidez from the car and walked him to where the U.S. marshals waited at the United States Border Patrol station in Calexico, California. The marshals and DEA took him into custody and transferred him to the Metropolitan Correctional Center in San Diego, where he remained pending trial. The Ninth Circuit noted in footnote 1 that shortly "after the apprehension and delivery of Verdugo-Urquidez to the United States, the six Mexican police officers reported to their American counterparts that they were receiving death threats and feared for their safety and that of their families."[4] The Mexican officers and their families migrated to the United States with permission. Meanwhile, a prosecutor in Baja California, Mexico, filed a "formal accusation" against them charging them with kidnapping.

Once Mr. Verdugo-Urquidez was in custody, Terry Bowen, a DEA agent assigned to the Calexico DEA office, decided to arrange for searches of Mr. Verdugo-Urquidez' Mexican residences, located in Mexicali and San Felipe. Agent Bowen believed that the searches would reveal evidence related to Mr. Verdugo-Urquidez' alleged narcotics trafficking activities and his alleged involvement in the Camarena kidnapping and torture-murder. On January 24, 1986, Agent Bowen telephoned Walter White, assistant special agent in charge of the DEA office in Mexico City, and asked him to seek authorization for the search from Florentino Ventura, director general of the Mexican Federal Judicial Police (MFJP). After several attempts to reach high-ranking Mexican officials, Agent White eventually contacted the director general, who authorized the searches and promised the cooperation of Mexican authorities. At no time did the DEA seek a search warrant from an American magistrate. Mexico has no equivalent constitutional requirement. Thereafter, DEA agents working together with officers of the MFJP searched Mr. Verdugo-Urquidez' properties in Mexicali and San Felipe and seized certain documents. In particular, the search of the Mexicali residence uncovered a "tally sheet," which the government believed reflected the quantities of marijuana smuggled by Mr. Verdugo-Urquidez or affiliates into the United States.

Mr. Verdugo-Urquidez' attorney moved to suppress the evidence obtained during the searches in Mexicali and San Felipe. The trial court granted the motion. The United States, through the U.S. attorneys prosecuting the case, appealed to the Ninth Circuit, which heard argument on December 10, 1987. The Ninth Circuit Court of Appeals issued its opinion on August 29, 1988, affirming the trial court's ruling, and holding that the Fourth Amendment required that the evidence seized during the warrantless searches in Mexico be excluded at trial. The United States government appealed again, this time to the United States Supreme Court. The Supreme Court heard argument on November 7, 1989, and rendered its opinions on February 28, 1990.

Chief Justice William Rehnquist delivered the opinion for a majority of the Court. President Richard Nixon appointed Rehnquist, a conservative from Arizona, to the Supreme Court in 1972, and President Ronald Reagan elevated him to Chief Justice in 1986 when Chief Justice Burger retired. Since then, the Rehnquist Court has taken as dramatic a shift to the right as the Warren Court took to the left, particularly in the context of civil rights and constitutional criminal procedure issues. Twelve years of appointments by Republican presidents (not including Nixon and Ford appointees, 1968–1976) altered the composition of the Supreme Court and the federal judiciary in general. Republican appointees on the Rehnquist Court in particular curtailed the scope of constraints against police actions that had arisen and been expanded during the Warren Court era.

Chief Justice Rehnquist's opinion starts by defining the question for the Court as "whether the Fourth Amendment applies to the search and seizure by United States agents of property that is owned by a nonresident alien and located in a foreign country." Chief Justice Rehnquist clearly answered that the Fourth Amendment does not apply to searches or seizures of aliens in other countries, reserving the balance of the opinion to explain the reasons for that conclusion. The Fourth Amendment states:

> The right of the people to be secure in their persons, houses, papers, and effects, against unreasonable searches and seizures, shall not be violated; and no Warrants shall issue but upon probable cause, supported by Oath or affirmation, and particularly describing the place to be searched, and the persons or things to be seized.

Chief Justice Rehnquist began his analysis of the Fourth Amendment by distinguishing it from the Fifth Amendment's privilege against self-incrimination, which was not at issue in that appeal, and where "a constitutional violation occurs only at trial." By contrast, according to Chief Justice Rehnquist, the Fourth Amendment prohibits unreasonable searches and seizures whether or not the evidence is to be used at a criminal trial, and a violation of the Fourth Amendment is "fully accomplished" at the time of an unreasonable governmental intrusion. According to Chief Justice Rehnquist, any alleged constitutional violation would have occurred solely in Mexico and therefore exclusion of evidence at trial in the United States should not apply.

Then Chief Justice Rehnquist went into the heart of his opinion, which followed the government's argument as to the phrase "the People" of the United States being a term of art in the Constitution. Chief Justice Rehnquist referred to sections of the Constitution using the phrase "the People" in portions of the First Amendment, the Second Amendment, the Ninth and Tenth Amendments, and clause 1 of section 2 of Article I, relating to the selection of members of the House of Representatives. He then stated that the term indicated "a class of persons who are part of a national community or who have otherwise developed sufficient connection with this country to be considered part of that community." By contrast, the Constitution uses the terms "person" and "accused" in the Fifth and Sixth Amendments, regulating procedure in criminal cases.

Chief Justice Rehnquist then noted that the Fourth Amendment was meant to restrict searches and seizures which might be conducted by the United States in *domestic* matters. Chief Justice Rehnquist then stated that the framers debated whether having a Fourth Amendment was necessary, and concluded that the "available historical data" indicated that the purpose of the Fourth Amendment was to protect the people of the United States against arbitrary action by their own government; "it was never suggested that the provision was intended to restrain the actions of the Federal Government against aliens outside of the United States territory." In further support of that view, Chief Justice Rehnquist noted that during the "undeclared war" with France in the late eighteenth century, where public armed vessels employed by the United States subdued, seized, and took armed French vessels, no one suggested that the Fourth Amendment restrained the authority of Congress or of United States agents to conduct those types of operations.

Chief Justice Rehnquist rejected the "global view taken by the Court of Appeals of the application of the Constitution" because not every constitutional provision applies to governmental activity even where the United States has sovereign power, citing *Balzac v. Porto [sic] Rico* (1922) and the *Insular Cases* (1901) (Chapter 2), as well as other cases holding that constitutional protections are not applicable to the territories. Given that only "fundamental" constitutional rights are guaranteed to inhabitants of those territories that are governed by Congress, Mr. Verdugo-Urquidez' claim that the protections of the Fourth Amendment extended to aliens in foreign nations was "even weaker." Chief Justice Rehnquist stated that the *Insular Cases* "foreclosed" the Court's consideration of the view "that every constitutional provision applies wherever the United States Government exercises its power." The Supreme Court's rejection of extraterritorial application of the Fifth Amendment in a case involving a Nazi during the post–World War II era was, according to Chief Justice Rehnquist, "emphatic," and since the Fifth speaks about "person," the same reasoning applied with greater force to the Fourth, which involves "the people."

Chief Justice Rehnquist further rejected Mr. Verdugo-Urquidez' and the Ninth Circuit's reliance on cases where the Supreme Court had held that aliens enjoy certain constitutional rights, such as *Plyler v. Doe* (1982) (Chapter 9), because those cases establish only that aliens are entitled to constitutional protections when they are in the United States and have "developed substantial connections with this country." Chief Justice Rehnquist found them inapplicable and contrasted those aliens with Mr. Verdugo-Urquidez, whom he described as "an alien who has had no previous significant voluntary connection with the United States." He similarly found inapplicable the case of *INS v. Lopez-Mendoza* (1984), where "a majority of Justices assumed that the Fourth Amendment applied to illegal aliens in the United States." Chief Justice Rehnquist limited any further reliance on the *Lopez-Mendoza* case, stating that the issue central to that case was not properly before the Court in *Verdugo-Urquidez,* the only issue being the applicability of the Exclusionary Rule to deportation proceedings: "Our statements in *Lopez-Mendoza* are therefore not dispositive of how the Court would rule on a Fourth Amendment claim by illegal aliens in the United States if such a claim were squarely before us." Regardless, according to Chief Justice Rehnquist, illegal aliens came "to the United States voluntarily and presumably had accepted some societal obligations," unlike Mr. Verdugo-Urquidez, who "had no voluntary connection with this country that might place him among 'the People' of the United States."

Chief Justice Rehnquist then turned to very practical political considerations that seem to be key to the decision. According to Chief Justice Rehnquist, the result of accepting Mr. Verdugo-Urquidez' claim and the Ninth Circuit's "global view" "would have significant and deleterious consequences for the United States in conducting activities beyond its boundaries." The rule adopted by the Ninth Circuit could apply not only to law enforcement operations abroad, but also to other foreign policy operations that might result in searches or seizures. Chief Justice Rehnquist noted that the United States "frequently employs Armed Forces outside this country—over 200 times in our history—for the protection of American citizens or national security. Application of the Fourth Amendment to those circumstances could significantly disrupt the ability of the political branches to respond to foreign situations involving our national interest." Following Mr. Verdugo-Urquidez' position, other aliens "with no attachment to this country" might bring actions for damages "to remedy claimed violations of the Fourth Amendment in foreign countries or in international waters." The Ninth Circuit's global view "would plunge them into a sea of uncertainty as to what might be reasonable in the way of searches and seizures conducted abroad." In conclusion Chief Justice Rehnquist and the four justices that joined the Court's opinion found that the text of the Fourth Amendment, its history, and the Supreme Court's cases discussing the application of the Constitution to aliens and extraterritorially required rejecting Mr. Verdugo-Urquidez' claim. The Fourth Amendment did not apply because, at the time of the search, "he was a citizen and resident of Mexico with no voluntary attachment to the United States, and the place searched was located in Mexico."

Chief Justice Rehnquist's final paragraph summarizes the practical considerations that are the lynchpins for his decision:

> For better or for worse, we live in a world of nation-states in which our Government must be able to "functio[n] effectively in the company of sovereign nations." Some who violate our laws may live outside our borders under a regime quite different from that that obtains in this country. Situations threatening to important American interests may arise half-way around the globe, situations that in the view of the political branches of our Government require an American response with armed force. If there are to be restrictions on searches and seizures that occur incident to such American action, they must be imposed by the political branches through diplomatic understanding, treaty, or legislation.

Therefore the Supreme Court reversed the Ninth Circuit's opinion and ordered that the information obtained during the seizure be allowed into evidence in Mr. Verdugo-Urquidez' criminal trial.

Justice Kennedy wrote a concurring opinion wherein he agreed that there had been no Fourth Amendment violation and analyzed the extraterritorial application of the Constitution by distinguishing between aliens and citizens, following from the "undoubted proposition that the Constitution does not create, nor do general principles of law create, any juridical relation between our country and some undefined, limitless class of noncitizens who are beyond our territory." Justice Kennedy did not agree with the argument that the reference to "the People" in the Fourth Amendment restricted its protections and agreed with the plurality opinion in *Reid v. Covert* (1957) that the first step is that the federal government may act only as the Constitution authorizes, whether its actions are foreign or domestic. Next, according to Justice Kennedy, constitutional protections must be viewed in light of "the undoubted power of the United States to take actions to assert its legitimate power and authority abroad." In other words, relying on the *Insular Cases* and other cases, there should be "no rigid and abstract rule that Congress, as a condition precedent to exercising power over Americans overseas, must exercise it subject to all the guarantees of the Constitution." The absence of local judges or magistrates available to issue warrants, the differing and perhaps unascertainable conceptions of reasonableness and privacy that prevail abroad, and the need to cooperate with foreign officials all are considerations that made the Fourth Amendment's warrant requirement "impracticable and anomalous," according to Justice Kennedy. Justice Kennedy therefore believed that the Fourth Amendment's warrant requirement did not apply to searches in Mexico, and he also noted that he found no due process violation to Mr. Verdugo-Urquidez in that case.

Justice Stevens issued a brief concurring opinion where he claimed that lawfully resident aliens in the United States are among those "people" entitled to the protection of the Bill of Rights, including the Fourth Amendment, and that Mr. Verdugo-Urquidez, as a person brought to the U.S. and held here against his will, fit that description. However, Justice Stevens agreed that the search conducted by the United States agents with the approval and cooperation of the Mexican authorities was not "unreasonable" as that term is used in the first clause of the Amendment. Justice Stevens did not believe that the Warrant Clause applied to searches of non-citizens' homes in foreign jurisdictions because American magistrates have no power to authorize search warrants in Mexico. Only two justices dissented, Justice Brennan and Justice Marshall. The dissenting opinion in *Verdugo-Urquidez* was one of Justice Brennan's final dissents. Passionate and nostalgic, the dissent summarized in many ways the reversal of the tide from the Warren Court's legacy, in which Brennan had played such a prominent role. Justice Brennan began his dissent: "Today the Court holds that although foreign nationals must abide by our laws even when in their own countries, our Government need not abide by the Fourth Amendment when it investigates them for violations of our laws." Then Justice Brennan summarized the recent trend in expansion of federal laws and the reach of U.S. laws internationally:

> Particularly in the past decade, our Government has sought, successfully, to hold foreign nationals criminally liable under federal laws for conduct committed entirely beyond the territorial limits of the United States that nevertheless has effects in this country. Foreign nationals must now take care not to violate our drug laws, our antitrust laws, our securities laws, and a host of other federal criminal statutes . . . enormous expansion of federal criminal jurisdiction outside our Nation's boundaries has led one commentator to suggest that our country's three largest exports are now "rock music, blue jeans, and United States law."[5]

According to Justice Brennan, the Constitution is the source of Congress' authority to criminalize conduct, of the executive's authority to investigate and prosecute criminal conduct, and it is the limit on the government's authority to investigate, prosecute, and punish criminal conduct, whether foreign or domestic. By contrast, Justice Brennan characterized the Court's ruling in *Verdugo-Urquidez* as creating "an antilogy: the Constitution authorizes our Government to enforce our criminal laws abroad, but when Government agents exercise this authority, the Fourth Amendment does not travel with them." Justice Brennan would have ruled that the Fourth Amendment is an unavoidable correlative of the government's power to enforce the criminal law. Justice Brennan contended that the most obvious connection between Mr. Verdugo-Urquidez and the United States that the majority ignored was that the government investigated and prosecuted him for violations of United States law and that he faced the prospect of spending the rest of his life in a United States prison. Justice Brennan then discussed the concept of "mutuality," which he attributed to President James Madison and other founders, whereby if the United States expects aliens to obey its laws, aliens should be able to expect that the United States will obey the Constitution when investigating, prosecuting, and punishing them. Justice Brennan contended that mutuality "is essential to ensure the fundamental fairness that underlies our Bill of Rights" and inculcates the values of law and order, because according to him, "lawlessness breeds lawlessness." Justice Brennan further stated that

> when United States agents conduct unreasonable searches, whether at home or abroad, they disregard our Nation's values. For over 200 years, our country has considered itself the world's foremost protector of liberties . . . Our national interest is defined by those values and by the need to preserve our own just institutions. We take pride in our commitment to a Government that cannot, on mere whim, break down doors and invade the most personal of places. We exhort other nations to follow our example. How can we explain to others—and to ourselves—that these long cherished ideals are suddenly of no consequence when the door being broken belongs to a foreigner?

Justice Brennan disagreed with the majority's view of "the People" and instead focused on the broader purposes in drafting the Constitution and the Bill of Rights, where "the Framers strove to create a form of Government decidedly different from their British heritage. Whereas the British Parliament was unconstrained, the Framers intended to create a Government of limited powers." Justice Brennan then said that "the Framers of the Bill of Rights did not purport to create rights. Rather, they designed the Bill of Rights to prohibit our Government from infringing rights and liberties presumed to be preexisting." Justice Brennan concluded: "It is thus extremely unlikely that the Framers intended the narrow construction of the term the people adopted by Chief Justice Rehnquist's opinion and the majority as well as contrary to the drafting history of the Fourth Amendment." Justice Brennan further took issue with Chief Justice Rehnquist's characterization of *Johnson v. Eisentrager* (1950), a case involving German nationals convicted of engaging in continued military activity against the United States after World War II, and the *Insular Cases* and *Balzac*, which Justice Brennan claimed were "limited to their facts long ago." Justice Brennan then challenged the practical concerns raised by Chief Justice Rehnquist about disrupting the political branches' ability to respond to foreign situations involving our national interest as "fanciful," in part because many sensitive operations abroad would involve exigent circumstances, a separate basis to exempt searches and seizures from the Fourth Amendment's warrant requirement. Agreeing with Mr. Verdugo-Urquidez' position in the case would not, according to Justice Brennan, mean that enemy aliens in wartime would be protected by the Constitution.

Justice Brennan and Justice Marshall would have affirmed the Ninth Circuit's ruling that the Fourth Amendment governed the search of Mr. Verdugo-Urquidez' Mexican residences, and that the evidence seized during the searches should have been excluded as evidence at trial because the officers did not obtain a warrant. According to the dissenters, the Warrant Clause would serve the same functions abroad as it does domestically, which are the "assurance of neutrality and a safeguard against overzealous law enforcement." The dissenters would have found, as a matter of United States constitutional law, that the warrant requirement serves "the need to protect those suspected of criminal activity from the unbridled discretion of investigating officers [which] is no less important abroad than at home."

Because seven justices voted in favor of admitting the seized evidence at the trial, the matter proceeded with the evidence obtained in the searches in Mexico.

C. The Significance of *Verdugo-Urquidez* and Post–*Verdugo-Urquidez* Developments to Latinos in the American Legal System

On first blush, *Verdugo-Urquidez* may seem to have little applicability to Latinos and the American legal system because it involves the rights of foreigners living in foreign countries, not Americans or aliens residing in the United States. However, the case is particularly relevant to Latinos in the American system because of how it conditions the applicability of constitutional protections on whether a person is part of "the People" of the United States or not. Also, Chief Justice Rehnquist's opinion suggests more limits to the applicability of the Fourth Amendment and perhaps other constitutional protections and safeguards for undocumented aliens inside the United States in addition to those outside the United States. Chief Justice Rehnquist's *Verdugo-Urquidez* opinion is significant for reaffirming the validity of *Balzac* and the *Insular Cases,* whose continuing validity the Warren Court had called into question, as noted in Justice Brennan's dissent. Therefore, the *Verdugo-Urquidez* opinion suggests that people in Puerto Rico are still not entitled to all constitutional protections directly through the application of the Constitution and that Puerto Rico itself is still governed under the Territory Clause, notwithstanding arguments to the contrary.

As in *Balzac* and other cases involving Hispanics, aliens, and others (such as Native Americans), the views espoused in Chief Justice Rehnquist's opinion defer to the political branches and support a view that gives Congress and the executive branch "plenary power" in handling the country's affairs. Subsequent cases from lower courts have followed the majority opinion's reasoning in *Verdugo-Urquidez*, further limiting the scope of constitutional protections. For instance, a recent opinion from a Utah federal district judge ruled that an undocumented alien who had been previously deported and committed a felony was not part of "the People" protected by the Fourth Amendment, even for searches committed *within* the United States (Utah).[6] In the post–September 11, 2001, world, Chief Justice Rehnquist's opinion for the Court in *Verdugo-Urquidez* reveals notable foresight.

Verdugo-Urquidez is also significant for Latinos and the American legal system in part because the case involved the prosecution and ultimate conviction for a high-profile Latino victim of a vicious crime in Mexico. Further, the United States government showed that it could, and would, prosecute those who it believed were high-ranking members of organized crime groups involved in drug smuggling. Just two years after the Court's ruling in *Verdugo-Urquidez*, the Supreme Court considered a significant and even more controversial case related to Mr. Camarena's torture and murder, *United States v. Alvarez-Machain* (1992). The United States government accused Dr. Humberto Alvarez-Machain, a doctor from Guanajuato, Mexico, of participating in the torture and murder of Mr. Camarena by allegedly "prolonging Camarena's life so that others could further torture and interrogate him."[7] The issue before the Supreme Court in *Alvarez-Machain* was whether the kidnapping of Dr. Alvarez-Machain by private bounty hunters hired by the United States' DEA to kidnap him in Mexico and physically take him to the United States violated public international law since Mexico has an extradition treaty with the United States. "The arrest of Alvarez took place without an extradition request by the United States, without the involvement of the Mexican judiciary or law enforcement, and under protest by Mexico."[8] In another opinion written by Chief Justice Rehnquist, the Court found no violation and ruled that the manner of the abduction did not prevent the government from prosecuting Dr. Alvarez-Machain and that the extradition treaty between Mexico and the United States did not prohibit the abduction.[9] Ultimately, the district judge granted a motion acquitting Dr. Alvarez-Machain, and he in turn sued the United States government, his "former captors," and the DEA agents in a federal court in California, asserting numerous common law and constitutional torts. He prevailed at trial, and the Ninth Circuit affirmed his verdict of approximately $25,000. In *Sosa v. Alvarez-Machain* (2004), the Supreme Court reversed the Ninth Circuit's opinion, holding that Dr. Alvarez-Machain could not recover under either the Federal Tort Claims Act or under the Alien Tort Statute.

Around the same time of the *Verdugo-Urquidez* case, another high-profile case involving Latin America arose in the American legal system, the criminal prosecution of Manuel Antonio Noriega.[10] Mr. Noriega, a Panamanian general, took control of Panama in 1989, shortly before the United States invaded Panama in Operation Just Cause, which resulted in the capture of Noriega by U.S. troops and his being taken from Panama to the United States, where he was indicted for narcotics trafficking offenses. He was tried in Miami and has remained incarcerated in the United States, serving his sentence.

In honor of Enrique Camarena, since 1993, the Office of the United States Attorney presents the Enrique Camarena award, which recognizes and honors law enforcement officers who significantly contribute in the field of drug prevention and personify Mr. Camarena's goal to make a difference.

Hernandez v. New York (1991)
and the Exclusion of Bilingual Jurors

A. Background

In 1954, a Mexican-American named Pete Hernandez successfully challenged exclusionary and discriminatory practices against Mexican-Americans in the selection of grand juries in *Hernandez v. Texas* (1954) (Chapter 3). Almost forty years later, Dionisio Hernandez (no relation) raised the issue of allegedly discriminatory practices against Hispanics in the selection of "petit" juries before the United States Supreme Court in a markedly different context and environment. In *Hernandez v. New York* (1991), the Supreme Court considered whether a prosecutor's intentional exclusion of bilingual Latino jurors because of their ethnicity/national origin and/or Spanish-speaking ability violated the Equal Protection Clause.

Just twenty years prior to the *Hernandez v. New York* opinion, the federally appointed United States Commission on Civil Rights (USCCR) found that Mexican-Americans were still underrepresented in petit and grand juries notwithstanding the Supreme Court's ruling in *Hernandez v. Texas* and other anti-discriminatory efforts.[1] While the judge instructs the jury on the law in any given case through the jury charge, the jury is supposed to determine the facts of the case through its verdict by answering the questions the judge provides in the jury charge. A jury's factual findings are not generally reviewable by judges.

The issue involved in *Hernandez v. New York* arose because prior to every trial, the trial judges or the attorneys (depending on the jurisdiction) question members of the *venire* panel about their views and whether or not the prospective jurors can be impartial and unbiased in deciding the particular case. This *voir dire* process means to "speak the truth."[2] In order to ensure a fair and impartial panel, some prospective jurors are struck "for cause." Jurors are generally struck "for cause" if they cannot be fair jurors in the particular case because they are biased for or against a party, admit that they have prejudged the merits of the case, and/or state they cannot render a fair and impartial verdict. In addition to striking jurors "for cause," parties may use *peremptory challenges*, which are additional strikes given to each party to use without providing an explanation for the strike, for a real or imagined partiality.

Exclusion of prospective jurors from serving on a jury is important for two primary reasons. First, individual citizens' rights to participate in the legal system are affected, and denying their right to participate solely because of their race, ethnicity, or other immutable category is problematic. Second, the parties' (particularly the criminal defendants') expectation and right to have jurors selected by a fair cross section of the community are at stake.[3] Juries have a unique role in the American legal system in that they are supposed to be the voice of the community. The Constitution mentions the right to a jury trial on four separate occasions.[4] For criminal defendants, the jury serves as a check to prevent oppression by the government and to safeguard against a corrupt or overzealous prosecutor, as well as against a compliant, biased, or eccentric judge.[5] The choice to have juries reflects "a profound judgment about the way in which law should be enforced and justice administered."[6] Over two hundred years ago, the French scholar Alexis de Tocqueville praised the role of the American jury system in promoting civic participation among the American colonists.[7] In recent years, however, criticism of the American jury system has increased. In 1970, the USCCR found that Mexican-Americans received harsher treatment at all stages of the criminal justice system. Puerto Ricans and other Latinos had historically faced similar discrimination in the administration of criminal justice. Accordingly, the issues of Latinos participating in the legal and political system as jurors and the issue of Latino victims and criminal defendants having a jury including their (at least ethnically speaking) "peers" were at the forefront in *Hernandez v. New York*.

B. *Hernandez v. New York* (1991): The Opinions

The State of New York accused Dionisio Hernandez of two counts of attempted murder and two counts of criminal possession of a weapon. According to the Kings County district attorney, on December 8, 1985, Mr. Hernandez chased and then shot a young woman friend named Charlene Calloway, and her mother, Ada Saline, as they left a restaurant on a Brooklyn street. Ms. Calloway suffered three gunshot wounds that severed two vertebrae in her neck. The district attorney stated that Mr. Hernandez also fired shots at Ms. Saline, but missed and instead hit two men in a nearby restaurant, who survived the shootings.

On December 31, 1985, a grand jury indicted Mr. Hernandez.[8] In November of 1986, the State of New York tried Mr. Hernandez in Kings County. Jury selection occurred from November 3 through November 7. Ten days after jury selection, on November 17, 1986, the jury convicted Mr. Hernandez. The trial judge sentenced Mr. Hernandez to concurrent terms of four to twelve years on attempted murder, and one and one-half to four and one to three on weapons charges. Mr. Hernandez unsuccessfully appealed to the Second Division of the New York Supreme Court, Appellate Division, which affirmed his conviction on May 16, 1988. Mr. Hernandez then appealed to the New York Court of Appeals (the highest criminal court in New York), which rejected his pleas of discrimination in jury selection and affirmed his conviction on February 22, 1990.

The United States Supreme Court heard argument on February 25, 1991. Three opinions were issued in *Hernandez v. New York.* Reagan appointee Justice Anthony Kennedy announced the Supreme Court's judgment and wrote the leading opinion, which Chief Justice Rehnquist, Justice David Souter (appointed by President George Bush in 1990), and Justice White joined. By 1991, the impact of the Reagan and Bush appointees had altered the Supreme Court. Of the nine Supreme Court justices considering *Hernandez v. New York,* seven had been appointed by Republican presidents and two had been appointed by Democratic presidents. The Warren Court of the 1950s and 1960s had been the most liberal Court in the twentieth century; the Burger Court of the 1970s through mid-1980s had shifted to the right; and the Rehnquist Court of the 1990s was the most conservative Court in the second half of the twentieth century.

The sole point the Court considered in *Hernandez v. New York* was Mr. Hernandez' contention that the prosecution violated the Constitution during jury selection by striking Latino jurors because of their ethnicity. The lawyer who argued the case at the Supreme Court for Mr. Hernandez, Kenneth Kimmerling, from the Puerto Rican Legal Defense and Education Fund, began his argument as follows:

> This case presents a narrow issue under the Court's decision in Batson v. Kentucky, an issue important not only *[sic]* the petitioner here but to every other Puerto Rican and Latino in this county.[9]

In the case Mr. Kimmerling referenced, *Batson v. Kentucky* (1986), the Supreme Court ruled that the intentional exclusion of black jurors by the prosecutor because of their race violated the Equal Protection Clause. The Court's 1986 *Batson* decision was "on the eve of Chief Justice Rehnquist's elevation to the Court's center seat" as Chief Justice.[10] *Batson,* a Burger Court opinion, overruled the liberal Warren Court's precedent holding that race-based peremptory strikes did not violate the Constitution, showing that the political alignment of the Court does not always dictate a result.[11]

The Supreme Court issued its decision in *Hernandez v. New York* on May 28, 1991, three months after oral argument. Justice Kennedy's plurality opinion stated early on that if the prosecutor in fact used peremptory challenges to exclude Latinos from the jury by reason of their ethnicity, that would constitute a violation of the Equal Protection Clause as interpreted by *Batson*. Although only three other justices joined Justice Kennedy, altogether seven of the nine justices agreed with this proposition. Therefore, *Hernandez v. New York* stands, at least in part, for the proposition that striking jurors because of their Latino/Hispanic ethnicity violates the Constitution's guarantee of equal protection.

However, Justice Kennedy clarified that the heart of the issue was whether the Court would find facts supporting Mr. Hernandez' contention of illegal discrimination by the prosecutor. *Hernandez v. New York* did not present a case of "direct evidence" of discrimination, where the allegedly discriminating party admitted in writing or orally of its discrimination based on ethnicity. Indirect cases alleging discrimination are far more common, since rarely do people who discriminate admit their discriminatory intent. In other words, the prosecutor did not admit that he had struck the potential Latino jurors *because* they were Latinos. Therefore, in order to prevail on his claim, Mr. Hernandez had to rely on indirect or circumstantial evidence to prove intentional discrimination in the jury selection in his case. In determining whether a prosecutor struck jurors based on race, the Supreme Court in *Batson* had adopted the three-part test the Court had previously created for, and adopted in, employment discrimination cases involving indirect discrimination, discussed in Chapter 7. The *Batson* test has three parts. First, the defendant or challenging party must make a relatively easy *prima facie* case that the allegedly discriminating party exercised the peremptory strikes on the basis of race. Then, if the party has made its *prima facie* case, the allegedly discriminating party must show the court a race-neutral purpose for the strikes. Lastly, the trial judge determines if the challenging party proved that purposeful discrimination was the reason for the strike.

After sixty-three potential jurors had been questioned and nine had been empanelled as jury members at Mr. Hernandez' trial in Kings County in November of 1986, Mr. Hernandez' trial counsel, Mr. Blaustein, objected that the prosecutor had used four peremptory challenges to exclude Latino potential jurors. Two of the Latino venirepersons challenged by the prosecutor, whose last names were Muñoz and Rivera, had brothers convicted of crimes, and the brother of one of those potential jurors was being prosecuted by the same district attorney's office for a probation violation. Mr. Hernandez did not press his *Batson* claim with respect to those prospective jurors, only the other two, whose last names were Mikus and Gonzalez. Mr. Blaustein made the following objection: "I'm going to make an objection at this time that he has rejected all Hispanics, Judge. We have no Hispanics on this jury because of the District Attorney's challenges, either peremptory or for cause." [12]

Under a typical *Batson* scenario, a defense attorney like Mr. Blaustein would have to make a *prima facie* showing of discrimination. However, in this case, Mr. Hernandez did not have to meet the first minimal step of making a *prima facie* case because once Mr. Hernandez' lawyer made his *Batson* objection, the prosecutor did not wait for a ruling on whether he established a *prima facie* case of discrimination, making the issue moot. Instead, the prosecutor volunteered his alleged non-discriminatory reasons for striking the jurors in question. In reviewing the second part of the *Batson* test, and in response to Mr. Hernandez' contention that the prosecutor's reasons for excluding the bilingual Latino jurors were not race-neutral, Justice Kennedy, on behalf of a plurality of the Court, determined that the proper standard in a *Batson* challenge assumes that the prosecutor's stated reasons are true. In order to be race-neutral, the prosecutor's explanation need only be based on something other than the juror's race or ethnicity. The reasons the prosecutor stated for striking the two Latino jurors at issue were as follows:

> Your honor, my reason for rejecting the—these two jurors—I'm not certain as to whether they're Hispanics. I didn't notice how many Hispanics had been called to the panel, but my reason for rejecting these two is I feel very uncertain that they would be able to listen and follow the interpreter.

After an interruption by Mr. Hernandez' attorney, the prosecutor continued:

> We talked to them for a long time; the Court talked to them, I talked to them. I believe that in their heart they will try to follow it, but I felt there was a great deal of uncertainty as to whether they could accept the interpreter as the final arbiter of what was said by each of the witnesses, especially where there were going to be Spanish-speaking witnesses, and I didn't feel, when I asked them whether or not they could accept the interpreter's translation of it, I didn't feel that they could. They each looked away from me and said with some hesitancy that they would try, not that they could, but that they would try to follow the interpreter, and I feel that in a case where the interpreter will be for the main witnesses, they would have an undue impact upon the jury.

Mr. Hernandez' lawyer moved for a mistrial based on the alleged misconduct of the prosecutor, which the trial judge denied. Justice Kennedy noted that later on, the prosecutor denied having a motive to exclude Latinos from the jury, in part because the four victims and all of the prosecution witnesses were Hispanic. The prosecutor stated that he thus had "absolutely no reason—there's no reason for me to want to exclude Hispanics." The prosecutor also stated that he believed that prospective Hispanic jurors might be more sympathetic toward the victims than toward the accused, or, in his words, "They might feel sorry for a guy who's had a bullet hole through him, he's Hispanic, so they may relate to him more than they'll relate to the shooter."

The heart of Mr. Hernandez' challenge to the "race-neutrality" of the prosecutor's strikes was that the high correlation between Spanish-language ability and Latino ethnicity in New York means that exercising a peremptory challenge on the ground that a Latino potential juror speaks Spanish is the same as striking a Latino juror based on his ethnicity. The briefs filed by the *amici curiae*, the Mexican American Legal Defense and Education Fund and the Commonwealth of Puerto Rico, made the same argument. Mr. Hernandez' lawyer also argued that the effect of the Supreme Court finding no discrimination in Mr. Hernandez' case would result in the exclusion solely on language-speaking (or actually, understanding) ability in every case because any honest bilingual juror would admit difficulty in accepting only the English translation of the Spanish testimony. Justice Kennedy rejected that argument because that prosecutor did not rely *solely* on language, but rather the demeanor of the two individuals during *voir dire*, which caused the prosecutor to "doubt their ability to defer to the official translation of Spanish-language testimony." Justice Kennedy accepted the prosecutor's reasons, which he found were not based on stereotypical assumptions about Latinos or bilinguals, but rather on the prosecutor's stated basis for these challenges, dividing potential jurors into two classes: those whose conduct during *voir dire* persuaded him they might have difficulty in accepting the translator's rendition of Spanish-language testimony and those who did not. According to Justice Kennedy, each category would include both Latinos and non-Latinos. "While the prosecutor's criterion might well result in the disproportionate removal of prospective Latino jurors, that disproportionate impact does not turn the prosecutor's actions into a *per se* violation of the Equal Protection Clause."

The district attorney's office cited a case from California as an example of the Pandora's box that could flow from allowing bilingual jurors to sit on a jury where some testimony will be in the non-English language. In that California case, the bilingual juror interrupted the trial and asked the trial judge if she could not ask a question about the interpretation of the Spanish word *"la vado"* as a bar rather than a restroom. The trial judge in the California case clarified that the jurors could ask questions directly. The interpreter stated that "the jurors are not to listen to the Spanish but to the English. I am a certified court interpreter." The juror responded by apparently calling the interpreter "an idiot." Although the juror indicated that she said it was "an idiom," she was dismissed.[13] The prosecution cited this case as an illustration of distractions that could occur with bilingual jurors in the jury box.

In *Hernandez v. New York*, the Supreme Court deferred to the judge's acceptance of the prosecutor's race-neutral explanation for striking the two jurors in question, rejecting the claim that the reasons were pretextual. Justice Kennedy stated that the Supreme Court "of course" had no opportunity to review the prosecutor's demeanor. He noted that the trial court could have rejected the pretext claim based on the prosecutor's claim that he did not know which jurors were Latinos, and that the ethnicity of the victims and prosecution witnesses tended to undercut any motive to exclude Latinos from the jury. Finally, Justice Kennedy tried to limit the Court's ruling in *Hernandez v. New York* by stating that the plurality's opinion did "not imply that exclusion of bilinguals from jury service is wise, or even that it is constitutional in all cases."

Justice O'Connor authored the second opinion in *Hernandez v. New York*, which concurred in the judgment. Justice Scalia joined Justice O'Connor's opinion. Justices O'Connor and Scalia agreed with the plurality opinion's conclusions on how they disposed of the case, but believed that Justice Kennedy's analysis was unnecessarily complex. Justice O'Connor noted that a rule that disproportionate effect might suffice to establish a *Batson* violation in the use of peremptory strikes would cause unacceptable delays and turn *voir dire* into a full-blown trial within a trial, "with statistical evidence and expert testimony on the discriminatory effect of any particular nonracial classification." Justices O'Connor and Scalia, both Reagan appointees, found that Mr. Hernandez failed to show that the prosecutor struck any juror *because of* their ethnicity. To Justices O'Connor and Scalia, the prosecutor's asserted justification for striking certain Hispanic jurors because of uncertainty about their ability to accept the official translation of trial testimony did not constitute strikes *because of* their ethnicity. Justice O'Connor noted, "No matter how closely tied or significantly correlated to race the explanation for a peremptory strike may be, the strike does not implicate the Equal Protection Clause unless it is based on race."

Three justices dissented from the Court's judgment in *Hernandez v. New York:* Justice Stevens, Justice Thurgood Marshall, and Justice Harry Blackmun. Although both Justice Stevens and Justice Blackmum had been appointed by Republican presidents, over their approximately three decades on the Court, they had increasingly voted in opposition to the opinions entered by the more conservative members of the Court on civil rights and constitutional criminal procedure issues. The dissenters believed that the Court wrongly concluded that *any* non-facially discriminatory justification made by a prosecutor defeats a *Batson* challenge. Unlike the other six justices, Justice Stevens, who authored the dissenting opinion, would have ruled that a "significant disproportionate impact will rarely qualify as a legitimate, race-neutral reason sufficient to rebut the *prima facie* case because disparate impact is itself evidence of discriminatory purpose." Justice Stevens also stated that a frivolous or illegitimate justification cannot rebut a *prima facie* case. Justice Stevens referred to Justice Kennedy's view as "vain and illusory," stating: "Frequently the most probative evidence of intent will be objective evidence of what actually happened." In other words, the most probative evidence of intent in Mr. Hernandez' case was that all Latinos were excluded from jury service by the prosecutor.

The three dissenting justices would have rejected the prosecutor's explanations for three reasons, taken together. First, the justification *inevitably* results in a disproportionate disqualification of Spanish-speaking prospective jurors. Second, the prosecutor's concern could easily have been accommodated by less drastic means such as instructing the jury to consider only the official translation and/or bringing to the attention of the judge any disagreements they might have with the translation. Third, if the prosecutor's concern was valid and substantiated by the record, it would have supported a challenge for cause. Finally, Justice Stevens and the dissenters proposed an "even more effective solution" of having the translator be the only person hearing the witness' words. The translator would simultaneously interpret testimony into English, permitting the jury to hear only the official English interpretation.

C. The Significance of *Hernandez v. New York* and Post-*Hernandez* Developments to Latinos in the American Legal System

In part, *Hernandez v. New York* extends *Batson's* rule on the exclusion of Latino jurors just as *Hernandez v. Texas* extends the *Strauder* rule to Mexican-Americans (see Chapter 3). However, that is only a small part of the significance of *Hernandez v. New York* to Latinos in the American legal system. *Hernandez v. New York* is as significant, if not more so, for Latinos in the American legal system as its Texas counterpart. In *Hernandez v. New York,* seven justices supported (at least in theory) the position that if Latinos were excluded on the basis of their ethnicity (or if language was merely a proxy for discrimination on that basis), that would violate the Equal Protection Clause, while at the same time, six justices supported the holding that the prosecution's use of peremptory strikes against the Latino bilingual jurors in that case *did not* violate the Equal Protection Clause. In practice, the distinction has been blurred. According to one federal judge who has written a treatise on the law of juries, the application of *Batson* "to the intentional exclusion of Spanish-speaking jurors has been especially problematic."[14]

Hernandez v. New York was widely, and quickly, criticized. For instance, Juan Cartagena, legal director for the Department of Puerto Rican Community Affairs, in June of 1991 referred to *Hernandez v. New York* as a "setback" to the cause of equal jury selection and asserted that it sanctioned discrimination based on language and national origin.[15] In defending his assistant district attorney's conduct in the case, the Kings County district attorney stated unequivocally that Cartagena was incorrect "because the case does not involve such deplorable conduct."[16] A spokesman for the National Council of La Raza stated that the organization thought the result and opinion in *Hernandez v. New York* was "completely outrageous . . . It makes knowing a second language a handicap."[17] A Tucson, Arizona, defense attorney reacted to the opinion by calling it "an obscene ruling . . . It's unfair to uphold this kind of practice when the import of it has strong racial overtones."[18] The day after the opinion was announced, Mr. Hernandez' attorney was quoted as follows:

> Prosecutors could readily rely on the reason this prosecutor gave to exclude Latinos from many, many juries around the country . . . The potential is scary because the Supreme Court leaves it up to the trial judge to decide on the credibility of the prosecutor. A trial judge is reluctant to say that a particular prosecutor is a liar and a racist when the prosecutor is going to come before him the next day and the day after that.[19]

Almost seventy years before *Hernandez v. New York*, the Supreme Court overturned the conviction of schoolteachers who had been criminally prosecuted for teaching German to students during World War I, when the United States was at war against Germany.[20] In one of those cases, *Meyer v. Nebraska* (1923), the Court ruled that teaching a non-English language was a fundamental constitutional right protected by the Fourteenth Amendment's Due Process Clause.[21]

Hernandez v. New York gives lawyers a clear way of eliminating Spanish-speaking bilinguals from a jury in cases where the testimony in part will be in Spanish, notwithstanding Justice Kennedy's cautionary language that *Hernandez v. New York* should not be read to "imply that exclusion of bilinguals from jury service is wise, or even that it is constitutional in all cases." A person must have English proficiency to serve on a jury in most United States jurisdictions and in federal courts. Justice Kennedy acknowledged that the Court's ruling created "a harsh paradox that one may become proficient enough in English to participate in trial, only to encounter disqualification because he knows a second language as well." Yet that may very well be the practical effect of Justice Kennedy's opinion, as several commentators have noted.[22]

The number of American citizens affected by the ruling in *Hernandez v. New York* is substantial and growing. According to the 1990 Census, almost 32 million Americans over age five spoke a language other than English at home, and the number of persons speaking Spanish at home exceeded 17 million.[23] In Kings County, where Mr. Hernandez' trial took place, the statistics in the record indicated that "virtually all Latinos speak Spanish at home." Moreover, at the time this case worked through the system, Judge Kaye of the New York Court of Appeals noted that New York's court system "employs 113 Spanish translators—presumably rendering accurate translations in court proceedings—who are engaged more than 250 times a day."

In 1989, President Bush "aggressively escalated" the "war on drugs" declared by President Reagan in 1982. In the late 1980s, crime rates were high and worrisome to many Americans. Hispanic/Latinos were no exception. As Randall Kennedy has written in the context of African-Americans, members of minorities are frequently the *victims* of violent criminal activity, and a major criticism of discriminatory treatment in the administration of criminal justice is the *underpunishment* of crimes against Latinos and/or other minorities. In 1989, for instance, Hispanics had higher victimization rates for personal crimes overall, violent crimes, and theft crimes, especially personal larceny with contact.[24] In *Hernandez v. New York,* the victims were Hispanic.

Apart from the increase of Latinos as victims of criminal activity, because much of the drug trade into the United States flows through Latin America and areas where many Hispanics live, the increased drug trade and the corresponding war on drugs has increased the number of Latino defendants. The "war on drugs" also increased the trend of federalizing criminal laws. Traditionally in American history, criminal matters were almost exclusively the province of state law and state courts. There have always been federal laws pertaining to treason, tax crimes, and violations of federal laws, but that was historically a small percentage of criminal matters. The "war on drugs," however, increased the federal government's role in criminal justice, a trend further expanded in the aftermath of the terrorist attacks of September 11, 2001. Accordingly, beginning in the 1980s, increasing numbers of Latinos and Latin Americans have been criminal defendants in federal (and other) criminal proceedings. Additional issues arising from the "war on drugs" that particularly impacted Latinos include racial profiling (see *United States v. Brignoni-Ponce* (1975)) (Chapter 8) and problems related to mandatory sentencing guidelines.

Excluding Latino jurors because of Spanish-speaking (or understanding) ability is even more problematic in the absence of widespread participation by Latinos in other facets of the criminal justice system. Some, including the USCCR, cite the absence of Latinos as lawyers, judges, police, and prosecutors as part of the reason for unequal treatment in the administration of justice.[25] In 1970, the USCCR found that in the five southwestern states of Arizona, California, Colorado, New Mexico, and Texas, only 2 of the 59 Federal District judges had a Spanish surname. At that time, of 961 state judges in those five states, only 32, or 3%, were Spanish surnamed.[26] In 1970, USCCR found in the same five southwestern states that of 590 state district attorneys and public prosecutors and their assistants, only 20, or slightly more than 3%, were Spanish surnamed. Of these 20, there were none in Arizona or Colorado, 1 in New Mexico, 8 in Texas, and 11 in California.

Although the number of Latinos participating in the criminal justice system as prosecutors, judges, and jurors increased in the last quarter of the twentieth century, the increase in absolute numbers did not necessarily translate into percentage increases. A statistical compilation at the time the Supreme Court considered *Hernandez v. New York* shows that while Hispanics constituted 7.5% of the workforce, they accounted for only 2.7% of all employed persons characterized as "lawyers and judges."[27] In 1991, according to *The Hispanic Almanac*, there were "85 Hispanic members of the federal tribunals," including those presiding in "Puerto Rico as well as U.S. magistrates and administrative law judges."[28] By 1991, the number of Latinos serving as police officers had also increased. Latinos now sit on the U.S. district courts and courts of appeals. One source in 1997 claimed that there were thirty Latinos on the federal judiciary out of hundreds of federal judges.[29] However, no Hispanic has ever been appointed to the Supreme Court.

The majority of the Supreme Court justices in *Hernandez v. New York* held that the prosecutor's use of peremptory strikes in that case did not violate the Equal Protection Clause because the prosecutor based the strikes on permissive, non-discriminatory criteria, mainly that the prospective jurors spoke Spanish and would not be able to accept the English translation of testimony from Spanish witnesses. The Supreme Court accepted the prosecutor's "race-neutral" explanation of "two categories" (those who persuaded the prosecutor that "they might have difficulty in accepting the translator's rendition of Spanish-language testimony" and those who did not) because the challenges rested neither on the intention to exclude Latino or bilingual jurors nor on stereotypical assumptions about Latinos or bilinguals. While not as direct in percentages, this dubious distinction sounds like a previous one drawn by the Supreme Court in a Title VII case where the Supreme Court rejected a sex discrimination challenge by a pregnant woman because the distinction was not based on "sex" or gender but rather on "pregnant persons" and "non-pregnant persons."[30]

In 1978, Congress subsequently overruled that opinion by enacting the Pregnancy Discrimination Act.[31]

Justice Stevens argued in dissent in *Hernandez v. New York* that language can be nothing more than a proxy for a discriminatory practice. Others have persuasively made this argument.[32] Although unique in its facts, *Hernandez v. New York* typifies how Spanish-language ability can be a proxy for discrimination. Discrimination against Latinos based on national origin or ethnicity may be more difficult to overtly detect because it may be masked by subtleties or other closely affiliated traits such as language, color, physical features, gestures, speech and accent, dress, surnames, places of residence or other "ethnic insignia" which may be the source of "surrogates" for discrimination against Hispanics.[33] Although color and "otherness" has been a basis for discrimination against Latinos, frequently discrimination is based on language, economic status, geographical residence, and/or citizenship—critical issues for Latinos in the American legal system. After the *Hernandez v. New York* opinions, the question in this context becomes the extent to which surrogates have to correlate to race or ethnicity to constitute discrimination *on the basis of* Latino ethnicity. Is 100% required, as in the pregnancy example above? Or should statistics showing a "supercorrelation" (using Deborah Ramirez' term) that 88% of Americans speaking Spanish are Latinos and that 75% of all Latinos speak Spanish suffice to establish "Spanish/English bilingualism as a proxy for Latino ethnicity?"

Juan Perea's detailed and thorough review of *Hernandez v. New York* has highlighted that the Supreme Court's opinion focused on the "problem" of a bilingual juror refusing to accept the official translation and questioning the accuracy of potentially inaccurate translations to testimony in the non-English language. Specifically, Perea asks: "But why should anyone in the courtroom, jurors, judge, attorneys, or parties, accept an incorrect or potentially incorrect rendering of a witness' testimony?"[34] The Supreme Court in *Hernandez v. New York,* and the American legal system generally, places a premium on the "official record" over accuracy or the discovery of the truth. In most jurisdictions, only the English-language record is preserved. As Ramirez points out in her study of *Hernandez v. New York,* the proper term is actually interpretation of the oral testimony, not translation, which applies to written materials. Errors in translation and interpretation are common, notwithstanding the sincere best efforts of translators and interpreters. For example, Perea notes that in the official transcript of the oral argument of *Hernandez v. New York* itself there are several apparent errors by the certified court reporter.[35] Since the law presumes that when the trial judge instructs the jury to "disregard" evidence, the jury will do so, there is no inherent reason to believe that bilingual jurors are less competent or able than other jurors to follow this legal fiction. Nevertheless,

Hernandez v. New York created the potential of singling out bilingual jurors and excluding otherwise qualified bilingual jurors from jury service, which has been realized at least in part in subsequent cases.[36] Post–*Hernandez v. New York* non–Supreme Court opinions from lower federal courts and state courts have split on the issue of whether language-based discrimination against bilinguals is a "suspect class" (like race or national origin) which requires a strict scrutiny of the challenged practice in order to pass constitutional muster.[37] As for Mr. Hernandez, records from New York's prisons indicate that he served a prison sentence in New York until he was released on parole.[38]

After *Hernandez v. New York,* the Supreme Court expanded *Batson's* prohibitions against unconstitutional uses of peremptory challenge strikes to civil cases, strikes made by criminal defendants, and strikes based on gender as well as race and national or ethnic origin.[39] Currently, *Batson's* principles apply to all parties in a jury trial. However, the long-term fate of the peremptory challenge itself and the fate of *Batson* remain uncertain.

Supporters of the peremptory challenge trace its long history in the Anglo-American legal system. For instance, Chief Justice Burger, citing a treatise from 1852, stated that "[l]ong ago it was recognized that [the peremptory] challenge is almost essential for the purpose of securing perfect fairness and impartiality in a trial."[40] Justice O'Connor's concurring opinion in *Hernandez v. New York* cited the nineteenth-century English legal scholar Sir William Blackstone, who described the peremptory challenge as an "arbitrary and capricious right" which "must be exercised with full freedom, or it fails of its full purpose." Justice Ruth Bader Ginsburg, appointed by President Clinton, has stated that the peremptory is "part of our common-law heritage. Its use in felony trials was already venerable in Blackstone's time."[41] Apart from vintage, supporters state that the peremptory challenge reinforces a defendant's right to be tried by an impartial jury, makes up for the limitations of *voir dire,* removes jurors antagonized during the *voir dire,* and legitimizes the process for litigants since they had a role in selecting the jury.[42]

Critics of peremptory challenges claim that lawyers use the peremptory challenge to exclude people based on characteristics such as their race, which was the primary reason for the *Batson* opinions. In one racially charged criminal case considered by the Supreme Court (*Swain v. Alabama* (1965)), the prosecutor removed all six black people from the jury, and the Court noted that no black person had ever served on a jury in Talladega County, Alabama, where Robert Swain, then nineteen, was tried and convicted of raping a white seventeen-year-old girl. *Batson* overruled *Swain's* holding.

The *Batson* cases have been widely criticized. In keeping with the arguments of the peremptory's advocates, some complain that *Batson* undermines the whole purpose of the peremptory, which is to allow a party to strike jurors for *any* reason.[43] Others criticize the expansion to non-prosecutors, who arguably are not "state actors" and are in fact fighting state prosecution.[44] Yet another criticism is that *Batson,* as interpreted, has created a purely precatory right since a violation may be virtually impossible to prove.[45] Toward the end of his career, Justice Thurgood Marshall advocated abolishing peremptory challenges.[46] In recent years, others have joined this position.[47] There have also been proposals for modifying, without abolishing, the peremptory system.[48]

In part, *Hernandez v. New York* questioned whether *Batson* has any "teeth." A more recent opinion from the Rehnquist Court has made this question more acute. In *Purkett v. Elem* (1995), the Supreme Court relied on *Hernandez v. New York* in holding that a race-neutral explanation need not be "persuasive" or even "plausible" because unless a discriminatory intent is "inherent" in the prosecutor's explanation, the reason offered will be deemed race neutral.[49] In *Purkett,* the prosecutor's explanation for striking black men from the criminal jury panel was that the prosecutor did not like the way they looked "with the way the hair is cut, both of them. And the mustaches and the beards look suspicious to me." One of the jurors in *Purkett,* according to the prosecutor, had "long curly hair" and the other had "a mustache and goatee type beard," and were the only two prospective jurors with facial hair.

More recently, in *United States v. Martinez-Salazar* (2000), involving a drug and weapons possession prosecution of a Latino defendant in Arizona, the Supreme Court concluded that no constitutional or rule-based right is violated if a trial judge makes an error in not striking a prospective juror for cause (the Court indicated that the juror should have been struck for stating a bias in favor of the prosecution) where the defendant strikes the biased juror through the use of a peremptory strike. The Court concluded that Mr. Martinez-Salazar received a fair trial because his lawyer struck the biased juror, although he was not required to do so. In other words, defendants faced with a biased prospective juror who the trial judge will not strike for cause now have the choice of either using a peremptory to strike that biased prospective juror or allowing the biased prospective juror to stay on the panel and urging reversal after a conviction, if convicted, by a jury including the biased juror. In 2003, the Supreme Court in *Miller-El v. Cockrell* reaffirmed *Batson* and the continuing existence of peremptory challenges.

Johnson v. DeGrandy (1994),
Cuban-Americans, and Voting Rights
in the American Legal System

A. Background

Miguel DeGrandy and other Hispanic voters filed suit in a federal court in Miami on the first day of Florida's 1992 legislative session, complaining that Florida officials (including the speaker of the house at the time, Bolley Johnson, the senate's president, and Governor Lawton Chiles) had malapportioned the voting districts in state elections in Florida. Mr. DeGrandy and his co-plaintiffs sought to maximize the influence of Cuban-American and other Hispanic voters in Florida to elect as many representatives from different districts to the Florida Senate and Florida House of Representatives. At oral argument before the Court, C. Allen Foster, counsel for Mr. DeGrandy and the other Hispanic plaintiffs, stated that maximization was not their goal; rather:

> What the plaintiffs are saying in this case is they want to be treated—when districts are drawn in neighborhoods where they live, they want to be treated the same way the Anglos are treated when districts are drawn in Anglo neighborhoods.

Footnote 6 of the Supreme Court's *Johnson* opinion "recognized" that the use of the black, Hispanic, and white categories was "neither mutually exclusive nor collectively exhaustive"; rather, the district court used them as "rough indicators of South Florida's three largest racial and linguistic minority groups." During the time leading up to the court challenges in *Johnson*, Cuban-American/Hispanic voters, black voters, and white voters tended to vote as three identifiable blocs in South Florida. This three-way division of electoral influence is found in other parts of the country as well. The Supreme Court had seen a similar tripartite division of interests between Latinos/Hispanics, blacks, and whites in the context of school desegregation and bilingual education in *Keyes v. Denver School District No. 1, Denver, Colorado* (1973). In South Florida, migration from Latin America in the second half of the twentieth century created this three-way division. The district court's opinion in *Johnson* indicated that 55% of Dade County's Hispanic population of 953,407 at the time were Cuban-Americans. However, non-Cuban Hispanics accounted for 40.7% of the Hispanic voters in Dade County. The district court noted that "over 300,000 Latin Americans moved into Dade County" during the 1980s, over 200,000 of which were either Cubans brought in the 1980 Mariel boatlift or Nicaraguans fleeing the Sandinista regime.

The formative events involving Cuban-Americans in the American legal system began on January 1, 1959, when Fidel Castro took over the reins of power in Cuba. Shortly thereafter he began consolidating complete control and imposing a Communist regime aligned with the Soviet Union, the arch-enemy of the United States during the Cold War. Not only is Cuba located ninety miles from Key West, Florida, but Cuba also had been traditionally a zone of American influence. In fact, during the nineteenth and early twentieth centuries, there were discussions of the United States annexing Cuba as a territory or state. Cuba obtained its independence from Spain after the Spanish-American War. From 1898 to 1911 Cuba remained a protectorate of the United States.

Cubans have lived in the United States since the eighteenth century, and significant Cuban-American communities existed in places like Tampa (including the founding of Ybor City) and Miami prior to Castro's rise to power, but Cuban migration to the United States increased dramatically after Castro. Apart from Miami and South Florida, Cubans fleeing Castro's regime also emigrated to the East Coast and other parts of the United States. For several reasons, the experience of Cuban-Americans has been different from that of other large Hispanic groups: the preferential immigration status the United States government provided to Cubans under the Cuban Adjustment Act; the strong political clout of many Cuban-Americans; and the traditional alignment of the Cuban-American community with the Republican Party (as opposed to other Hispanic/Latino groups, generally associated with the Democratic Party), largely due to the more aggressively anti-Communist stance of the Republican Party and President John F. Kennedy's conduct during the Bay of Pigs invasion. For these and other reasons, relatively few cases directly involving Cuban-Americans have made their way to the Supreme Court. The Supreme Court refused to consider perhaps the best-known case, that of Elian Gonzalez. Several landmark Supreme Court cases have involved expropriation and nationalization of properties owned by Americans in Cuba. In one such case,

Banco Nacional de Cuba v. Sabbatino (1964), the Supreme Court used a judicial abstention, or avoidance doctrine, called the Act of State doctrine to refuse to examine the validity of the Castro Cuban government's taking of property from private parties even though the claimants invoked a violation of international law. The Act of State doctrine is based on the principle that courts in the United States should not examine the validity or legality of acts by foreign sovereign governments in their own territory. Over time, the Court limited the expansive abstention of *Sabbatino* in cases such as *First National City Bank v. Banco Nacional de Cuba* (1972) and *Alfred Dunhill of London, Inc. v. Republic of Cuba* (1976). A Cuban-American also had his claim considered by the Court in *Matthews v. Diaz* (1976), where the Court denied this Cuban resident alien and others' equal protection challenge to a federal law requiring a continuous residency period to obtain Medicare benefits from the federal government.

In *Johnson*, Mr. DeGrandy and the other Hispanic plaintiffs challenged Florida's apportionment scheme for electing state representatives in both houses of Florida's state government's legislative branch under the Voting Rights Act (VRA) of 1965. The main purpose of the VRA was to eradicate discrimination in voting and to ensure fair minority representation in electing representatives in the democratic process throughout the United States. All types of impediments to minority voting had been implemented throughout the twentieth century, ranging from the mild and subtle to intimidation, coercion, and blatant, racially based gerrymandering, particularly against African-Americans, as exemplified by the Alabama law in the landmark case of *Gomillion v. Lightfoot* (1960), which involved a "28 sided polygon" designed explicitly to remove all but a handful of black voters from the Tuskegee city limits. Congress initially passed the VRA with a five-year period, but extended the VRA's applicability in 1970 for another five years, in 1975 for another seven years, in 1982 for ten years, and again in 1992 for fifteen years (until 2007). Prior to 1980, a person suing under the VRA could prevail by proving that a challenged law or procedure resulted in a denial to a racial or language minority of equal participation in elections. However, in *City of Mobile v. Bolden* (1980), the Supreme Court added the requirement that VRA plaintiffs had to show discriminatory *intent* by the legislators enacting the challenged law. In 1982, Congress amended section 2 of the VRA to overrule *Bolden*'s intent requirement and reinstate the results-oriented test based on a "totality of the circumstances." The leading post-*Bolden* case interpreting this part of the 1982 VRA amendments was *Thornburg v. Gingles* (1986), where the Court established three elements that a person suing under the VRA challenging an at-large system must establish. The three *Gingles* conditions or factors are that the minority group (1) is large enough and compact enough to constitute a majority in a single-member district; (2) is politically cohesive; and (3) has a preferred candidate that is usually defeated by white bloc voting.

Section 5 of the VRA, also mentioned in *Johnson*, requires jurisdictions subject to its mandate to obtain a preclearance from either the United States Department of Justice or the United States District Court of the District of Columbia. To obtain preclearance, the governmental entity must establish that neither the purpose nor the effect of an election change is to deny or abridge minority voters' rights. Even if a jurisdiction does not acquire preclearance, the jurisdiction can make a claim to a three-judge federal panel in Washington, D.C.

Apart from Mr. DeGrandy's challenge, black voters together with state NAACP branches filed suit in another court challenging Florida's apportionment scheme. Those claims were consolidated with the suit filed by Mr. DeGrandy. While the lawsuit was pending, Florida's state legislature adopted a new reapportionment plan on April 10, 1992, called Senate Joint Resolution 2-G (SJR 2-G). As required under Florida's Constitution, Florida's attorney general, Robert Butterworth, petitioned the Florida Supreme Court for a declaratory judgment affirming the plan's validity under state and federal law. The Florida Supreme Court upheld the validity of SJR 2-G. Attorney General Butterworth also sought preclearance from the Department of Justice as required under VRA section 5. As noted in footnote 2 of the Supreme Court's opinion, Florida submitted SJR 2-G to the Department of Justice for preclearance pursuant to section 5 of the VRA. Although five Florida counties were subject to section 5's preclearance requirement, Dade County was not one of them. According to the Court, when "the Attorney General of the United States refused to preclear the plan's Senate districts for the Hillsborough County area and the state legislature refused to revise the plan, the Supreme Court of Florida ordered the adjustments necessary to obtain preclearance . . . [it is] the version of SJR 2-G so adjusted that is at issue in this litigation."

Once SJR 2-G was upheld, Mr. DeGrandy and the other plaintiffs that filed with him, as well as the NAACP plaintiffs (as the Supreme Court referred to them) amended their complaints to charge that the apportionment "unlawfully fragments cohesive minority communities and otherwise impermissibly submerges their right to vote and to participate in the electoral process." The United States Department of Justice also sued the state of Florida and Florida officials, claiming that SJR 2-G diluted the voting strength of blacks and Hispanics in two parts of Florida in violation of section 2 of the VRA. The United States' complaint alleged that SJR 2-G diluted the votes of the Hispanic population in an area largely covered by Dade County (including Miami) and the black population in an area covering much of Escambia County (including

Pensacola). The district court consolidated that case with Mr. DeGrandy's case and the claims brought by the NAACP plaintiffs. On July 1, 1992, after a five-day trial and a hearing on what remedies the court should order, the court found that SJR 2-G's plans for electing state house districts violated section 2 of the VRA because "more than [SJR 2-G's] nine Hispanic districts may be drawn without having or creating a regressive effect upon black voters." The district court, seeking to maximize the number of minority districts, ordered the implementation of Mr. DeGrandy's plan, which called for eleven majority-Hispanic house districts. As to the challenges to SJR 2-G's drawing of districts for senate elections, the district court also found a violation of section 2 of the VRA, but found that no new districts could be drawn because any attempt to create an additional (fourth) majority-Hispanic district would be "at the expense of black voters in the area." Accordingly, Justice Souter characterized the district court's findings as having no practical effect "because the court held that remedies for the blacks and the Hispanics were mutually exclusive; it consequently deferred to the state legislature's work as the 'fairest' accommodation of all the ethnic communities in South Florida."

A case prior to *Johnson,* at the district court level, involved a challenge to Florida's congressional districts and was resolved independently of *Johnson.* In *DeGrandy v. Wetherell* (N.D. Fla. 1992), the three-judge panel (Judges Hatchett, Stafford, and Vinson) found a "longstanding history of official discrimination against minorities [which] has influenced Florida's electoral process," including poll taxes, segregation, and other tactics. That court noted the absence of Hispanic representation in both the state senate in Florida and in the United States Congress, where as of 1992, only one Hispanic Congressman had served from Florida. The district court noted that all parties to the suit agreed that "racially polarized voting exists throughout Florida to varying degrees" and found that Hispanics in South Florida (as well as African-Americans) formed a large enough and politically cohesive enough group. The district court also found that in Dade County, "Hispanics and African-Americans were each politically cohesive among themselves but were not at all cohesive—and were often at odds—in relation to each other." The district court also stated that "party competitiveness in Florida's congressional districts is an important goal because Florida has developed into a strong two-party state."

The parties did not dispute the expert testimony of Dr. Dario Moreno that the "nature of tripartite politics in Dade means that only when Hispanics have a super majority can a Latin candidate win." What constituted a "Hispanic supermajority" was central to the dispute because at issue were whether two additional districts could be drawn in Dade County to create "Hispanic" seats.

B. *Johnson v. DeGrandy* (1994): The Opinions

The Florida state agencies and representatives appealed to the United States Supreme Court, who heard argument on October 4, 1993. The Court issued its ruling on June 30, 1994. Justice Souter, a moderate Republican from New Hampshire appointed by President George Bush in 1990, delivered the Court's opinion. Justice Souter characterized the cases as involving the meaning of, and the facts required to show, vote dilution when single-member legislative districts are challenged under VRA section 2. Seven justices joined in the Court's ruling that *Johnson* presented no VRA section 2 violation. The two dissenters also found no violation, but for different reasons—they did not believe these types of claims could ever be brought. Justice Souter described the situation in *Johnson* as one where "in spite of continuing discrimination and racial bloc voting, minority voters form effective voting majorities in a number of districts roughly proportional to the minority voters' respective shares in the voting-age population." According to Justice Souter's opinion:

> While such proportionality is not dispositive in a challenge to single-member districting, it is a relevant fact in the totality of circumstances to be analyzed when determining whether members of a minority group have "less opportunity than other members of the electorate to participate in the political process and to elect representatives of their choice."

Before addressing the substantive VRA issues at stake in *Johnson,* Justice Souter rejected Florida's contention that because the Florida Supreme Court had ruled on the legality of the SJR-2G plan, Mr. DeGrandy and the other plaintiffs were precluded from challenging the claim in federal court. According to Justice Souter, the claim preclusion doctrine (called *res judicata*) did not bar Mr. DeGrandy's claims, those of the other private plaintiffs, or the claims of the United States. After deciding that jurisdictional challenge, the Court considered the merits of the vote dilution claims covering the house districts. Justice Souter wrote that "the crux" of Florida's argument was that because Hispanics have the power under SJR 2-G "to elect candidates of their choice in a number of districts that mirrors their share of the Dade County area's voting-age population (i.e., 9 out of 20 House districts); this power, according to the State, bars any finding that the plan dilutes Hispanic voting strength." Florida sought to reverse the district court's ruling because, according to Florida, the district court misapplied prior VRA cases from the Supreme Court as requiring a maximization of the number of Hispanic-controlled districts. Since Florida relied, in part, on cases from the Court's prior term, *Voinovich v. Quilter* (1993) and *Growe v. Emison* (1993), Justice Souter clarified that *Johnson* involved "two quite different questions." First, whether Hispanics are sufficiently numerous and geographically compact to be a majority in additional single-member districts, as required by the first *Gingles* factor. Second, if Mr. DeGrandy and the other plaintiffs established all three *Gingles* conditions, whether an analysis of the "totality of the circumstances" supported a finding of vote dilution when Hispanics could be expected to elect their chosen representatives in substantial proportion to their percentage of the area's population. Justice Souter's opinion analyzes each factor in turn.

Justice Souter noted that Mr. DeGrandy's plan for the Dade County area provided for eleven reasonably compact districts, each with a voting-age population at least 64% Hispanic. Florida claimed that the Hispanic super-majorities could not elect representatives of their choice in all eleven districts "without cross-over votes from other ethnic groups," claiming that half of the Hispanic voting-age residents of the region were not citizens. By contrast, the district court had accepted Mr. DeGrandy and the other plaintiffs' arguments that the super-majorities compensated for the ineligibility factor, many being recent immigrants. The Court did not make a ruling on this point, stating: "We can leave this dispute without a winner." Instead, the Court assumed for purposes of its analysis, without making a ruling, that the Hispanics in South Florida satisfied the first *Gingles* condition of establishing that Hispanics were sufficiently large and geographically compact to constitute a majority in these districts.

Justice Souter then clarified that the district court wrongly found a section 2 violation based solely on its finding that the plaintiffs had established all three *Gingles* conditions, that there had been historic discrimination against Hispanics, and that more could (and therefore should) have been done to create additional Hispanic super-majority districts. Justice Souter's opinion for the Court in *Johnson* then established and clarified that establishing the three *Gingles* conditions was necessary, but not sufficient, to establish a violation of section 2. As the general reason for requiring more, the Court stated that

> ultimate conclusions about equality or inequality of opportunity were intended by Congress to be judgments resting on comprehensive, not limited, canvassing of relevant facts. Lack of electoral success is evidence of vote dilution, but courts must also examine other evidence in the totality of circumstances, including the extent of the opportunities minority voters enjoy to participate in the political processes.

Justice Souter found that the district court misjudged the relative importance of the *Gingles* factors and historical discrimination when compared with evidence tending to show that despite these, SJR 2-G provided minority voters with an equal measure of political and electoral opportunity. The Supreme Court's opinion does not take issue with the evidence of historical discrimination against Hispanic voters "continuing in society generally to the present day." Rather the Court found that notwithstanding that history, the proposed redistricting scheme of SJR 2-G demonstrated rough proportionality of minority representation of Hispanics in Dade County compared to the minority's share of voting-age population. Therefore, the Court could "not see how these district lines, apparently providing political effectiveness in proportion to voting-age numbers, deny equal political opportunity." Specifically, the Court cited the record establishing that Hispanics constitute 50% of the voting-age population in Dade County and under SJR 2-G would make up supermajorities in nine of the eighteen house districts in the county. The Court found that SJR 2-G thwarted "the historical tendency to exclude Hispanics, not encourage or perpetuate it," and found "no grounds for holding in this case that SJR 2-G's district lines diluted the votes cast by Hispanic voters."

Justice Souter also rejected arguments that the heavily Hispanic Kendall and Kendall Lakes areas were illegally "packed" and "fragmented" to dilute Hispanic voting. The Court concluded "only that lines could have been drawn elsewhere, nothing more. But some dividing by district lines and combining within them is virtually inevitable and befalls any population group of substantial size." According to Justice Souter, calling the line-drawing "packing" and "fragmenting" without more did not establish vote dilution where proportionality existed.

Justice Souter then rejected the district court's reading of the VRA and its case law as requiring the maximization of minority voting power. To make the point that maximization is not required by section 2 of the VRA, the Court used a hypothetical of one thousand voters in ten districts and a scenario of extreme distortion. In the Court's flowery language:

> One may suspect vote dilution from political famine, but one is not entitled to suspect (much less infer) dilution from mere failure to guarantee a political feast. However prejudiced a society might be, it would be absurd to suggest that the failure of a districting scheme to provide a minority group with effective political power 75 percent above its numerical strength indicates a denial of equal participation in the political process. Failure to maximize cannot be the measure of [section] 2.

The Court also rejected, as contrary to the "totality of circumstances" test, Florida's proposed definitive rule that "as a matter of law, no dilution occurs whenever the percentage of single-member districts in which minority voters form an effective majority mirrors the minority voters' percentage of the relevant population." Justice Souter found the need for the "totality of the circumstances approach" based on "the demonstrated ingenuity of state and local governments in hobbling minority voting power . . . a point recognized by Congress when it amended the statute in 1982," quoting from the Senate's record. In other words, local and state governments could continue to find mechanisms to discriminate against minority voters even if their representative numbers were "proportionate." As support, the Court looked to past practices and "past reality." According to the Court's opinion, in

> a substantial number of voting jurisdictions, that past reality has included such reprehensible practices as ballot box stuffing, outright violence, discretionary registration, property requirements, the poll tax, and the white primary; and other practices censurable when the object of their use is discriminatory, such as at-large elections, runoff requirements, anti-singleshot devices, gerrymandering, the impeachment of office-holders, the annexation or deannexation of territory, and the creation or elimination of elective offices.

The Court also rejected Florida's proportionality argument for two additional reasons. First, such a rule would be based on "an unexplored premise of highly suspect validity: that, in any given voting jurisdiction (or portion of that jurisdiction under consideration), the rights of some minority voters under 2 may be traded off against the rights of other members of the same minority class." In other words, the most blatant racial gerrymandering in half of a county's single-member districts would be irrelevant if offset by political gerrymandering in the other half, so long as proportionality became determinative. Second, governmental entities would tend to strive for proportionality to shield themselves from challenges under section 2 of the VRA "even in circumstances where they may not be necessary to achieve equal political and electoral opportunity." While Justice Souter described "the lesson of *Gingles*" as a recognition that in the United States, "racial and ethnic cleavages sometimes necessitate majority-minority districts to ensure equal political and electoral opportunity," he noted that in some other communities, minority citizens can form coalitions with voters from other racial and ethnic groups and elect candidates of their choice without being a numerical majority. In summary, Justice Souter wrote, "No single statistic provides courts with a short-cut to determine whether a set of single-member districts unlawfully dilutes minority voting strength."

Justice Souter then rejected the United States' suggestion that proportionality ought to be an affirmative defense. Since Florida did not argue statewide proportionality in the district court, that issue could not properly be brought before the Court. Further, the parties had agreed on the appropriate geographical scope for analyzing the alleged section 2 violation and devising its remedy, namely Dade County and Escambia County areas. The Court noted that Mr. DeGrandy and the other plaintiffs who sued with him "even voluntarily dismissed their claims of Hispanic vote dilution outside the Dade County area."

The Court found that none of the plaintiffs had established a violation of the VRA, specifically, they provided insufficient evidence of vote dilution in the drawing of house districts in the Dade County area; the Supreme Court therefore reversed the district court's opinion as to the portion where it declared Florida's House of Representatives scheme unconstitutional.

The Court also found, based on a "totality of circumstances" analysis, no vote dilution in senate elections and insufficient evidence to establish that either blacks or Hispanics in Dade County had produced evidence otherwise indicating that under SJR 2-G voters in either minority group had "less opportunity than other members of the electorate to participate in the political process and to elect representatives of their choice." Part of the Court's reasoning was that within the seven-district Dade County area, blacks and Hispanics enjoyed "rough proportionality." Specifically, Justice Souter noted:

> The voting-age population in the seven-district area is 44.8% Hispanic and 15.8 percent black. Record, U.S. Exh. 7. Hispanics predominate in 42.9 percent of the districts (three out of seven), as do blacks in 14.3 percent of them (one out of seven). While these numbers indicate something just short of perfect proportionality (42.9 percent against 44.8; 14.3 percent against 15.8), the opposite is true of the five districts located wholly within Dade County.

The Court found no VRA violation as to electing state senators, either. Since the district court left SJR 2-G's plan for Florida state senate districts undisturbed, the Court affirmed that portion of the district court's opinion.

Justice O'Connor wrote a particularly lucid and concise concurring opinion, noting:

> The critical issue in this case is whether 2 of the [VRA] requires courts to "maximize" the number of districts in which minority voters may elect their candidates of choice. The District Court, applying the maximization principle, operated "on the apparent assumption that what could have been done to create additional Hispanic super-majority districts should have been

done." . . . The Court today makes clear that the District Court was in error, and that the [VRA] does not require maximization.

Justice O'Connor's concurrence highlights that the Court's opinion did not just reject the maximization principle, but provided a guideline for future voting rights claims, with its "central teaching" being that proportionality "defined as the relationship between the number of majority-minority voting districts and the minority group's share of the relevant population—is always relevant evidence in determining vote dilution, but is never itself dispositive."

Justice Kennedy also wrote a separate opinion concurring with the Court's holding. The gist of Justice Kennedy's opinion was a warning to legislators, courts, Department of Justice officials, and others involved in redistricting not to engage in exclusively race-based proportionate representation schemes. Justice Kennedy agreed with the Court that the district court's "maximization theory" wrongly applied section 2 of the VRA and that there was no violation of the VRA in *Johnson*. Justice Kennedy's opinion then examines "whether proportionality, ascertained by comparing the number of majority-minority districts to the minority group's proportion of the relevant population, is relevant in deciding whether there has been vote dilution under 2 in a challenge to election district lines." First, Justice Kennedy noted that the "statutory text does not yield a clear answer." Justice Kennedy cited the relevant portion of the VRA, which states that one circumstance which may be considered in determining whether there has been vote dilution is the "extent to which members of a protected class have been elected to office in the State or political subdivision." The VRA clarifies that the law does not create a "quota" or a right to have "members of a protected class elected in numbers equal to their proportion in the population." Justice Kennedy noted the distinction between the VRA's language relating to "the number of minorities elected to office, not the number of districts in which minorities constitute a voting majority." Not only are they not synonymous, according to Justice Kennedy, but "it would be an affront to our constitutional traditions to treat them as such. The assumption that majority-minority districts elect only minority representatives, or that majority-white districts elect only white representatives, is false as an empirical matter." More fundamentally, Justice Kennedy found such an assumption as reflecting "the demeaning notion that members of the defined racial groups ascribe to certain 'minority views' that must be different from those of other citizens." After discussing other court rulings, Justice Kennedy agreed with the majority's decision, reflected in Justice Souter's opinion, that proportionality is relevant, but the lack of proportionality is not "dispositive" proof of vote dilution, nor is the presence of proportionality "a safe harbor" precluding challenges of vote dilution. Justice Kennedy then discussed the practical problem that he foresaw, mainly that an absence of "proportionality" might lead a governmental entity to "engage in race-based redistricting and create a minimum number of districts in which minorities constitute a voting majority," or that the Department of Justice (particularly in light of President Bill Clinton's election two years earlier in 1992) might require proportionality "as a condition of granting preclearance, under 5 of the Act." Justice Kennedy then cited opinions from prior Supreme Court cases (including his own prior dissents and concurrences), cautioning that governmental actions of that type, in his view, "tend to entrench the very practices and stereotypes the Equal Protection Clause is set against." He further wrote that generally "the sorting of persons with an intent to divide by reason of race raises the most serious constitutional questions," which would require a strict scrutiny review of the constitutionality of the drawing of electoral and political boundaries. Justice Kennedy then noted the Court's ruling the year before in *Shaw v. Reno* (1993), where the Court wrote that racial gerrymandering, even for the supposed benefit of minorities or for remedial purposes, "may balkanize us into competing racial factions; it threatens to carry us further from the goal of a political system in which race no longer matters—a goal that the Fourteenth and Fifteenth Amendments embody, and to which the Nation continues to aspire." Justice Kennedy noted that *Shaw* alluded to, but left unresolved, the question of whether "the intentional creation of majority-minority districts, without more, always gives rise to an equal protection claim." Justice Kennedy cautioned also that "explicit race-based districting embarks us on a most dangerous course. Redistricting must comply with the overriding demands of the Equal Protection Clause." Because there were no constitutional claims or issues under the Equal Protection Clause raised in *Johnson*, Justice Kennedy concurred with the Court's judgment and all of the opinion except for the portions discussing proportionality.

Justice Clarence Thomas, the second African-American justice appointed to the Supreme Court (by President Bush in 1991), and Justice Antonin Scalia, the predominant conservative on the Court since his appointment in 1986 by President Ronald Reagan, dissented. Justice Thomas had served as Chairman of the Equal Employment Opportunity Commission (EEOC) under President Reagan. In 1994, at the time of the *Johnson* opinion, Justice Thomas frequently joined Justice Scalia in voting on decisions. The dissenters did not reject the majority's opinion because they would have supported Mr. DeGrandy or the other plaintiffs. Instead, the dissenters would have vacated the district court's judgment declaring Florida's apportionment scheme as unconstitutional and would have instructed the district judge to dismiss all of the consolidated claims in *Johnson* for failure to state a cognizable claim under section 2 of the VRA.

The reasoning was that, to Justice Thomas' and Justice Scalia's view, an apportionment plan (like the one at issue in *Johnson*) is not a "standard, practice, or procedure" that could *ever* be challenged under section 2 of the VRA.

C. The Significance of *Johnson* and Post-*Johnson* Developments to Latinos in the American Legal System

Johnson is an important contribution to the Court's case law interpreting the VRA, particularly section 2. The Court found no violation of section 2 because the relative strengths of the particular minority communities as voting majorities were roughly proportionate to the minority voters' share of the voting-age population; yet the Court's opinion suggests that proportionality is a relevant fact in the "totality of the circumstances" analysis.

Like other voting rights cases involving Hispanics, such as *Lopez v. Monterey County* (1999), *Johnson* demonstrates that by sheer numbers, Hispanic voters are having greater electoral influence than ever before, regardless of the VRA. Apart from local and federal elections, this reality is highlighted in presidential elections by the concentration of Latinos/Hispanics in states with substantial electoral representation (California, Texas, New York, Illinois). Stating that Florida's voters (or the Supreme Court) were influential to the result of the 2000 presidential elections would be an understatement.

Just as the Court ruled in *Johnson v. DeGrandy* that section 2 does not require maximizing majority-minority districts, the following year the Court ruled in *Miller v. Johnson* (1995) in an opinion written by Justice Kennedy that section 5 of the VRA also does not require the creation of majority-minority districts wherever possible. Later cases have supported Justice Kennedy's warnings in *Johnson*. *Bush v. Vera* (1996) and *Shaw v. Hunt* (1996), referred to as racial gerrymandering cases, where lines were drawn with race as a predominant factor, establish the general proposition that because the Constitution (including the Equal Protection Clause) has supremacy over laws of Congress, including the VRA, race cannot be the sole or primary consideration in drawing electoral districts and could not survive a strict scrutiny analysis. In the area of voting rights, particularly the VRA, the Rehnquist Court has reflected an antipathy to redistricting plans the Court has perceived as race-based preferences, quotas, or any system benefiting minority voters, similar to the antipathy the Rehnquist Court has generally shown toward affirmative action cases,[1] with the notable exception of *Grutter v. Bollinger* (2003), the 5–4 decision upholding the University of Michigan Law School's plan. In the voting rights area, Tinsley Yarbrough has noted that the Rehnquist Court's approach reflects "an assumption that racial bias is largely a relic of the past . . . [and] that race-conscious remedies for discrimination are themselves inherently inconsistent with . . . the notion of a color-blind Constitution."[2]

Unlike other areas, the voting rights area reflects a "zero-sum" situation where district lines necessarily result in benefits to one group or groups (whether they be racially, politically, or otherwise defined) to the detriment of others.

Johnson also highlighted the degree to which African-Americans and Hispanics were cohesive within but not across their respective communities:

> Hispanics and African-Americans were each politically cohesive among themselves but were not at all cohesive—and were often at odds—in relation to each other . . . There is a high degree of tension in Dade County between the African-American population and the Hispanic population . . . Furthermore, while African-Americans tend to vote Democratic, Hispanic voters tend to vote Republican.

The district court cited examples where either the Hispanic voters or the African-American voters would combine with white voters to defeat the other minority group's candidate. Quite possibly, if voting patterns in the United States continue to reflect ethnic/racial "bloc" voting, this kind of scenario involving all types of ethnically conflicting interests could continue.

Much of the oral argument at the Supreme Court focused on whether the Court should look at just Dade County, or all of Florida in determining redistricting. In rebuttal, Joel Klein on behalf of Florida stated that the "one undisputed fact" on this point was that outside of Dade County, the only other Hispanic house member in Florida was a Democrat from the Tampa area in Hillsborough County. Therefore, according to Mr. Klein, "[t]he idea that there's [statewide] cohesion is simply untenable." The Court even asked questions at oral argument to James Feldman, who argued on behalf of the United States, as to who constitutes the protected Hispanic group. Mr. Feldman described the "defining characteristic" as the Spanish heritage and the rights of "language minorities and the problems that have been caused by discrimination against people on the basis of the fact that they speak a different language." As for Mr. DeGrandy, he later served as a representative in Florida's House of Representatives. Redistricting resurfaces after every decade's census. In 2002, Florida's house speaker, Tom Feeney, hired Mr. DeGrandy, a Miami attorney, along with other law firms, to assist in the 2002 redistricting challenges.

Alexander v. Sandoval (2001),

Title VI, and the Court's Refusal to Consider

the Validity of English-Only Laws or Rules

A. Background

Although English is the language of the United States, consistent with the concept of a limited federal government, the United States Constitution (written in English) is silent with respect to a government-mandated "official" language. States and other jurisdictions subject to United States control and rule (e.g., Puerto Rico) have had official languages over the last 230 years. At various times, English-language orthodoxy has been viewed as synonymous with, or at least a necessary component of, being "American" or a patriotic American. For instance, during the World War I and post–World War I eras, the anti-German sentiment throughout portions of the United States led to discrimination against German-Americans and laws designed to limit the teaching of German (or other languages) to young children. In *Meyer v. Nebraska* (1923) and *Bartels v. Iowa* (1923), the Supreme Court reversed convictions of teachers who taught German in schools, and ruled that the Due Process Clause and the First Amendment of the Constitution included the protection to teach non-English languages in schools.

About forty years later, as part of the Civil Rights Act of 1964, Congress passed Title VI, which forbids discrimination on the basis of race, color, or national origin in the provision of "any program or activity" covered by Title VI, which applied to services provided by state or local governments receiving federal funds. In *Lau v. Nicholas* (1974), the Court concluded that Title VI forbade discrimination against non-English-language-proficient children (in that case Chinese students in the San Francisco school district) and mandated that under Title VI, non-English-language-proficient children receive bilingual education or instruction in their native language. Beginning in the 1970s, with increased immigration from Asia and Latin America, proposals emerged to make English the "official" language of the United States. One of the more vocal and high-profile advocates has been U.S. English and its former president, Linda Chavez. President George W. Bush nominated Ms. Chavez to be the Secretary of Labor, but her candidacy failed when allegations surfaced that she had hired an undocumented alien from Guatemala.[1] Employers began increasingly to include "English-only" policies in the workplace, which were challenged in courts under Title VII and other laws, with divergent results. However, to date, the Supreme Court has not considered any English-only policies in the workplace.

The Supreme Court accepted certiorari in *Arizonans for Official English v. Arizona* (1997), a case involving a challenge by a state employee to Arizona's constitutional amendment making English its official language. The Court declined to rule directly on the issues, concluding that the suit became moot when the state government employee resigned from her post.[2] In another case challenging Arizona's official English law, the Arizona Supreme Court declared it unconstitutional.[3] Like Arizona, Alabama amended its constitution to declare English "the official language of the state of Alabama." In accordance with that constitutional amendment, approved by the voters in 1990, Alabama officials decided to administer state driver's license examinations only in English. Alabama's position was that the English-only license examination policy was necessary to advance public safety.

By accepting federal funding from the federal government, specifically the United States Department of Justice (DOJ) and Department of Transportation (DOT), Alabama became subject to federal laws, including the restrictions of Title VI of the Civil Rights Act of 1964. Section 602 of Title VI authorizes federal agencies "to effectuate the provisions of [sec. 601] . . . by issuing rules, regulations, or orders of general applicability," and the DOJ in an exercise of this authority promulgated a regulation forbidding funding recipients to "utilize criteria or methods of administration which have the effect of subjecting individuals to discrimination because of their race, color, or national origin."

Martha Sandoval filed a class action suit against James Alexander, director of the Alabama Department of Public Safety (DPS), in federal court in the Middle District of Alabama, contending that because the DPS accepted grants of financial assistance from the federal government, Alabama's English-only policy violated Title VI's prohibition against national origin discrimination. On May 6, 1997, Ms. Sandoval's attorneys filed a motion for class certification that the district court granted on October 17, 1997, without objection from the governmental defendants. The trial began on February 17, 1998, and lasted about a week. The district court issued its corrected opinion on June 5, 1998, agreeing with Ms. Sandoval and granting her the injunctive relief she sought, preventing DPS from enforcing the English-only policy and ordering the department to accommodate non-English speakers. On November 30, 1999, the Eleventh Circuit Court of Appeals affirmed the trial court's rulings. Both courts rejected Alabama's argument that Title VI did not provide respondents a cause of action to enforce the regulation. *Alexander* turns, in part, on the difference between intentional, direct discrimination based on an action against a person or persons, on the one hand, and *disparate impact* claims, on the other. "Disparate impact" claims, which arise often in the context of claims of employment discrimination, involve facially neutral policies that disproportionately target or impact a group based on race, national origin, or other prohibited criteria.

B. *Alexander v. Sandoval* (2001): The Opinions

The Court heard argument on January 16, 2001, and the Court issued its opinions on April 24, 2001. Justice Scalia delivered the opinion of the Court for four other justices. Justice Scalia defined the issue before the Court as "whether private individuals may sue to enforce disparate-impact regulations promulgated under Title VI of the Civil Rights Act of 1964." Justice Scalia then limited the scope of the opinion and the review, writing that the Court was not inquiring whether the DOJ regulation was authorized by section 602, or whether the courts below were correct to hold that the English-only policy had the effect of discriminating on the basis of national origin. Instead, the "petition for writ of certiorari raised, and we agreed to review, only the question posed in the first paragraph of this opinion: whether there is a private cause of action to enforce the regulation."

Justice Scalia then set out the background of the case and began the discussion of Title VI. Although prior cases had involved Title VI, Justice Scalia called it "perhaps an understatement" that the Court's precedents "have not eliminated all uncertainty regarding its commands." Justice Scalia then set forth, amidst disagreement on Title VI issues, three aspects of Title VI that "must be taken as given." First, private individuals may indisputably sue to enforce section 601 of Title VI and obtain both injunctive relief and damages. Second, section 601 prohibits only intentional discrimination. Justice Scalia cited the leading affirmative action/"reverse discrimination" case of *Regents of the Univ. of Cal. v. Bakke* (1978). Third, the Court assumed for purposes of deciding the Sandoval case "that regulations promulgated under §602 of Title VI may validly proscribe activities that have a disparate impact on racial groups, even though such activities are permissible under §601." Justice Scalia assumed without deciding that the DOJ and DOT regulations prohibiting activities having a disparate impact on the basis of race were valid, since Alabama officials had not challenged them.

Ms. Sandoval's lawyers argued that if the Court were to reject a private cause of action to enforce disparate-impact regulations, the Court would have to ignore the actual language of two prior Supreme Court cases, *Guardians Ass'n. v. Civil Service Commission of the City of New York* (1983) and *Cannon v. University of Chicago* (1979). Justice Scalia, who was a professor at the University of Chicago Law School prior to his appointment to the Court by President Reagan, disagreed and noted that "in any event, this Court is bound by holdings, not language." Justice Scalia stated that *Cannon* had been decided on the assumption that the University of Chicago had intentionally discriminated against Ms. Cannon, thereby holding that Title IX created a private right of action to enforce its ban on intentional discrimination. According to Justice Scalia, this private right recognized in *Cannon* did not extend to claims based on disparate impact. Justice Scalia then noted that no prior opinion of the Supreme Court had ever explicitly stated that the private right of action claimed by Ms. Sandoval existed.

According to the Court's opinion, *Lau* forbade funding recipients to take actions which had the effect of discriminating on the basis of race, color, or national origin. Justice Scalia stated that the Court in *Alexander* faced the "question avoided by *Lau.*" Justice Scalia stated that since the Court in opinions rendered after *Lau* rejected *Lau*'s interpretation of section 601 as reaching beyond intentional discrimination, "[i]t is clear now that the disparate-impact regulations do not simply apply §601—since they indeed forbid conduct that §601 permits—and therefore clear that the private right of action to enforce §601 does not include a private right to enforce these regulations." According to the Court's opinion, the right of a person to sue based on a disparate-impact claim under Title VI requires an explicit intent and law created by Congress to "create not just a private right but also a private remedy." The Court noted that without finding such intent, the Supreme Court or other courts may not imply a cause of action if Congress did not intend to do so, regardless of "how desirable that might be as a policy matter, or how compatible with the statute." In 1964, the Court explained that it was the Court's duty to be "alert to provide such remedies as are necessary to make effective the congressional purpose" expressed by a statute; Justice Scalia stated that in 1975 the Court developed a different standard and "abandoned that understanding." Justice Scalia then wrote that "[h]aving sworn off the habit of venturing beyond Congress's intent, we will not accept [Ms. Sandoval's] invitation to have one last drink." The Court's opinion analogizes claims under Title VI to claims under the Securities Act of 1934, under which the Court rejected implied private rights of action.

The Court stated that in determining whether Congress intended there to be a private right of action to enforce a law, the Court begins with the "text and structure" of the law, Title VI in this case. Noting that section 602 authorizes federal agencies "to effectuate the provisions of [sec. 601] . . . by issuing rules, regulations, or orders of general applicability," the Court found it "immediately clear" that the "'rights-creating' language so critical to the Court's analysis in *Cannon* of §601 . . . is completely absent from §602." Justice Scalia found the focus of section 602 "twice removed from the individuals who will ultimately benefit from Title VI's protection. Statutes that focus on the person regulated rather than the individuals protected create 'no implication of an intent to confer rights on a particular class of persons.'" According to the Court, section 602 "is yet a step further removed: it focuses neither on the individuals protected nor even on the funding recipients being regulated, but on the agencies that will do the regulating." As Justice Scalia stated, the "express provisions of one method of enforcing a substantive rule suggests that Congress intended to preclude others." The Court found "no evidence anywhere to suggest that Congress intended to create a private right to enforce regulations promulgated under §602." The Court likewise rejected contentions that the regulation might aid in interpreting congressional intent and that the subsequent amendments "ratified" the Court's prior opinions finding an implied private right of action to enforce disparate-impact regulations. Therefore, the Court concluded that Congress did not intend to create a private right of action like the one Ms. Sandoval had filed. Therefore, the Supreme Court reversed the judgment of the Eleventh Court of Appeals and ruled against Ms. Sandoval and the class members.

Three justices joined Justice Stevens' dissenting opinion. The other dissenters were Justice Souter, and President Bill Clinton's two appointees, Justice Ruth Bader Ginsburg and Justice Steven Breyer. Justice Stevens began his opinion by stating that in 1964, as part of the groundbreaking and comprehensive Civil Rights Act, Congress prohibited recipients of federal funds from discriminating on the basis of race, ethnicity, or national origin. Pursuant to powers expressly delegated by that act, the federal agencies and departments responsible for awarding and administering federal contracts immediately adopted regulations prohibiting federal contractees from adopting policies that have the "effect" of discriminating on those bases. At the time these regulations came into effect, prevailing principles of statutory construction assumed that Congress intended a private right of action if necessary to protect individual rights granted by federal law. According to Justice Stevens' dissent, "Relying both on this presumption and on independent analysis of Title VI, this Court has repeatedly and consistently affirmed the right of private individuals to bring civil suits to enforce rights guaranteed by Title VI. A fair reading of those cases, and coherent implementation of the statutory scheme, requires the same result under Title VI's implementing regulations."

According to Justice Stevens:

> Today, in a decision unfounded in our precedent and hostile to decades of settled expectations, a majority of this Court carves out an important exception to the right of private action long recognized under Title VI. In so doing, the Court makes three distinct, albeit interrelated, errors. First, the Court provides a muddled account of both the reasoning and the breadth of our prior decisions endorsing a private right of action under Title VI, thereby obscuring the conflict between those opinions and today's decision. Second, the Court offers a flawed and unconvincing analysis of the relationship between §§601 and 602 of the Civil Rights Act of 1964, ignoring more plausible and persuasive explanations detailed in our prior opinions. Finally, the Court badly misconstrues the theoretical linchpin of our decision in *Cannon v. University of Chicago* (1979), mistaking that decision's careful contextual analysis for judicial fiat.

While conceding that the majority correctly stated that the Court had never used the words that a "private right of action exists to enforce the disparate-impact regulations promulgated under §602," Justice Stevens wrote that in the opinion of the four dissenters that right *did* exist, and had been assumed in prior opinions from the Court, which the opinion examined. Only Justice Stevens and Chief Justice Rehnquist were members of the Court both in 2001, at the time of *Alexander,* and in 1979, when the Court decided *Cannon.* Justice Stevens interpreted *Lau* as follows: "When this Court faced an identical case 27 years ago, all the Justices believed that private parties could bring lawsuits under Title VI and its implementing regulations to enjoin the provision of governmental services in a manner that discriminated against non-English speakers." According to Justice Stevens' dissent, nothing in the *Lau* majority's opinion suggested a difference between a private action under section 601 and a private action under section 602. Justice Stevens also quoted a portion of *Cannon* where the Court had stated in 1979 that "[w]e have no doubt that Congress intended to create Title IX remedies comparable to those available under Title VI and that it understood Title VI as authorizing an implied private cause of action for victims of the prohibited discrimination." Justice Stevens challenged the majority's interpretation that intentional discrimination was required, stating that the opinion recognized a private right of action for victims of all prohibited discrimination, not just some. Justice Stevens also noted that "*Cannon* was itself a disparate-impact case." Justice Stevens also discussed the *Guardian* case and interpreted it to "strongly imply" a private right of action. Taking these three precedents, including the unanimous *Lau* opinion, Justice Stevens found the answer "overdetermined" in favor of allowing Ms. Sandoval's claim to proceed. In footnote 1 to his dissenting opinion, Justice Stevens noted that the overwhelming number of lower federal appellate courts that had considered the issue had either "explicitly or implicitly held that a private right of action exists to enforce all of the regulations issued pursuant to Title VI, including the disparate-impact regulations." According to Justice Stevens, "Even absent my continued belief that Congress intended a private right of action to enforce both Title VI and its implementing regulations, I would answer the question presented in the affirmative and affirm the decision of the Court of Appeals as a matter of *stare decisis.*"

Justice Stevens then criticized Justice Scalia's statutory analysis as doing "violence to both the text and the structure of Title VI. Section 601 does not stand in isolation, but rather as part of an integrated remedial scheme. Section 602 exists for the sole purpose of forwarding the anti-discrimination ideals laid out in §601." The dissenters found the Court's opinion "even more troubling" because prior cases had

already adopted a simpler and more sensible model for understanding the relationship between the two sections. For three decades, we have treated §602 as granting the responsible agencies the power to issue broad prophylactic rules aimed at realizing the vision laid out in §601, even if the conduct captured by these rules is at times broader than that which would otherwise be prohibited.

The dissenters described as not only reasonable, but also "inspired," Congress' approach of allowing agencies the first opportunity to try to remedy the "complex determination of what sorts of disparate impacts upon minorities constituted sufficiently significant social problems" without the necessity of specific legislation as opposed to regulations. Justice Stevens found additional support in the so-called "*Chevron* doctrine," based on the landmark case of *Chevron, U.S.A., Inc. v. Natural Resources Defense Council, Inc.* (1984). The *Chevron* doctrine provides that in many contexts, the Supreme Court defers and lower courts defer as controlling to the interpretations made by the agencies charged with administering statutes unless the interpretation of the statute by the agency is unreasonable. According to the dissenters, only one private cause of action exists under Title VI, which applies to both section 601 and section 602 claims.

Justice Stevens' dissenting opinion chastised the majority's claim that "As much as we would like to help those disadvantaged by discrimination, we must resist the temptation to pour ourselves 'one last drink'" by stating that "[o]verwrought imagery aside, it is the majority's approach that blinds itself to congressional intent." According to the dissenters, Congress, not the Court, created the cause of action, and Congress ratified the Court's rulings in *Cannon* by amending Title VI in 1986 and 1988 and not overruling those opinions. The dissenters also noted that "Congress does not legislate in a vacuum" and that in 1964, when Congress passed Title VI, the Court's analysis, and the law at the time, was to imply private causes of action whenever statutes designed to protect a particular class did not contain specific enforcement mechanisms. Justice Stevens found that the "present majority's unwillingness to explain its refusal to find the reasoning in *Cannon* persuasive suggests that today's decision is the unconscious product of the majority's profound distaste for implied causes of action rather than an attempt to discern the intent of the Congress that enacted Title VI of the Civil Rights Act of 1964." The dissenters found the Court's disclaimer that it did not venture beyond Congress' intent as hollow and inaccurate.

C. The Significance of *Alexander* and Post-*Alexander* Developments to Latinos in the American Legal System

Alexander is significant to Latinos in the American legal system for various reasons. First, Latinos are generally protected from racial, national origin, or ethnic discrimination by Title VI as well as Title VII. The 5–4 decision by the Court prohibiting people from trying to enforce these rights themselves against policies by state and other governmental agencies that while facially neutral have a discriminatory effect on Latinos limits the "teeth" or enforcement mechanisms of Title VI. In the history of the United States, state officials have at times been actively involved in, or at least complicit with, discriminatory treatment toward Hispanics and others.

In 2004, Senator Ted Kennedy and other lawmakers presented to Congress a proposed bill referred to as the Civil Rights Act of 2004, seeking to modify Title VI and overruling *Alexander*, which did not pass. The proposed bill also sought to overrule *Hoffman Plastic Compounds, Inc. v. National Labor Relations Board* (2002), a case where a 5–4 majority of the Rehnquist Court (in an opinion authored by Chief Justice Rehnquist) ruled that undocumented aliens could not recover in claims where employers have violated the Fair Labor Standards Act of 1938. According to one commentator, the *Hoffman Plastic Compounds* opinion demonstrates the antipathy of the Rehnquist Court toward aliens, and a majority that "seems willfully ignorant of the realities of life for many poor and struggling people."[4] The proposed congressional bill sought a result for Title VI similar to that which Congress accomplished during the first President George Bush's term, when Congress passed the Civil Rights Act of 1991, which amended Title VII of the Civil Rights Act to overrule Rehnquist Court decisions that had interpreted Title VII's protections quite narrowly.

Second, *Alexander* typifies cases where the Court has avoided ruling directly on the controversial issue of whether the Constitution's silence on English as an "official" language of the United States means that the Constitution prohibits a state or other government from so adopting an official language or not. As in *Arizonans for Official English* in 1997, rather than addressing the issue of the constitutionality of English-only rules or laws directly, the Court decided *Alexander* on a procedural issue, mainly that Ms. Sandoval and the other class members lacked the standing (or right) to assert a claim that the English-only law discriminated again her and others on the basis of national origin, contrary to Title VI's protections. In fact, Lisa Kloppenberg devoted the first chapter of her book *Playing It Safe* to the *Arizonans for Official English* case. Alabama and Arizona are not alone in raising issues of English-only and Latinos' drivers' licenses.[5] The issue of licensing aliens surfaced in the California election that recalled Governor Gray Davis, as well. Several other states have adopted English-only laws. The rise in English-only rules in the workplace also increased throughout the 1990s and into the twenty-first century, as noted briefly in Chapter 7.[6] Some who seek to codify English as an official language may be trying to promote unity. Others in the English-only movement are motivated by more than just a desire to "assimilate" Americans; rather, they seek to use these laws to keep the United States from being a "mongrel nation"—invoking the racial supremacy of a prior era of popular nativism.[7] Laws or rules seeking to mandate English, whether imposed by government officials or by private citizens, frequently have discriminatory effects on Latinos, including the deprivation of governmental benefits. Steven Bender has used the term "language vigilantes" to refer to non-governmental persons or businesses that seek to impose English orthodoxy on speakers of languages other than English in places such as school and work.[8] As an example, Kloppenberg has noted that the woman who sued to challenge the Arizona English-only law, Maria Kelly Yngiuez, was subject to harassment after she filed that suit, including someone shooting through her window and sending hate mail.[9] Nativist sentiment reappeared in public life in the United States during the 1990s. Nativist impulses affect not only immigrants but also residents, and even citizens, who may be discriminated against on the basis of the way they look, the way they speak, or even on the basis of their name. Hopefully in the twenty-first century, the Supreme Court will not defer to political forces that may be catering to new nativist influences, as the Court did at the beginning of the twentieth century by creating the Territorial Incorporation Doctrine (Chapter 2). That the Court will be presented the opportunity to consider the propriety of attempts to limit constitutional rights and safeguards of Latinos and other Americans, as in the case of Ms. Sandoval, is virtually certain.

Conclusion

Landmark decisions are generally those that significantly change existing law. Another sense of "landmark" involves features of land, such as monuments or other markers setting up boundaries or having historical significance. This book has dealt with both senses of the term "landmark." Within the larger category of landmark cases that have significantly changed existing law, the focus has been on those that either directly involved Latinos/Hispanics (e.g., *Miranda*) or established the markers by which Latinos/Hispanics have been categorized and treated in the American legal system.

In *Botiller v. Dominguez* (1889), the Fuller Court (1888–1910) effectively ruled that good title to land in California under Mexican land grants was insufficient to protect the rights of those who did not comply with a federal recording statute, notwithstanding the Treaty of Guadalupe Hidalgo. In *Balzac v. Porto [sic] Rico* (1922), the Court ruled that the right to trial by jury was not fundamental enough to apply to Puerto Rico, thus reaffirming the Territorial Incorporation Doctrine, which provided legal sanction to the American government owning colonies and governing the territories as property, and the inhabitants therein as subjects, rather than as equal citizens.

The Warren Court (1953–1969), for all of its shortcomings, provided Latinos/Hispanics legal precedents supporting their claims to equal and fair treatment in the American legal system, particularly in public life, the legal and political process, and the criminal justice system. *Hernandez v. Texas* (1954) challenged the binary black-white view of the Equal Protection Clause and recognized that Mexican-Americans, like other Latino/Hispanic groups, have been subject to discrimination and that they thus had the right to assert claims of equal protection violation that courts should take seriously. *Katzenbach v. Morgan* (1966) changed the landscape by suggesting that statutory schemes involving protections to minorities, including Latinos/Hispanics, were a floor to protection of their rights; this paved the way for bilingual ballots and other mechanisms for empowering disenfranchised Latino/Hispanic voters. *Miranda v. Arizona* (1966) established the standard to which governmental officers would be held during in-custody interrogations.

The Burger Court (1969–1986) largely constrained the Court's expansion of recognizing obligations in protecting civil rights and government responsibilities toward citizens and aliens, including Latinos/Hispanics and others, with the notable exception of children of undocumented aliens in *Plyler v. Doe* (1982). By contrast, in *San Antonio ISD v. Rodriguez* (1973), a landmark case in the area of public education, the Court held that education was not a fundamental right under the United States Constitution, contrary to language in prior Court cases, and found that poor people were not a suspect class. *Plyler* may limit *Rodriguez* in cases where the state completely deprives a person of a right or benefit that it provides to others. The Burger Court also decided *Espinoza v. Farah Mfg. Co.* (1973), the Supreme Court's landmark case during the first forty years of Title VII of the Civil Rights Act, on the meaning of the term "national origin," which the Court interpreted to exclude discrimination based on alien status. *United States v. Brignoni-Ponce* (1975) sets the standard that stopping someone far from the Mexico-U.S. border solely because that person "looks Mexican" is unreasonable. However, as the Court's opinion set out, looking Mexican may be constitutionally permissible as part of a profile for law enforcement.

In the Rehnquist Court (1986–2005), *INS v. Cardoza-Fonseca* (1987) became a landmark in the area of political asylum, recognizing a lesser burden for those seeking to remain in the United States as refugees. Many people from Latin America have used *Cardoza-Fonseca*'s ruling in seeking to remain in the United States. *U.S. v. Verdugo-Urquidez* (1990) limits the applicability of the Fourth Amendment's protections and exemplifies the Rehnquist Court's move to the right. Like *Brignoni-Ponce, Hernandez v. New York* (1991) stands in part for the proposition that discriminating against Latinos/Hispanics violates the Constitution. *Hernandez v. New York* also reflects the fact that by 1991, the Supreme Court primarily used the term "Hispanic/Latino" rather than the terms for country of origin, consistent with the trend in the United States to refer to people from the various Spanish-speaking groups under these broader categories. While decrying discrimination against Latinos/Hispanics, *Hernandez v. New York*'s exception of allowing discrimination against Spanish bilingual jurors runs the risk of swallowing up the rule. *Johnson v. DeGrandy* (1994) addressed complexities likely to continue to arise involving tri-ethnic situations in voting rights; the Court basically found that rough proportionality sufficed to defeat a history of discriminatory treatment in voting under the Voting Rights Act. Finally, *Alexander v. Sandoval* (2001) limits the rights of Hispanic/Latinos and other private citizens and residents to challenge discriminatory practices in the area of services provided by state and local agencies under Title VI of the Civil Rights Act of 1964 and leaves open the question of the legality and constitutionality of English-only rules and laws for another day.

Latinos and American Law does not include, by any means, all of the significant cases involving Latinos/Hispanics in the American legal system. Several other landmark cases have been mentioned or cited. However, this survey of influential cases spanning three centuries should provide a historical background from which to understand how legal issues have generally affected Latinos/Hispanics in the United States.

Demographics alone suggests the likelihood of more cases involving Latinos reaching the Supreme Court in the future. Historically, the people now called Hispanics have been largely an afterthought or marginal in the legal process. This is particularly true at the national level. The traditional absence of political representation accounts for some of this, as does the pre–*Hernandez v. Texas* binary view of race.

In cases involving Latinos, the Supreme Court has varied from being outright hostile to Hispanic claimants to accommodating interests particular to Hispanics. Some of the landmark cases, like *Hernandez v. New York* and *Brignoni-Ponce*, also reflect a pattern of formally proclaiming a commitment to equality for Latinos while creating exceptions that engulf the proclamations. Particularly disturbing are cases like *Balzac* and the *Insular Cases*, which branded formal inequalities into settled constitutional law, or, as the Chief Justice of the First Circuit Court of Appeals, Juan Torruella, has described it, a "doctrine of separate and unequal" in the case of Puerto Rico.

As of 2005, no Hispanic has ever served as a justice on the United States Supreme Court. Some have suggested that this statement is incorrect either because Justice Benjamin Cardozo was of Portuguese descent or because Justice Antonin Scalia is of Italian descent. However, neither of these groups is generally considered Hispanic/Latino. In 2005, President George W. Bush made a landmark appointment in naming Alberto Gonzalez as the attorney general of the United States, the first Hispanic to serve in that position. Mr. Gonzalez' appointment as attorney general is another clear signal that Hispanics have become more prominent in the political and legal realms of the United States. While governor of Texas, President George W. Bush had appointed Attorney General Gonzalez to the Texas Supreme Court, and there has been speculation that Mr. Gonzalez may be named as the first Latino candidate to the Supreme

Court as one of President George W. Bush's likely second-term Supreme Court appointments. Such an appointment would likely increase the profile of Latinos in the American legal system, whether that individual be Mr. Gonzalez or someone else.[1]

Latinos and American Law has featured cases involving the Court's interpretation of laws passed by Congress as well as constitutional issues. While the legislative branch can reverse the Court on the former, the Court is the last word on constitutional interpretation. Therefore, absent an amendment by the rare and purposefully cumbersome constitutional amendment process, changes in constitutional law generally occur only in response to watershed political changes or by changes to the Court's personnel. Accordingly, the composition of the U.S. Supreme Court should be a matter of interest to anyone interested in constitutional law.

I deliberately organized *Latinos and American Law* chronologically, making it more historical than "thematic" in order to focus on what actually happened rather than any argument about what should have happened. Accordingly, the book, like history, points in various directions and mirrors changes in political opinion. Nevertheless, some broad patterns and implications emerge. For one, with regard to Latinos, the Court has historically been generally a conservative institution, with some exceptions. Further, the Court has adopted what may have initially been controversial, but are now generally accepted, broad principles of non-discrimination and equality. And, the current political and historical landscape renders it likely that immigrant-related cases, cases involving law enforcement, and interpretations of the geographical expansion of constitutional protections will continue to resurface in the first quarter of the twenty-first century.

Some will criticize a work like this one on the notion that Americans should focus on things that unite us, not on those that divide us. Relatedly, I have heard criticisms about Latinos/Hispanics "refusing" to be part of the melting pot. In my view, the "melting pot" is in part a function of its specific, individual ingredients; adding different ingredients frequently changes the entire "recipe." This book has reviewed how the institution at the summit of the American legal system, the Supreme Court, has treated issues affecting the lives of millions of Latinos, as well as how the Court has at times retreated from directly or fairly addressing those issues. Increasingly, people proclaim that Hispanics are the "largest minority" group in the United States, and people have noted that several states have become or will become "majority-minority" (e.g., not Anglo) states. The number of Latinos in the United States exceeds 40 million and grows daily as a combined result of birth rates and immigration. The legal system, and its impact on this long-standing and growing segment of American society, is critical to the future of Latinos and all Americans in the United States.

Ultimately, the legal system, and those who serve in the system that make, interpret, and enforce the laws, must ensure fair treatment to all Americans. Without an intent of equal application of rules and laws, all that remains is pure politics. The founders drafted the United States Constitution with the goal of creating a government accountable to its citizens and based on the rule of law, not the will of monarchs or other rulers. These ideals are expressed in the Constitution and the Pledge of Allegiance, which speaks to one indivisible nation under God, "with liberty and justice for all." As we move into the twenty-first century, one hopes the Supreme Court will not repeat some of its historic rulings with respect to Latinos. As noted in this book, the U.S. Supreme Court condoned the taking of family ranches from Mexican landowners; the jailing of a Puerto Rican newspaper editor who criticized a local colonial governor, without a trial by jury; the prevention of Spanish-speaking citizens from fulfilling their civic obligation of serving as jurors, solely on the basis that they spoke Spanish; and the discrimination against residents who may not be proficient in English in activities as basic as obtaining a driver's license.

As the color of the United States changes, will the quality of its justice change? Does the ethnic composition of the United States change our understanding of who "the People" are and who are merely "persons"? Undoubtedly the serious threats posed by international terrorism and the national interests in controlling the United States' borders and egress will warrant constant, effective governmental action. However, will these and other legitimate security concerns translate into unjustified actions against United States citizens and others who do not seek to harm the country? Will certain Americans receive diminished constitutional protections? Hopefully by examining our past, we can do better in the future.

Notes

Introduction

1. *Black's Law Dictionary* 1414 (7th ed. 1999).
2. For instance, in Mexico, according to the doctrine of *jurisprudencia obligatoria*, once the Mexican supreme court has made the same ruling five consecutive times, it becomes settled law. Stephen Zamora, José Ramón Cossío, Leonel Pereznieto, José Roldán-Xopa, and David Lopez, *Mexican Law* 96–98 (2004).
3. Apart from ethnicity and national origin, some of the characteristics that significantly distinguish Hispanics and the people within the Latino/Hispanic categorizations can be gleaned through the book's content, such as geographic location, political aspirations and ideologies, gender, class, immigration history and status, and nationality. Some Latinos have family members who have resided in territory known as the United States for three hundred years, others only a few days. Frank D. Bean and María Tienda, *Hispanic Population of the United States* 104–134 (1987).
4. Some people do seem to care about the particular term or label. According to one writer, "Hispanic" is a term "concocted by federal bureaucrats [and] barrio political entrepreneurs when it suits their purposes." Peter Skerry, *Mexican-Americans: The Ambivalent Minority* 25 (1993). Some note that preferences for either "Latino" or "Hispanic" may relate to locale or geography. As Earl Shorris points out: "*Hispanic* is preferred in the Southeast and much of Texas. New Yorkers use both *Hispanic* and *Latino*. Chicago, where no nationality has attained a majority, prefers *Latino*. In California, the word *Hispanic* has been barred from the *Los Angeles Times*, in keeping with strong feelings of people in that community. Some people in New Mexico prefer *Hispano*." Earl Shorris, *Latinos: A Biography of the People* xvi–xvii (1992).
5. "Although common ancestral ties to Spain and/or Latin America as well as frequent usage of the Spanish language, might seem to imply an underlying

cultural similarity among peoples of Hispanic origin, the diverse settlement and immigration experiences of Mexicans, Puerto Ricans, Cubans, and other Hispanic groups have created distinct subpopulations with discernible demographic and economic characteristics. Persisting socioeconomic differences among these groups not only challenge the idea that the term 'Hispanic' [or Latino] is appropriate as an ethnic label, they also suggest that a careful scrutiny of the historical commonalities and divergences among these groups [is] relevant to understanding their contemporary sociodemographic situations." Bean and Tienda, *Hispanic Population* at 7.

6. Shorris, *Latinos* at 12.
7. Linda Chavez, *Out of the Barrio: Toward a New Politics of Hispanic Assimilation* 62 (1991).
8. *Tijerina v. Henry*, 398 U.S. 922, 923–924 (1970) (Douglas, J., dissenting).
9. See, e.g., Derrick Bell, *Race, Racism and American Law* 66–74 (3rd ed. 1992).

Chapter 1

1. I prefer citing the case in the manner traditionally used for referencing cases between people, as opposed to the style typically used for referencing cases *in rem* that involve property disputes.
2. David M. O'Brien, *Constitutional Law and Politics: Civil Rights and Civil Liberties* 36 (Vol. 2. 1991).
3. Treaty of Guadalupe Hidalgo, 9 Stat. 922, T.S. 207 (1848). See generally Richard Griswold del Castillo, *The Treaty of Guadalupe Hidalgo: A Legacy of Conflict* (1990).
4. Griswold del Castillo, *The Treaty of Guadalupe Hidalgo* at 62.
5. Douglas Brinkley, *A History of the United States* 151 (1998).
6. Akhil Reed Amar, *The Bill of Rights* 288 (1998).
7. Kermit L. Hall (ed.), *The Oxford Companion to the Supreme Court of the United States* 548 (1992).
8. Amar, *The Bill of Rights* at 288.
9. Juan F. Perea, Richard Delgado, Angela P. Harris, and Stephanie M. Wildman, *Race and Races: Cases and Resources for a Diverse America* 283–284 (2000), citing Christopher David Ruiz Cameron, One Hundred Fifty Years of Solitude: Reflections on the End of the History Academy's Dominance of Scholarship on the Treaty of Guadalupe Hidalgo, 5 *SW. J. L. & Trade Am.* 83, 97 (1998).
10. According to one source, only 813 claims were made to the commission under the act, 604 of which were confirmed. George Ochoa, *Atlas of Hispanic-American History* 93 (2001).
11. Perea et al., *Race and Races* at 278–280, 284–290.
12. Land grant claims continued late into the twentieth century. See, e.g., *Alliance of Descendants of Texas Land Grants v. United States*, 37 F.3d 1478 (Fed. Cir. 1994).
13. Griswold del Castillo, *The Treaty of Guadalupe Hidalgo* at 67.

Chapter 2

1. José Trías Monge, *Puerto Rico: The Trials of the Oldest Colony in the World* 26 (1997).
2. Trías Monge, *Puerto Rico* at 27.
3. Olga Jiménez de Waggenheim, *El Grito de Lares: Sus Causas y Sus Hombres* 159–217 (1980).
4. Trías Monge, *Puerto Rico* at 5.
5. Trías Monge, *Puerto Rico* at 23; Juan R. Torruella, *The Supreme Court and Puerto Rico: The Doctrine of Separate and Unequal* 11 (1985).
6. See generally, José Cabranes, *Citizenship and the American Empire* (1979); Torruella, *The Supreme Court and Puerto Rico*. Among academic works analyzing the factors affecting U.S. relations with the territories see Michael H. Hunt, *Ideology and U.S. Foreign Policy* (1987).
7. Racial or national origin issues were implicated in the 1898 war as well. As Harvard professor Archibald Coolidge states in a book published in the early twentieth century: "In considering the causes of war, we should remember . . . that the relations between Spain and the United States had never been really cordial, nor was there any reason why they should have been. The Americans had inherited the anti-Spanish prejudices of their English ancestors." Archibald C. Coolidge, *The United States as a World Power* 122 (1912).
8. Under American rule, the name of the island was "officially" Porto Rico for some time. *Balzac v. Porto [sic] Rico*, 258 U.S. 298, 42 S. Ct. 343 (1922).
9. For a thorough analysis of the *Insular Cases* and the academic debate, see Torruella, *The Supreme Court and Puerto Rico* at 24–31. There has been renewed interest in legal academia in the *Insular Cases* (see, e.g., Christine Duffy Burnett and Burke Marshall, *Foreign in a Domestic Sense: Puerto Rico, American Expansion, and the Constitution* (2001); Sanford Levinson, Why the Canon Should Be Expanded to Include the Insular Cases and the Saga of American Expansionism, 17 *Const. Comment* 241 (Summer 2000).
10. "The Congress shall have Power to dispose of and make all needful Rules and Regulations respecting the Territory or other Property belonging to the United States." U.S. Const. art. IV, sec. 3.
11. "New States may be admitted by the Congress into this Union; but no new State shall be formed or erected within the Jurisdiction of any other State; nor any State be formed by the Junction of two or more States, or Parts of States, without the Consent of the Legislatures of the States concerned as well as of the Congress." U.S. Const. art. IV, sec. 3.
12. *Thompson v. Utah*, 170 U.S. 343, 346–347 (1898).
13. Torruella, *The Supreme Court and Puerto Rico* at 3 n. 1.
14. The "Territorial Incorporation Doctrine" should not be confused with the incorporation of the Bill of Rights against the states. According to Neuman, it is "unfortunate that tradition has associated the word 'incorporate' with both

the applicability of the Bill of Rights to federal action in the territories and the applicability of the Bill of Rights to actions of the states. In the first case, the reference is to incorporating a territory into the United States, and in the second to incorporating the Bill of Rights into the Fourteenth Amendment." Gerald L. Neuman, Whose Constitution? 100 *Yale L.J.* 909, 958 n. 287 (Jan. 1991). The use of the term "incorporation" in both instances is not so unfortunate in my view since this usage highlights the strong links between the two debates.

15. Before the Spanish-Cuban-American War, "the distinction between acquisition and incorporation was not regarded as important, or at least it was not fully understood and had not aroused great controversy. Before that, the purpose of Congress might well be a matter of mere inference . . . but in these latter days, incorporation is not to be assumed without express declaration, or an implication so strong as to exclude any other view." *Balzac,* 258 U.S. at 306, 311.

16. *Downes v. Bidwell,* 182 U.S. 244, 373 (1901) (Fuller, C. J., dissenting).

17. Simeon E. Baldwin, The Constitutional Questions Incident to the Acquisition and Government by the United States of Island Territory, 12 *Harv. L. Rev.* 393, 415 (1899) (emphasis added).

18. Talcott H. Russell, Results of Expansion, 9 *Yale L.J.* 239, 240–242 (1900) (emphasis added).

19. Brinkley, *History of the United States* at 335.

20. Brinkley, *History of the United States* at 335–336.

21. Sandra Day O'Connor, *The Majesty of the Law: Reflections of a Supreme Court Justice* 119 (2003).

22. O'Connor, *The Majesty of the Law* at 119. By contrast, during the 1991–2000 period, 19% were decided by one vote, usually 5–4.

23. Brinkley, *History of the United States* at 361–363.

24. On the trial, see Vincent Buranelli, *The Trial of Peter Zenger* (1957); and James Alexander, *A Brief Narrative of the Case and Trial of John Peter Zenger* (1963). On the significance of the trial see Akhil Reed Amar, The Bill of Rights and the Fourteenth Amendment, 101 *Yale L.J.* 1193, 1277, 1282 (1992); Amar, *The Bill of Rights* at 87, 236–237.

25. Consisting of headlines claiming "Traitor, Seducer, and Perjurer. Sensational Allegations Against Commissioner Legarda. Made of Record and Read in English—Spanish Reading Waived. Wife would have killed him. Legarda Pale and Nervous." The article dealt with the testimony of Don Benito Legarda, a member of the Philippine Commission who testified for the prosecution against the editor of another paper named Valdez. *Dorr,* 195 U.S. at 149. More recently, the Samoan right to trial by jury in Samoa was also implicated in the First Amendment context since that case involved Jake King, the publisher of the weekly *Samoan News,* the only newspaper in American Samoa. Stanley Laughlin Jr., The Application of the Constitution in United States Territories: American Samoa, a Case Study, 2 *U. Haw. L. Rev.* 337, 341 (1980–1981). The trial judge was the

head of the Samoan Supreme Court. That case was an income tax evasion case, not a libel prosecution.

26. This rationale has disturbing similarities with later cases involving Puerto Rico and federal assistance to Puerto Ricans. In *Harris v. Rosario*, 446 U.S. 651, 652 (1980) and *Califano v. Torres*, 435 U.S. 1 (1978), the Court said that one of the three rational factors permitting discriminatory federal funding to United States citizens in Puerto Rico was that "greater benefits could disrupt the Puerto Rican economy." Some problems with this rationale are highlighted by Justice Thurgood Marshall in dissent: "This rationale has troubling overtones. It suggests that programs designed to help the poor should be less fully applied in those areas where the need may be the greatest, simply because otherwise the relative poverty of recipients compared to other persons in the same geographic area will somehow be upset." *Harris*, 446 U.S. at 655–656 (Marshall, J., dissenting).

27. "Congress has thought that a people like the Filipinos or the Porto [*sic*] Ricans, trained to a complete judicial system which knows no juries, living in compact and ancient communities, with definitely formed customs and political conceptions, should be permitted themselves to determine how far they wish to adopt this institution of Anglo-Saxon origin." *Balzac*, 258 U.S. at 310.

28. Ronald Fernandez, *The Disenchanted Island: Puerto Rico and the United States in the Twentieth Century* 55–56 (1992); Pedro A. Malavet, *America's Colony: The Political and Cultural Conflict between the United States and Puerto Rico* 93 (2004). English was imposed as the language of instruction in the schools in Puerto Rico. Compare with *Meyer v. Nebraska*, 262 U.S. 390, 397–403, 43 S. Ct. 625, 626–627 (1923); *Bartels v. Iowa*, 262 U.S. 404, 409–411, 43 S. Ct. 628, 629–630 (1923).

29. *Dorr*, 195 U.S. at 155 (Harlan, J., dissenting).

30. Torruella, *The Supreme Court and Puerto Rico* at 99 (jury trials in Puerto Rico since 1899). See generally, Carmelo Delgado Cintron, *Derecho y Colonialismo: La Trayectoria Histórica del Derecho Puertorriqueño* (1988).

31. Laughlin, *Constitution in American Samoa* at 372.

32. This language comes from a speech by General Nelson Miles upon arriving in Puerto Rico with the United States' invasion force in 1898, when he said: "We have not come to make war upon the people of a country that for centuries has been oppressed, but, on the contrary, to bring you protection, not only to yourselves but to your property, to promote your prosperity, and to bestow upon you the immunities and blessings of the liberal institutions of our government . . . This is not a war of devastation, but one to give all within the control of its military and naval forces the advantages and blessings of enlightened civilization." Arturo Morales Carrión, *A Political and Cultural History of Puerto Rico* 132 (1983); Kal Waggenheim and Olga Jiménez de Waggenheim, *The Puerto Ricans: A Documented History* 95 (1994).

33. Akhil Reed Amar, The Bill of Rights as a Constitution, 100 *Yale L.J.* 1131, 1190 (1991); Amar, *The Bill of Rights* at 96.

34. For example, in *Elk v. Wilkins,* 112 U.S. 94, 99–104 (1884), the Supreme Court held that Indians, even assimilated ones, were not citizens of the United States and could not vote in elections despite the clear and unequivocal language of the Fourteenth and Fifteenth Amendments. In *United States v. Kagama,* 118 U.S. 375, 379–381 (1886), the Supreme Court held that Indians were within the geographical limits of the United States and subject to the plenary powers of Congress.

35. Sarah H. Cleveland, Powers Inherent in Sovereignty: Indians, Aliens, Territories, and the Nineteenth Century Origins of Plenary Power over Foreign Affairs, 81 *Tex. L. Rev.* 1, 14 (Nov. 2002). Cleveland writes that the "nativist and nationalist impulses combined particularly powerfully in the *Insular Cases,*" noting that Justice Henry Brown, who authored one of the key *Insular Cases* and *Plessy,* opened his autobiography with the statement that in his pure, English family, there "has been no admixture of blood for 250 years" (266 n. 1773).

36. *Duncan v. Louisiana,* 391 U.S. 145, 186 (1968) (Harlan, J., dissenting).

37. *Duncan,* 391 U.S. at 155–156 (citations omitted).

38. David M. Helfeld, How Much of the United States Constitution and Statutes are Applicable to the Commonwealth of Puerto Rico? *First Circuit Judicial Conference,* 110 F.R.D. 449, 458 (1985).

39. *Torres v. Puerto Rico,* 442 U.S. 465, 475–476 (1979) (Brennan, J., concurring).

40. See, e.g., *U.S. v. Kole,* 164 F.3d 164, 167 (3rd Cir. 1998).

41. Richard Weisskoff, *Factories and Foodstamps: The Puerto Rico Model of Development* (1985).

42. "No person shall be held to answer for a capital, or otherwise infamous crime, unless on a presentment or indictment of a Grand Jury, except in cases arising in the land or naval forces, or in the Militia, when in actual service in time of War or public danger." U.S. Const. amend. V.

43. *Dorr,* 195 U.S. at 156. (Harlan, J., dissenting).

44. *Downes,* 182 U.S. at 382–383 (Harlan, J., dissenting).

45. *Igartua de la Rosa v. U.S.,* 107 F. Supp. 2d 140 (D.P.R. 2000), and 113 F. Supp. 2d 228, 242 (D.P.R. 2000), rev'd, 229 F.3d at 85.

46. *U.S. v. Acosta-Martinez,* 106 F. Supp. 2d 311, 321 (D.P.R. 2000).

47. *Igartua de la Rosa,* 107 F. Supp. 2d at 148–149. There has been a recent resurgent scholarly interest in the constitutional issues. See, e.g., Torruella, *The Supreme Court and Puerto Rico;* Trías Monge, *Puerto Rico;* and Christina Duffy Burnett and Burke Marshall (eds.), *Foreign in a Domestic Sense: Puerto Rico, American Expansion, and the Constitution* (2001).

Chapter 3

1. Lucas A. Powe Jr., *The Warren Court and American Politics* xv (2000).

2. The relatively brief U.S. Constitution has four provisions relating to jury trials. As Akhil Amar has pointed out, the paradigmatic image underlying the Bill of Rights is the jury. The jury serves important societal functions for both the

individual defendant and society as a whole. Amar, The Bill of Rights as a Constitution at 1190. According to the Supreme Court, the criminal defendant is protected by the jury as a check: to "prevent oppression by the Government"; to safeguard "against the corrupt or overzealous prosecutor and against the compliant, biased, or eccentric judge," *Duncan,* 391 U.S. at 156. Society benefits from the jury system because it enables the ordinary citizen to participate in government, and it checks the power of distant authorities.

3. *Duncan,* 391 U.S. at 156–158.

4. Powe, *The Warren Court* at 27, 44–45.

5. Clare Sheridan, Another White Race: Mexican Americans and the Paradox of Whiteness in Jury Selection, *Law and History Review* (Spring 2003) at 9 nn. 14–15. http://www.history cooperative.org/journals/1hr/21.1/forum she ridan.html (Dec. 12, 2003).

6. See generally Guadalupe San Miguel Jr., *Let All of Them Take Heed: Mexican Americans and the Campaign for Educational Equality in Texas, 1910–1981* (1987).

7. *ISD v. Salvatierra,* 33 S.W. 791 (Tex. Civ. App.—San Antonio 1930); Sheridan, Another White Race at n. 79.

8. Sheridan, Another White Race at n. 19.

9. Stephen A. Saltzburg and Daniel J. Capra, *American Criminal Procedure: Cases and Commentary* 904 (4th ed. 1992).

10. *Ciudadanos Unidos de San Juan v. Hidalgo County Grand Jury Commissioners,* 622 F.2d 807, 810 (5th Cir. 1980).

11. *Ovalle v. State,* 13 S.W.3d 774, 777–782 (Tex. Crim. App. 2000).

12. Beatriz De la Garza, *A Law for the Lion: A Tale of Crime and Injustice in the Borderlands* 93–97 (2003).

13. See Randall Kennedy, *Race, Crime, and the Law* 69–73 (1998).

14. U.S. Commission on Civil Rights, *Mexican Americans and the Administration of Justice in the Southwest* 2, 12–13 (1970).

15. See, e.g., Nancy E. Walker, J. Michael Senger, Francisco A. Villaruel, and Angela M. Arboleda, *Lost Opportunities: The Reality of Latinos in the U.S. Criminal Justice System* (2004); Alfredo Mirandé, *Gringo Justice* 1–3, 20–22, 29 (1987).

Chapter 4

1. The Fifteenth, Seventeenth, Nineteenth, and Twenty-Fourth Amendments (and general principles of the Fourteenth Amendment). The Fifteenth Amendment forbids denial or abridgement of the franchise "on account of race, color, or previous condition of servitude"; the Seventeenth deals with popular election of members of the Senate; the Nineteenth provides for equal suffrage for women; the Twenty-Fourth outlaws the poll tax as a qualification for participation in federal elections. The Twelfth and Twenty-Seventh also address voting issues.

2. See generally Roy L. Brooks, Gilbert P. Carrasco, and Michael Selmi, *Civil Rights Litigation* 561–562, 685 (2000).
3. 79 Stat. 439, 42 U.S.C. 1973b(e) (1964 ed.).
4. Powe, *The Warren Court* at 263.
5. William Cohen, Congressional Power to Interpret Due Process and Equal Protection, 27 *Stan. L. Rev.* 606 (1975).
6. Laurence H. Tribe, *American Constitutional Law* 341 (2nd ed. 1988).
7. Tribe, *American Constitutional Law* at 341–342.
8. Chavez, *Out of the Barrio* at 46.
9. 42 USC sec. 1973b(f)(2).
10. 42 USC sec. 1973b(f)(1).
11. Brooks et al., *Civil Rights Litigation* at 975.

Chapter 5

1. See, e.g., Walter Prescott Webb, *The Texas Rangers: A Century of Frontier Defense* (1993).
2. See, e.g., Rodolfo Acuña, *Occupied America: A History of Chicanos* 38–43 (3rd ed. 1988); Mirandé, *Gringo Justice* at 20.
3. Griswold del Castillo, *The Treaty of Guadalupe Hidalgo* at 62–86.
4. Griswold del Castillo, *The Treaty of Guadalupe Hidalgo* at 68–72.
5. According to a statement attributed to Cheno Cortina: "Some laws were intended to protect our rights against the attacks from other men while the gringos assembled in shadowy councils attempted and executed the robbery and burning of the homes of our brothers . . . other officials who were entrusted with our land titles, refused to return them under false and frivolous pretenses . . . Many of us have been robbed of our property, jailed, persecuted, murdered, and hunted like wild beasts because our work was fruitful. Their avarice was incited and led them to frightful crimes against our people. These monsters are not punished because gringos do not apply their law against gringos and use it to persecute Mexicans because, they say, our people are not worthy to belong to the human race." Amando Morales, *Ando Sangrando: A Study of Mexican-American Police Conflict* 12 (1972). See also David Montejano, *Anglos and Mexicans in the Making of Texas, 1836–1986,* 63–70 (1987); Mirandé, *Gringo Justice* at 17–22.
6. Arnoldo DeLeón, *The Tejano Community,* 1836–1900, 23–43 (1982).
7. "Not only were Mexicans bamboozled by the political factions, but they were victimized by the law. One law applied to them and another, far less rigorous, to the political leaders and to the prominent Americans." Carey MacWilliams, *North from Mexico* 110 (1949), cited in Morales, *Ando Sangrando* at 12.
8. According to George Marvin, "the killing of Mexicans . . . through the border [during the Mexican Revolution 1910–1917, 1925] is almost incredible . . . Some rangers have degenerated into common man killers. There is no penalty for killing, for nobody along the border would ever convict a white man for shooting

a Mexican. . . . Reading over the Secret Service records makes you feel almost as though there were an open game season on Mexicans along the border." Carey MacWilliams, *North from Mexico* 110 (1949), cited in Morales, *Ando Sangrando* at 13.

9. Morales, *Ando Sangrando* at 1.
10. See, e.g., Morales Carrión, *A Political and Cultural History of Puerto Rico* at 257–258; Mario T. Garcia, *Mexican Americans* 36 (1986); San Miguel, *Let All of Them Take Heed* at 114–115.
11. Morales, *Ando Sangrando* at 16.
12. Beatrice Griffith, *American Me* 22 (1948).
13. Peter Irons and Stephanie Guitton (eds.), *May It Please the Court* 214 (1993).
14. Irons and Guitton, *May It Please the Court* at 214.
15. Powe, *The Warren Court* at 209, 497–499.
16. *Mapp v. Ohio*, 367 U.S. 643 (1961) (incorporating exclusionary rule); but see *Terry v. Ohio*, 392 U.S. 1 (1968) (creating "stop and frisk" exception).
17. *In re Oliver*, 333 U.S. 257 (1948) (public trial); *Pointer v. Texas*, 380 U.S. 400 (1965) (confront witness); *Parker v. Gladden*, 385 U.S. 363 (1966) (impartial jury); *Kopfer v. North Carolina*, 386 U.S. 213 (1967) (speedy trial); *Washington v. Texas*, 388 U.S. 14 (1967) (compulsory process for obtaining witness); *Duncan v. Louisiana*, 391 U.S. 145 (1968) (right to jury trial in nonpetty cases).
18. *Gideon v. Wainwright*, 372 U.S. 335 (1963) (right to counsel in felony cases), and *Argersinger v. Hamlin*, 407 U.S. 25 (1972) (right to counsel in all criminal cases involving jail term).
19. Irons and Guitton, *May It Please the Court* at 216.
20. Irons and Guitton, *May It Please the Court* at 220.
21. Irons and Guitton, *May It Please the Court* at 220.
22. O'Brien, *Constitutional Law and Politics* at 36 (1991).
23. Powe, *The Warren Court* at 394 (emphasis in original).
24. Saltzburg and Capra, *American Criminal Procedure* at 523.
25. *Chavez v. Martinez*, 538 U.S. 760 (2003).
26. *Dickerson v. United States*, 530 U.S. 428, 442–444 (2000).
27. *Griffin v. California*, 380 U.S. 609 (1965).
28. *Portuondo v. Agard*, 529 U.S. 61 (2000) (Ginsburg, J., dissenting).
29. Powe, *The Warren Court* at 411.
30. Powe, *The Warren Court* at 411.

Chapter 6

1. See, e.g., Richard Kluger, *Simple Justice* (1975); San Miguel, *Let All of Them Take Heed*.
2. See, e.g., Gerald Gunther, *Constitutional Law* 738 (12th ed. 1991); Tribe, *American Constitutional Law* at 1492.
3. Earl M. Maltz, *The Chief Justiceship of Warren Burger 1969–1986* 19 (2000).

4. Robert L. Manteuffel, Comment, The Quest for Efficiency: Public School Funding in Texas, 43 *S.W.L.J.* 1119, 1123 (1990).
5. Wilbourn E. Benton, *Texas Politics,* 17–23 (5th ed. 1984); Montejano, *Anglos and Mexicans* at 103–155.
6. Manteuffel, Quest for Efficiency, at 1123–1125.
7. Gail F. Levine, Note, Meeting the Third Wave: Legislative Approaches to Recent Judicial School Finance Rulings, 28 *Harv. J. Leg.* 507, 514 (1991).
8. Tribe, *American Constitutional Law* at 1451.
9. Guadalupe Salinas, Mexican-Americans and the Desegregation of Schools in the Southwest, 8 *U. Hou. L. Rev.* 929, 948–949 (1971).
10. Maltz, *The Chief Justiceship of Warren Burger* at 22.
11. See, e.g., Scott Rutledge, Commentary: Constitutional Law: School Daze, *Tex. Lawyer,* Oct. 25, 1993, at 18.
12. *Edgewood I.S.D. v. Kirby (Kirby I),* 777 S.W.2d 391, 392 (Tex. 1989).
13. The "language of article VII, section 1 imposes on the legislature an affirmative duty to provide for [effective] public free schools." *Kirby I, 777* S.W.2d at 394.
14. *Edgewood I.S.D. v. Kirby (Kirby II),* 804 S.W.2d 491 (Tex. 1991).
15. *Carrollton Farmers v. Edgewood I.S.D.,* 826 S.W.2d 489 (Tex. 1992).
16. William Murchison, Commentary: The Layman's Eye: Lani's Lessons, *Tex. Lawyer,* June 21, 1993, at 14.
17. 433 U.S. 267 (1977).

Chapter 7

1. See generally Acuña, *Occupied America;* Emilio Zamora, *The World of the Mexican Worker in Texas,* 30–31, 131–132, 149 (1993).
2. Juan Perea, Ethnicity and Prejudice: Reevaluating National Origin Discrimination under Title VII, 35 *William & Mary L. Rev.* 805, 860 n. 277 (1994), citing President's Committee on Civil Rights, To Secure These Rights 55 (1947).
3. *Ugalde v. McKenzie Asphalt,* 990 F.2d 239, 241 (5th Cir. 1993); *Wheelcox v. Phillip Morris,* 1997 U.S. Dist. LEXIS 1292, *29 (E.D. La. 1997); *Cruz v. Coach Stores,* 202 F. 3d 560, 568 (2nd Cir. 2000); *Union Pacific R.R. Co. v. Loa,* 153 S.W. 3d 162, 169 (Tex. Civ. App.—El Paso 2004).
4. Alex M. Saragoza, Concepción R. Juárez, Abel Valenzua Jr., and Oscar González, History and Public Policy: Title VII and the Use of the Hispanic Classification, 5 *La Raza L.J.* 1 (1992).
5. Perea, Ethnicity and Prejudice at 821 n. 90, referencing the fact that the length of the debate inspired the title of the book; Charles Whalen and Barbara Whalen, *The Longest Debate: A Legislative History of the 1964 Civil Rights Act* (1985).
6. *Griggs v. Duke Power Co.,* 401 U.S. 424, 429–430 (1971).
7. A second major statutory provision which is also frequently invoked in the employment discrimination context: Section 1981. 42 U.S.C. sec. 1981 is part of the Civil Rights Act of 1866, which gives people certain rights, most prominently,

the right "to make and enforce contracts" on the same basis as white citizens. Section 1981 applies to both public and private discrimination. *Jones v. Alfred Mayer Co.*, 392 U.S. 409 (1968).

8. See, e.g., Mary Romero, Twice Protected? Assessing the Impact of Affirmative Action on Mexican-American Women, 5 *Ethnicity and Public Policy Series: Ethnicity and Women* 135, 137–147, 152 (1982); Zamora, *The World of the Mexican Worker* at 26; Judith A. Winston, An Anti-Discrimination Legal Construct That Disadvantages Working Women of Color, 79 *Cal. L. Rev.* 775 (1991).

9. 29 CFR sec. 1606.1(d) (1972).

10. Citing 110 *Cong. Rec.* 2549 (1964).

11. Exec. Order No. 1997, H.R. Doc. No. 1258, 63d Cong., 3d Sess. 118 (1914); see 5 U.S.C. sec. 3301; 5 CFR sec. 338.101 (1972).

12. 398 U.S. 922 (Douglas, J., dissenting).

13. Perea, Ethnicity and Prejudice at 822, 824.

14. 29 CFR sec. 1606.7, 1606.8.

15. Perea, Ethnicity and Prejudice at 809, 859–861.

16. J. Alfred Southerland, *National Origin Discrimination Based on Accent and Manner of Speaking* 5 (1987). On accent discrimination, see Mari J. Matsuda, Voices of America: Accent Discrimination, Law, and a Jurisprudence for the Last Reconstruction, 100 *Yale L.J.* 1329, 1333–1356 (1991).

17. *Jurado v. Eleven-Fifty Co.*, 813 F.2d 1406, 1410 (9th Cir. 1987).

18. Bill Piatt, *¿Only English?* 62 (1990) referring to *Jurado and Zamora v. Local 11*, 817 F.2d 566 (9th Cir. 1987).

19. *Garcia v. Spun Steak Co.*, 998 F.2d 1480, 1483 (9th Cir.), reh'g denied, 13 F.3d 296, 298 n. 3 (9th Cir. 1993) (Reinhardt, J., dissenting from denial of en banc).

20. *García v. Gloor*, 609 F.2d 156 (5th Cir.) vacated, 618 F.2d 264, 267 (5th Cir. 1980); *Gutierrez v. Municipal Court*, 838 F.2d 1031 (9th Cir. 1989), vacated as moot.

21. See 29 C.F.R. sec. 1606.7(b) (1991).

22. 490 U.S. 642 (1989).

23. *Wards Cove*, 490 U.S. at 663 n. 4 (Stevens, J., dissenting).

24. Compare with *LULAC v. Woods*, 993 F.2d 83 (5th Cir. 1993).

25. *Wards Cove*, 490 U.S. at 656–663.

26. Pub. L. 102–166 (1991). Tom Kenworthy and Ann Devroy, Rights Leaders, Bush Trade Heated Salvos; House Nears Vote on Controversial Legislation, *Washington Post*, June 4, 1991, A-1.

27. 118 U.S. 356 (1886).

28. 100 Stat. 3359 (1986).

29. Acuña, *Occupied America* at 370–371 n. 24.

Chapter 8

1. *U.S. v. Galvan-Torres*, 350 F.3d 456 (5th Cir. 2003); *U.S. v. Montero-Camurgo*, 208 F.3d 1122, 1129–1140 (9th Cir. 2000).

2. Alfredo Mirandé, Is There a Mexican Exception to the Fourth Amendment? 55 *Fla. L. Rev.* 365 (2003).
3. *City of Indianapolis v. Edmond,* 531 U.S. 32, 38–39, 121 S. Ct. 447, 452 (2000).
4. *United States v. Montoya de Hernandez,* 473 U.S. 531, 545, 105 S. Ct. 3304, 3313 (1985) (Brennan, J., dissenting).

Chapter 9

1. See, e.g., Peter H. Schuck and Rogers M. Smith, *Citizenship without Consent: Illegal Aliens in the American Polity* (1985).
2. Maltz, *The Chief Justiceship of Warren Burger* at 57.
3. See, e.g., Robert G. McCloskey (revised by Sanford Levinson), *The American Supreme Court* 240 (4th ed. 2005).
4. MALDEF Vows to Continue Case against PROP. 200, Press Release, MALDEF at www.maldef.org/news.
5. *Friendly House v. Napolitano,* (9th Cir. 419 F.3d 930 2005).

Chapter 10

1. Kevin Johnson, Hard Look at Asylum, 2 *Utah L. Rev.* 279, 289 (1991).
2. The United States is also a signator to the convention against torture. United Nations Convention against Torture and Other Cruel, Inhuman, or Degrading Treatment or Punishment, art. 1, 3 (1985); 8 CFR sec. 208.16(c)(2).
3. 8 U.S.C. sec. 1101(a)(42).
4. Johnson, Hard Look at Asylum at 291 n. 43, citing 126 *Cong. Rec.* 4,501 (1980).
5. Sarah Ignatius, National Asylum Study Project: An Assessment of the Asylum Process of the Immigration and Naturalization Service 17 (1993), in Richard A. Boswell, *Immigration and Nationality Law: Cases and Materials* at 256 n. 21 (3rd ed. 2000).
6. Boswell, *Immigration and Nationality Law* at 590–591.
7. *Gonzalez v. Reno,* 212 F.3d 1338 (11th Cir. 2000).

Chapter 11

1. U.S. Federal Bureau of Investigation, *Uniform Crime Reports for the United States* (1991); U.S. Department of Justice, Bureau of Justice Statistics, *Sourcebook of Criminal Justice Statistics* (1991).
2. See generally William J. Eaton, Senate Backs Virtual Ban on Handguns for Juveniles, *L.A. Times,* November 10, 1993, at A1.
3. 139 *Cong. Rec.* S14974-03 (1993).
4. 856 F.2d 1214, 1216 n. 1 (1988).

5. V. Rock Grundman, The New Imperialism: The Extraterritorial Application of United States Law, 14 *Int'l Law* 257 (1980).
6. *U.S. v. Esparza-Mendoza*, 265 F. Supp. 2d 1254, 1270–1273 (D. Utah 2003).
7. 504 U.S. at 669–670.
8. *Alvarez-Machain v. United States*, 331 F.3d 604, 608 (9th Cir. 2003).
9. 504 U.S. 655, 659–661 (1992).
10. *United States v. Noriega*, 746 F. Supp. 1506 (S.D. Fla. 1990).

Chapter 12

1. U.S. Commission on Civil Rights, *Mexican Americans* at iii, 36–46.
2. *Black's Law Dictionary* 1575 (6th ed. 1990).
3. Although there is no constitutional mandate that any defendant be tried by a jury "of his/her peers," that phrase has made its way into the general discussion of juries, and is at least partly tied to an influential opinion involving jury trial rights authored by Justice Byron White in 1968. *Duncan*, 391 U.S. at 156. There is, however, a constitutional requirement that a jury be comprised from a "fair cross-section of the community" under the Sixth Amendment. *Taylor v. Louisiana*, 419 U.S. 522, 526–531 (1974) (systematic exclusion of women violates fair cross section requirement).
4. As Akhil Amar has pointed out, the jury is the "paradigmatic image underlying the Bill of Rights." Amar, The Bill of Rights as a Constitution at 1190.
5. *Duncan*, 391 U.S. at 149–162. Society benefits from the jury system because it enables the ordinary citizen to participate in government, and it checks the power of distant authorities.
6. *Duncan*, 391 U.S. at 154.
7. Alexis de Tocqueville, *Democracy in America* 334–437 (Schroder, 1st ed. 1961), cited in *Powers v. Ohio*, 499 U.S. 400, 406 (1991).
8. The following dates appear in the joint appendix filed by the parties with the Supreme Court. Joint Appendix, 1990 WL 10022982, Chronological Docket Dates at *1a.
9. Transcript of oral argument in *Hernandez v. New York*, 1991 WL 636571 at *3.
10. Tinsley E. Yarbrough, *The Rehnquist Court and the Constitution* 230 (2000).
11. *Swain v. Alabama*, 380 U.S. 202, 221–222 (1965).
12. Joint Appendix, 1990 WL 10022982, Transcript of New York State Supreme Court Decision on Claim of Jury Discrimination at *3a.
13. *U.S. v. Perez*, 658 F.2d 654 (9th Cir. 1981).
14. Nancy Gertner and Judith Mizner, *The Law of Juries* para. 4–19 (1997).
15. See Charles J. Hynes, The DA Didn't Discriminate, *Newsday*, June 25, 1991, 90.
16. Hynes, The DA Didn't Discriminate at 90.
17. Bob Dart, Supreme Court Allows Ban on Bilingual Jurors, *Austin American-Statesman*, May 29, 1991, A-1.

18. Joe Salkowski, Lawyers Differ over Ruling on Bilingual Jurors, *The Arizona Daily Star,* May 30, 1991, 1B.
19. Aaron Epstein, Decision May Lead to Increased Exclusion of Bilingual Jurors, *L.A. Daily News,* May 29, 1991, N 10.
20. *Meyer,* 262 U.S. at 397–403; *Bartels v. Iowa,* 262 U.S. at 409–411.
21. Juan Perea's Demography and Distrust chronicles the development of language rights and language discrimination as well as the multilingual history of the states of the United States and the various official languages that some states have had at different times in the country's history. Juan F. Perea, Demography and Distrust: An Essay on American Languages, Cultural Pluralism, and Official English, 77 *U. Minn. L. Rev.* 269 (1992).
22. Juan Perea, *Hernandez v. New York:* Courts, Prosecutors and the Fear of Spanish, 21 *Hofstra L. Rev.* 1, 15–46, 52–57 (1992); Alfredo Mirandé, Now That I Speak English, No Me Dejan Hablar [I'm Not Allowed to Speak]: The Implications of *Hernandez v. New York,* 18 *Chicano-Latino L. Rev.* 115 (1996).
23. Perea, *Hernandez v. New York* at 52–53.
24. Alfred N. Garwood (ed.), *Hispanic Americans: A Statistical Sourcebook* 210–213 (1992).
25. U.S. Commission on Civil Rights, *Mexican Americans* at 83.
26. U.S. Commission on Civil Rights, *Mexican Americans* at 84. Arizona had 0 out of 61, Texas had 3 out of 236, and New Mexico had the highest percentage with 18 out of 57.
27. Garwood, *Hispanic Americans* at 136–137. By comparison, Hispanics constituted 19.7% of domestic workers, 16.7% of cleaning and building service occupations, and 14.2% of farming, forestry, and fishing occupations.
28. Nicolás Kanellos, *The Hispanic Almanac: From Columbus to Corporate America* 233 (1994).
29. Richard Delgado, Rodrigo's Fifteenth Chronicle: Racial Mixture, Latino-Critical Scholarship, and the Black-White Binary, 75 *Tex. L. Rev.* 1181, 1197 (1997).
30. *General Electric Co. v. Gilbert,* 429 U.S. 125, 134–147 (1976).
31. See *California Federal Sav. & Loan Ass'n v. Guerra,* 479 U.S. 272, 276–277 (1987), referencing how the Pregnancy Discrimination Act, 42 U.S.C. sec. 200e(k), over-ruled Gilbert.
32. Deborah A. Ramirez, Excluded Voices: The Disenfranchisement of Ethnic Groups from Jury Service, 1993 *Wis. L. Rev.* 761, 776–794 (1993); Perea, *Hernandez v. New York* at 43–58. 29 C.F.R. sec. 1606.7(a) and (b); see also Malavet, *America's Glory* at 22 (language as a "cultural marker" for discrimination against Latinos). The EEOC has also classified discrimination based on "linguistic characteristics" as unlawful under Title VII because of the close relationship between language and national origin. 29 C.F.R. sec. 1606.1; see *Fragante v. City and County of Honolulu,* 888 F.2d 591, 595 (9th Cir. 1989).
33. Perea et al., *Race and Races* at 575.

34. Perea, *Hernandez v. New York* at 39.
35. Perea, *Hernandez v. New York* at 27.
36. See, e.g., *Pemberthy v. Beyer*, 19 F.3d 857, 862 (3rd Cir. 1994); *People v. Almendarez*, 639 N.E.2d 619, 623 (Ill. App. Ct. 1994); *U.S. v. Zapata Rodriguez*, 2001 WL 194758 at *5 (N.D. Tex. 2001); *Chavarria v. State*, 2000 WL 567072 at *1 (Tex. App.—Dallas 2002, pet. ref'd); Gertner and Mizner, *The Law of Juries* at para. 4–20 n. 58, para. 4–21 n. 59.
37. See, e.g., Donna F. Coltharp, Speaking the Language of Exclusion: How Equal Protection and Fundamental Rights Analysis Permits Language Discrimination, 28 *St. Mary's L.J.* 149, 172–177 (1996).
38. New York State Department of Correctional Services, Inmate Information— Location/Status/Legal Dates/etc. at http://nycsdocslookup.docs.state.ny.us/GCA00900/Wiq3/WINQ130.
39. *Georgia v. McCollum*, 505 U.S. 42, 50–57 (1992); *Edmonson v. Leesville Concrete Co.*, 500 U.S. 614, 628–631 (1991); *J.E.B. v. Alabama*, 511 U.S. 129, 143 (1994). In *United States v. Martinez-Salazar* (2000), the Supreme Court interpreted its ruling in *Hernandez v. New York* to prohibit discrimination based on "ethnic origin." *Martinez-Salazar*, 528 U.S. at 315.
40. *Batson v. Kentucky*, 476 U.S. 79, 118–119 (1986) (Burger, C. J., dissenting) citing W. Forsyth, *History of Trial by Jury* 175 (1852).
41. *Martinez-Salazar*, 528 U.S. 304, 311 (2000), citing 4 W. Blackstone, *Commentaries* 346–348 (1769).
42. *Martinez-Salazar*, 528 U.S. at 311; Gertner and Mizner, *The Law of Juries* at para. 4–5, 4–6.
43. *Powers*, 499 U.S. at 424–430.
44. *McCollum*, 505 U.S. at 68–70 (O'Connor, J., dissenting; Scalia, J., dissenting).
45. See, e.g., David Cole, Two Systems of Criminal Justice, in *The Politics of Law: A Progressive Critique* (ed. David Kairys) 421–424 (3rd ed. 1998); Perea, *Hernandez v. New York*.
46. *Batson*, 476 U.S. at 102–108 (Marshall, J., concurring).
47. *Rice v. Collins*, 126 S. Ct. 969, 977 (2006) (Breyer, J., concurring); *Edmonson*, 860 F.2d 1308, 1316 (5th Cir. 1988) (Gee, J., dissenting); *Wagment v. State*, 67 S.W.3d 851, 867 (Tex. Crim. 2001) (Meyer, J., concurring); *People v. Hernandez*, 75 N.Y.2d 350, 359, 552 N.E.2d 621, 625, 553 N.Y.S. 85, 89 (1990) (Titone, J., concurring); Morris B. Huffman, Peremptory Challenges Should Be Abolished: A Trial Judge's Perspective, 64 *U. Chi. L. Rev.* 809 (1997); Perea, *Hernandez v. New York* at 50; Albert W. Alschuler, The Supreme Court and the Jury, 56 *U. Chi. L. Rev.* 153 (1989); Gertner and Mizner, *The Law of Juries* at para. 4-58, 4-59, nn. 152–153; Eliminating a Safe Haven for Discrimination: Why New York Must Ban Peremptory Challenges from Jury Selection, 3 *J.L. & Policy* 605 (1995).
48. Gertner and Mizner, *The Law of Juries* at para. 4-56, 4-58.
49. *Purkett v. Elem*, 514 U.S. 765, 767–769 (1995).

Chapter 13

1. See, e.g., *City of Richmond v. J. A. Croson Co.*, 488 U.S. 469 (1989); *Adarand Constructors, Inc. v. Peña*, 515 U.S. 200 (1995); *Gratz v. Bollinger*, 539 U.S. 244 (2003).
2. Tinsley E. Yarbrough, *The Rehnquist Court and the Constitution* at 260 (2000).

Chapter 14

1. Linda Chavez, The Nanny Problem Takes Down Another Nominee, www .townhall.com/columnists/lindachavez/printlc20041216.shtml (Dec. 16, 2004) ("I have special reason to be concerned. My own nomination to be secretary of labor was derailed in 2001 when it became public that a decade earlier I had taken into my home and given modest financial assistance to a battered and abused woman from Guatemala, who at the time was illegally living in the United States.").
2. *Arizonans for Official English v. Arizona*, 520 U.S. 43, 73–80 (1997).
3. *Ruiz v. Hull*, 957 P.2d 984, 990, 1000–1003 (Ariz. 1998).
4. William Taylor, Racial Equality: The World according to Rehnquist, in *The Rehnquist Court: Judicial Activism on the Right* (ed. Herman Schwartz) 53–54 (2002).
5. Lisa A. Kloppenberg, *Playing It Safe: How the Supreme Court Sidesteps Hard Cases and Stunts the Development of Law* 17 (2001).
6. See, e.g., Raymond Tatalovich, Official English as Nativist Backlash, in Juan F. Perea (ed.), *Immigrants Out! The New Nativism and the Anti-Immigrant Impulse in the United States* 79 (1997); Carlos R. Soltero and Keith Strama, English-Only Rules in the Workplace in Texas, 64 *Tex. B.J.* 130 (Feb. 2001).
7. Kloppenberg, *Playing It Safe* at 20–21. As one example, Kloppenberg quotes John Tanton, the founder of U.S. English: the increasing Hispanic population, he noted, will cause "those with their pants up [to] get caught by those with their pants down."
8. Bender, Direct Democracy at 145–146; Malavet, *America's Colony* at 22.
9. Kloppenberg, *Playing It Safe* at 17.

Conclusion

1. See, e.g., Kevin Johnson, On the Appointment of a Latina/o to the Supreme Court, 5 *Harv. Latino L. Rev.* 1 (Spring 2002).

Bibliography

Acuña, Rodolfo. *Occupied America: A History of Chicanos* (3rd ed. 1988).

Amar, Akhil Reed. The Bill of Rights as a Constitution. 100 *Yale L.J.* 1131 (1991).

———. The Bill of Rights and the Fourteenth Amendment. 101 *Yale L.J.* 1193 (1992).

———. *The Bill of Rights* (1998).

Anker, Deborah E. *The Law of Asylum in the United States* (2nd ed. 1992).

Baldwin, Simeon E. The Constitutional Questions Incident to the Acquisition and Government by the United States of Island Territory. 12 *Harv. L. Rev.* 393 (1899).

Bean, Frank D., and María Tienda. *Hispanic Population of the United States* (1987).

Bell, Derek. *Race, Racism and American Law* (3rd ed. 1992).

Bender, Steven W. Direct Demography and Distrust: The Relationship between Language Law Rhetoric and the Language Vigilantism Experience, *Harv. Lat. L. Rev.* 2 (1997).

Berk-Seligson, Susan. *The Bilingual Courtroom: Court Interpreters in the Judicial Process* (1990).

Black's Law Dictionary (6th ed. 1990).

Black's Law Dictionary (7th ed. 1999).

Boswell, Richard A. *Immigration and Nationality Law: Cases and Materials* (3rd ed. 2000).

Brinkley, Douglas. *A History of the United States* (1998).

Brooks, Roy L., Gilbert Paul Carrasco, and Michael Selmi. *Civil Rights Litigation* (2000).

Cabranes, José. *Citizenship and the American Empire* (1979).

Chavez, Linda. *Out of the Barrio: Toward a New Politics of Hispanic Assimilation* (1991).

Cleveland, Sarah H. Powers Inherent in Sovereignty: Indians, Aliens, Territories, and the Nineteenth Century Origins of Plenary Power over Foreign Affairs, 81 *Tex. L. Rev.* 1 (Nov. 2002).

Cobb, Kim. Catch-22 on the Border. *Houston Chronicle,* May 12, 1994, 8A.

Coltharp, Donna F. Speaking the Language of Exclusion: How Equal Protection and Fundamental Rights Analysis Permits Language Discrimination. 28 *St. Mary's L.J.* 149 (1996).

Crenshaw, Kimberlé. Demarginalizing the Intersection of Race and Sex: A Black Feminist Critique of Antidiscrimination Doctrine, Feminist Theory, and Anti-racist Politics. *U. Chi. Legal. F.* 139 (1989).

Dart, Bob. Supreme Court Allows Ban on Bilingual Jurors. *Austin American-Statesman,* May 29, 1991, A-1.

De la Garza, Beatriz. *A Law for the Lion: A Tale of Crime and Injustice in the Border-lands* (2003).

DeLeón, Arnoldo. *The Tejano Community, 1836–1900* (1982).

Delgado Cintron, Carmelo. *Derecho y Colonialismo: La Trayectoria Histórica del Derecho Puertorriqueño* (1988).

Delgado, Richard. Rodrigo's Fifteenth Chronicle: Racial Mixture, Latino-Critical Scholarship, and the Black-White Binary. Book Review of *All Rise: Reynaldo G. Garza, The First Mexican American Federal Judge,* 75 *Tex. L. Rev.* 1181 (1997).

Douglas, William O. *The Court Years 1939–1975: The Autobiography of William O. Douglas* (1980).

Duffy Burnett, Christina, and Burke Marshall. *Foreign in a Domestic Sense: Puerto Rico, American Expansion, and the Constitution* (2001).

Dunn, Timothy J. *The Militarization of the U.S.-Mexico Border 1978–1992* (1996).

Edgewood of San Antonio News. Vol. 10. Special Edition. Nov. 1989.

Epstein, Aaron. Decision May Lead to Increased Exclusion of Bilingual Jurors. *L.A. Daily News,* May 29, 1991, N 10.

Fallon, Joseph. Funding Hate: Foundations and the Radical "Hispanic" Lobby. *The Social Contract* (Fall 2000).

Fernandez, Ronald. *The Disenchanted Island: Puerto Rico and the United States in the Twentieth Century* (1992).

Fuentes, Carlos. *Hispanicization of America* (1992).

García, Mario. *Mexican-Americans: Leadership, Ideology, and Identity* (1989).

Garwood, Alfred N., ed. *Hispanic Americans: A Statistical Sourcebook* (1992).

Gertner, Nancy, and Judith Mizner. *The Law of Juries* (1997).

Glazier, Nathan, and Daniel Patrick Moynihan. *Beyond the Melting Pot* (1955).

Gómez Quiñones, Juan. *Chicano Politics: Reality and Promise* (1990).

Griswold del Castillo, Richard. *The Treaty of Guadalupe Hidalgo: A Legacy of Conflict* (1990).

Guinn, David, M., Christopher W. Chapman, and Kathryn S. Kenchtel. Redistricting in 2001 and Beyond: Navigating the Narrow Channel between the Equal Protection Clause and the Voting Rights Act. 51 *Baylor L. Rev.* 225 (1999).

Gunther, Gerald. *Constitutional Law* (12th ed. 1991).

Hall, Kermit, ed. *The Oxford Companion to the Supreme Court of the United States* (1992).

Hans, Valerie P., and Neil Vidmar. *Judging the Jury* (1986).

Helfeld, David M. How Much of the United States Constitution and Statutes Are Applicable to the Commonwealth of Puerto Rico? *First Circuit Judicial Conference,* 110 F.R.D. at 458 (1985).

Hoops, Stephanie. *English-Only in an Era of Waning Immigration.* www.medill .nwu.edu/docket/99-1908fx.html.

Hunt, Michael H. *Ideology and U.S. Foreign Policy* (1987).

Hynes, Charles J. The DA Didn't Discriminate. *Newsday* 90 (June 25, 1991).

Irons, Peter. *A People's History of the Supreme Court* (1999).

Irons, Peter, and Stephanie Guitton, eds. *May It Please the Court* (1993).

Jiménez de Waggenheim, Olga. *El Grito de Lares: Sus Causas y Sus Hombres* (1980).

Johnson, Kevin. Hard Look at Asylum. 2 *Utah L. Rev.* 279 (1991).

Kairys, David, ed. *The Politics of Law: A Progressive Critique* (1998).

Kanellos, Nicolás. *The Hispanic Almanac: From Columbus to Corporate America* (1994).

Kennedy, Randall. *Race, Crime, and the Law* (1998).

Kent Curtis, Michael. *No State Shall Abridge: The Fourteenth Amendment and the Bill of Rights* (1986).

Kluger, Richard. *Simple Justice* (1975).

Laughlin, Stanley Jr. The Application of the Constitution in United States Territories: American Samoa, a Case Study. 2 *U. Haw. L. Rev.* 337, 341 (1980–1981).

Levine, Gail F. Meeting the Third Wave: Legislative Approaches to Recent Judicial School Finance Rulings, 28 *Harv. J. Leg.* 507 (1991).

Levinson, Sanford. Why the Canon Should Be Expanded to Include the Insular Cases and the Saga of American Expansionism. 17 *Const. Comment* 241 (Summer 2000).

Haney López, Ian F. *Racism on Trial: The Chicano Fight for Justice* (2003).

Kloppenberg, Lisa A. *Playing It Safe: How the Supreme Court Sidesteps Hard Cases and Stunts the Development of Law* (2001).

Mackinnon, Catharine A. *Feminism Unmodified* (1987).

Malavet, Pedro A. *America's Colony: The Political and Cultural Conflict between the United States and Puerto Rico* (2004).

Maltz, Earl M. *The Chief Justiceship of Warren Burger 1969–1986* (2000).

Manteuffel, Robert L. Comment. The Quest for Efficiency: Public School Funding in Texas, 43 *S.W.L.J.* 1119 (1990).

Marshall, Thurgood. No Call to Glory. *Vand. L. Rev.* (1989).

Matsuda, Mari J. Voices of America: Accent Discrimination, Law, and a Jurisprudence for the Last Reconstruction. 100 *Yale L.J.* 1329 (1991).

McCloskey, Robert G. *The American Supreme Court* 240 (4th ed. 2005).

McWilliams, Carey. *North From Mexico: The Spanish-Speaking People of the United States* (updated by Matt S. Meier); (1990).

Merryman, John Henry. *The Civil Law Tradition: An Introduction to the Legal Systems of Western Europe and Latin America* (2nd ed. 1985).

Mirandé, Alfredo. *Gringo Justice* (1987).

———. Now that I Speak English, No Me Dejan Hablar [I'm Not Allowed to Speak]: The Implications of *Hernandez v. New York*. 18 *Chicano-Latino L. Rev.* 115 (1996).

———. Is There a Mexican Exception to the Fourth Amendment? 55 *Fla. L. Rev.* 365 (2003).

Montejano, David. *Anglos and Mexicans in the Making of Texas, 1836–1986* (1987).

Moore, Joan, and Pachón, Harry. *Hispanics in the United States* (1985).

Morales, Amando. *Ando Sangrando: A Study of Mexican-American Police Conflict* (1972).

Morales Carrión, Arturo. *A Political and Cultural History of Puerto Rico* (1983).

Murchison, William. Commentary: The Layman's Eye: Lani's Lessons. *Tex. Lawyer*, June 21, 1993, at 14.

Neuman, Gerald L. Whose Constitution? 100 *Yale L.J.* 909 (Jan. 1991).

Newman, Roger K. *Hugo Black: A Biography* (2nd ed. 1997).

O'Brien, David M. *Constitutional Law and Politics: Civil Rights and Civil Liberties* (Vol. 2. 1991).

———. *Storm Center: The Supreme Court in American Politics* (6th ed. 2003).

Ochoa, George. *Atlas of Hispanic-American History* (2001).

Padilla, Felix M. *Latino Ethnic Consciousness* (1985).

Perea, Juan F. Demography and Distrust: An Essay on American Languages, Cultural Pluralism, and Official English. 77 *U. Minn. L. Rev.* 269 (1992).

———. *Hernandez v. New York*: Courts, Prosecutors and the Fear of Spanish. 21 *Hofstra L. Rev.* 1 (1992).

———. Ethnicity and Prejudice: Reevaluating National Origin Discrimination under Title VII. 35 *William & Mary L. Rev.* 805 (1994).

———, ed. *Immigrants Out! The New Nativism and the Anti-Immigrant Impulse in the United States* (1997).

Perea, Juan F., Richard Delgado, Angela P. Harris, and Stephanie M. Wildman. *Race and Races: Cases and Resources for a Diverse America* (2000).

Piatt, Bill. ¿*Only English? Law and Language Policy in the United States* (1990).

Powe, Lucas A., Jr. *The Warren Court and American Politics* (2000).

Ramirez, Deborah A. Excluded Voices: The Disenfranchisement of Ethnic Groups from Jury Service. *Wis. L. Rev.* 761 (1993).

Randolph, Carman F. Constitutional Aspects of Annexation. 12 *Harv. L. Rev.* 291, 304 (1898).

Rodríguez, Clara E. *Changing Race: Latinos, the Census, and the History of Ethnicity in the United States* (2000).

Romero, Mary. Twice Protected? Assessing the Impact of Affirmative Action on Mexican-American Women. 5 *Ethnicity and Public Policy Series: Ethnicity and Women* 135 (1982).

Roos, Peter. Bilingual Education: The Hispanic Response to Unequal Educational Opportunity. 42 *Law & Contemp. Problems* 111 (Fall 1978).

Ruiz Cameron, Christopher David. One Hundred Fifty Years of Solitude: Reflections on the End of the History Academy's Dominance of Scholarship on the Treaty of Guadalupe Hidalgo. 5 *SW. J. L. & Trade Am.* 83 (1998).

Russell, Talcott H. Results of Expansion, 9 *Yale L.J.* 239 (1900).

Salinas, Guadalupe. Mexican-Americans and the Desegregation of Schools in the Southwest, 8 *U. Hou. L. Rev.* 929 (1971).

Salkowski, Joe. Lawyers Differ over Ruling on Bilingual Jurors. *Arizona Daily Star,* May 30, 1991, 1B.

Saltzburg, Stephen A., and Daniel J. Capra. *American Criminal Procedure: Cases and Commentary* (4th ed. 1992).

San Miguel, Guadalupe, Jr. *Let All of Them Take Heed: Mexican Americans and the Campaign for Educational Equality in Texas, 1910–1981* (1987).

Saragoza, Alex M., Concepción R. Juárez, Abel Valenzua Jr., and Oscar González. History and Public Policy: Title VII and the Use of the Hispanic Classification. 5 *La Raza L.J.* 1 (1992).

Savage, David G. *Turning Right: The Making of the Rehnquist Supreme Court* (1993).

Schuck, Peter H., and Rogers M. Smith. *Citizenship without Consent: Illegal Aliens in the American Polity* (1985).

Schwartz, Herman. *The Rehnquist Court: Judicial Activism on the Right* (2002).

Sedillo Lópcz, Antoinette. *Latinos in the United States: Latino Employment, Labor Organizations, and Immigration.* (Vol. 4. 1995).

Sheridan, Clare. Another White Race: Mexican Americano and the Paradox of Whiteness in Jury Selection. *Law and History Review* (Spring 2003) at 9 nn. 14–15. http://www.historycooperative.org/journals/1hr/21.1/forum sheridan.html (Dec. 12, 2003).

Shorris, Earl. *Latinos: A Biography of the People* (1992).

Skerry, Peter. *Mexican-Americans: The Ambivalent Minority* (1993).

Soltero, Carlos R. The Supreme Court Should Overrule the Territorial Incorporation Doctrine and End One Hundred Years of Judicially Condoned Colonialism. 22 *Chicano-Latino L. Rev.* 1 (Spring 2001).

Soltero, Carlos R., and Keith Strama. English-Only Rules in the Workplace in Texas. 64 *Tex. Bar J.* 130 (Feb. 2001).

Southerland, J. Alfred. *National Origin Discrimination Based on Accent and Manner of Speaking* (1987).

Starr, Kenneth W. *First among Equals: The Supreme Court in American Life* (2002).

Stone, Geoffrey R., Louis M. Seidman, Cass R. Sunstein, and Mark V. Tushnet. *Constitutional Law* (2nd ed. 1991).

Taylor, William. Racial Equality: The World according to Rehnquist. In *The Rehnquist Court: Judicial Activism on the Right* (ed. Herman Schwartz, 2002).

Torruella, Juan R. *The Supreme Court and Puerto Rico: The Doctrine of Separate and Unequal* (1985).

Trías Monge, José. *Puerto Rico: The Trials of the Oldest Colony in the World* (1997).

Tribe, Laurence H. *American Constitutional Law* (2nd ed. 1988).

U.S. Commission on Civil Rights. *Mexican Americans and the Administration of Justice in the Southwest* (1970).

U.S. Department of Justice, Bureau of Justice Statistics. *Sourcebook of Criminal Justice Statistics* (1991).

U.S. Federal Bureau of Investigation. *Uniform Crime Reports for the United States* (1991).

Valencia, Reynaldo Anaya, Sonia R. García, Henry Flores, and José Roberto Juárez Jr. *Mexican Americans and the Law* (2004).

Waggenheim, Kal, and Olga Jiménez de Waggenheim. *The Puerto Ricans: A Documented History* 95 (1994).

Wilkins, David E. *American Indian Sovereignty and the U.S. Supreme Court: The Masking of Justice* (1997).

Winston, Judith A. An Anti-Discrimination Legal Construct That Disadvantages Working Women of Color. 79 *Cal. L. Rev.* 775 (1991).

Yarbrough, Tinsley E. *The Rehnquist Court and the Constitution* (2000).

Zamora, Emilio. *The World of the Mexican Worker in Texas* (1993).

Zamora, Stephen, José Ramón Cossío, Leonel Pereznieto, José Roldán-Xopa, and David Lopez. *Mexican Law* (2004).

List of Cases

Featured Supreme Court Cases and Lower Court Companion Cases

Botiller v. Dominguez, 130 U.S. 238 (1889).
  Botiller v. Dominguez, 13 Pac. Rep. 685 (Cal. 1887).
Balzac v. Porto [sic] Rico, 258 U.S. 298, 42 S. Ct. 343 (1922).
  People v. Balzac, 28 P.R.R. 139 (1920).
Hernandez v. Texas, 347 U.S. 475, 74 S. Ct. 667 (1954).
  Hernandez v. State, 160 Tex. Crim. 72, 251 S.W.2d 531 (Tex. Crim. 1952).
Katzenbach v. Morgan, 384 U.S. 641, 86 S. Ct. 1717 (1966).
  Morgan v. Katzenbach, 247 F. Supp. 196 (D.D.C. 1965).
Miranda v. Arizona, 384 U.S. 436, 86 S. Ct. 1602 (1966).
  State v. Miranda, 98 Ariz. 18, 401 P.2d 721 (Ariz. 1965).
San Antonio ISD v. Rodriguez, 411 U.S. 1, 93 S. Ct. 1278 (1973).
  Rodriguez v. San Antonio ISD, 337 F. Supp. 280 (W.D. Tex. 1971).
Espinoza v. Farah Mfg. Co., 414 U.S. 86, 94 S. Ct. 334 (1973).
  Espinoza v. Farah Mfg. Co., 462 F.2d 1331 (5th Cir. 1972).
  Espinoza v. Farah Mfg. Co., 343 F. Supp. 1205 (W.D. Tex. 1971).
United States v. Brignoni-Ponce, 422 U.S. 873, 95 S. Ct. 2574 (1975).
  United States v. Brignoni-Ponce, 499 F.2d 1109 (9th Cir. 1974).
Plyler v. Doe, 457 U.S. 202, 102 S. Ct. 2382 (1982).
  Doe v. Plyler, 628 F.2d 448 (5th Cir. 1980).
  Doe v. Plyler, 458 F.Supp. 569 (5th Cir. 1978).
INS v. Cardoza-Fonseca, 480 U.S. 421, 107 S. Ct. 1207 (1987).
  Cardoza-Fonseca v. INS, 767 F.2d 1448 (9th Cir. 1985).
U.S. v. Verdugo-Urquidez, 494 U.S. 259, 110 S. Ct. 1056 (1990).
  U.S. v. Verdugo-Urquidez, 856 F.2d 1214 (9th Cir. 1988).

Hernandez v. New York, 500 U.S. 352, 111 S. Ct. 1859 (1991).
   People v. Hernandez, 75 N.Y.2d 350, 552 N.E.2d 621, 553 N.Y.S. 85 (1990).
   People v. Hernandez, 140 A.D.2d 542, 528 N.Y.S. 625 (1988).
Johnson v. DeGrandy, 512 U.S. 997, 114 S. Ct. 2647 (1994).
   DeGrandy v. Wetherell, 815 F. Supp. 1550 (N.D. Fla. 1992).
Alexander v. Sandoval, 523 U.S. 275, 121 S. Ct. 1511 (2001).
   Sandoval v. Hagan, 197 F.3d 484 (11th Cir. 1999).
   Sandoval v. Hagan, 7 F. Supp. 2d 1234 (M.D. Ala. 1998).

Other Supreme Court Cases

Adarand Constructors, Inc. v. Peña, 515 U.S. 200 (1995).
Alfred Dunhill of London, Inc. v. Republic of Cuba, 425 U.S. 682 (1976).
Almeida-Sanchez v. United States, 413 U.S. 266 (1973).
Apodaca v. Oregon, 406 U.S. 404 (1972).
Arizonans for Official English v. Arizona, 520 U.S. 43 (1997).
Argersinger v. Hamlin, 407 U.S. 25 (1972).
Baker v. Carr, 369 U.S. 186 (1962).
Banco Nacional de Cuba v. Sabbatino, 376 U.S. 398 (1964).
Bartels v. Iowa, 262 U.S. 404 (1923).
Batson v. Kentucky, 476 U.S. 79 (1986).
Brown v. Board of Education, 347 U.S. 483 (1954).
Bush v. Vera, 517 U.S. 952 (1996).
Califano v. Torres, 435 U.S. 1 (1978).
California Federal Sav. & Loan Ass'n v. Guerra, 479 U.S. 272 (1987).
Cannon v. University of Chicago, 441 U.S. 677 (1979).
Cardona v. Power, 384 U.S. 672 (1966).
Castañeda v. Partida, 430 U.S. 482 (1977).
Chavez v. Martinez, 538 U.S. 760 (2003).
Cherokee Nation v. Georgia, 30 U.S. (5 Pet.) 1 (1831).
Chevron, U.S.A., Inc. v. Natural Resources Defense Council, Inc., 467 U.S. 837
   (1984).
City of Indianapolis v. Edmond, 531 U.S. 32 (2000).
City of Mobile v. Bolden, 446 U.S. 55 (1980).
City of Richmond v. J. A. Croson Co., 488 U.S. 469 (1989).
Cooper v. Aaron, 358 U.S. 1 (1958).
Dickerson v. United States, 530 U.S. 428 (2000).
Dorr v. United States, 195 U.S. 138 (1904).
Downes v. Bidwell, 182 U.S. 244 (1901).
Duncan v. Louisiana, 391 U.S. 145 (1968).
Edmonson v. Leesville Concrete Co., 500 U.S. 614 (1991).
Elk v. Wilkins, 112 U.S. 94 (1884).
Escobedo v. Illinois, 378 U.S. 478 (1964).

McCulloch v. State of Maryland, 17 U.S. 316 (1819).
McDonnell Douglas Corp. v. Green, 411 U.S. 792 (1973).
Meyer v. Nebraska, 262 U.S. 390 (1923).
Miller-El v. Cockrell, 537 U.S. 322 (2003).
Milliken v. Bradley, 418 U.S. 717 (1974).
Milliken v. Bradley, 433 U.S. 267 (1977).
Missouri ex rel Gaines v. Canada, 305 U.S. 337 (1938).
More v. Steinbach, 127 U.S. 70 (1888).
Oklahoma Tax Comm'n. v. Citizens Band Potawatimi Indian Tribe of Oklahoma, 498 U.S. 505 (1991).
Oregon v. Mitchell, 400 U.S. 112 (1970).
Palko v. Connecticut, 302 U.S. 319 (1937).
Parker v. Gladden, 385 U.S. 363 (1966).
Patterson v. McLean Credit Union, 491 U.S. 164 (1989).
Plessy v. Ferguson, 163 U.S. 537 (1896).
Pointer v. Texas, 380 U.S. 400 (1965).
Portuondo v. Agard, 529 U.S. 61 (2000).
Powers v. Ohio, 499 U.S. 400 (1991).
Price Waterhouse v. Hopkins, 490 U.S. 228 (1989).
Purkett v. Elem, 514 U.S. 765 (1995).
Regents of the Univ. of California v. Bakke, 438 U.S. 265 (1978).
Reid v. Covert, 354 U.S. 1 (1957).
Roe v. Wade, 410 U.S. 113 (1973).
Scott v. Sandford, 60 U.S. 393 (1856).
Shaw v. Hunt, 517 U.S. 899 (1996).
Shaw v. Reno, 509 U.S. 630 (1993).
Sosa v. Alvarez-Machain, 542 U.S. 697 (2004).
South Carolina v. Katzenbach, 383 U.S. 301 (1966).
Strauder v. West Virginia, 100 U.S. 303 (1879).
Swain v. Alabama, 380 U.S. 202 (1965).
Sweatt v. Painter, 339 U.S. 629 (1950).
Taylor v. Louisiana, 419 U.S. 522, 95 S. Ct. 692 (1974).
Terry v. Ohio, 392 U.S. 1 (1968).
Thompson v. Utah, 170 U.S. 343 (1898).
Thornburg v. Gingles, 478 U.S. 30 (1986).
Tijerina v. Henry, 398 U.S. 922 (1970).
Torres v. Puerto Rico, 442 U.S. 465 (1979).
U.S. v. Alvarez-Machain, 504 U.S. 655 (1992).
United States v. Kagama, 118 U.S. 375 (1886).
United States v. Kras, 409 U.S. 434 (1973).
United States v. Martinez-Fuerte, 428 U.S. 543 (1976).
United States v. Martinez-Salazar, 528 U.S. 304 (2000).
United States v. Montoya de Hernandez, 473 U.S. 531 (1985).

United States v. Ojeda-Rios, 495 U.S. 257 (1990).
United States v. Ortiz, 422 U.S. 891 (1975).
U.S. v. Sokolow, 490 U.S. 1, 109 S. Ct. 1581 (1989).
Wards Cove Packing Co. v. Atonio, 490 U.S. 642 (1989).
Washington v. Texas, 388 U.S. 14 (1967).
Yick Wo v. Hopkins, 118 U.S. 356 (1886).

Other Federal Cases

Alliance of Descendants of Texas Land Grants v. United States, 37 F.3d 1478 (Fed. Cir. 1994).
Alvarez-Machain v. United States, 331 F.3d 604 (9th Cir. 2003) (reversed).
American Baptist Churches v. Thornburg, 712 F. Supp. 756 (N.D. Cal. 1989).
American Baptist Churches v. Thornburg, 760 F. Supp. 796 (N.D. Cal. 1991).
Aspira of New York, Inc. v. Board of Ed. of City of New York, 394 F. Supp. 1161 (S.D.N.Y. 1975).
Belian v. Texas A&M Univ. Corpus Christi, 987 F. Supp. 517, 522 (S.D. Tex.), aff'd, 132 F.3d 1453 (5th Cir. 1997).
Bodenheimer v. PPG Industries, Inc., 5 F.3d 955 (5th Cir. 1993).
Bolanos-Hernandez v. INS, 767 F.2d 1277 (9th Cir. 1985).
Carter v. City of Miami, 870 F.2d 578 (11th Cir. 1989).
Ciudadanos Unidos de San Juan v. Hidalgo County Grand Jury Commissioners, 622 F.2d 807 (5th Cir. 1980).
Cruz v. Coach Stores, 202 F. 3d 560 (2nd Cir. 2000).
Damon v. Fleming Supermarkets of Florida, Inc., 196 F.3d 1354 (11th Cir. 1999).
DeGrandy v. Wetherell, 794 F. Supp. 1076 (N.D. Fla. 1992).
Fragante v. City and County of Honolulu, 888 F.2d 591 (9th Cir. 1989), cert. denied, 494 U.S. 1081, 110 S. Ct. 1811 (1990).
Friendly House v. Napolitano, 2005 WL 1869490 No. 05-15005 (9th Cir. Aug. 9, 2005).
García v. Gloor, 609 F.2d 156 (5th Cir.) vacated, 618 F.2d 264 (5th Cir. 1980).
Garcia v. Spun Steak Co., 998 F.2d 1480(9th Cir.), reh'g denied, 13 F.3d 296 (9th Cir. 1993).
Gonzalez v. Reno, 212 F.3d 1338 (11th Cir. 2000).
Gonzalez v. Reno, 86 F. Supp. 2d 1167 (S.D. Fla. 2000).
Guerra v. Manchester Terminal Corp., 350 F. Supp. 529 (S.D. Tex. 1972).
Gutierrez v. Municipal Court, 838 F.2d 1031 (9th Cir. 1989), vacated as moot.
Igartua de la Rosa v. U.S., 107 F. Supp. 2d 140 (D.P.R. 2000), and 113 F. Supp. 2d 228, 242 (D.P.R. 2000), rev'd, 229 F.3d 80 (1st Cir. 2000).
Jurado v. Eleven-Fifty Co., 813 F.2d 1406 (9th Cir. 1988).
LULAC v. Wilson, 131 F.3d 1297 (9th Cir. 1997).
LULAC v. Wilson, 997 F. Supp. 1244 (C.D. Cal. 1997).
LULAC v. Woods, 993 F.2d 80 (5th Cir. 1993).

Maldonado-Maldonado v. Pantasia Mfg. Co., 983 F. Supp. 58 (D.P.R. 1997).

Pemberthy v. Beyer, 19 F.3d 857 (3d Cir. 1994).

Prado v. Luria & Son, Inc., 975 F. Supp. 1349 (S.D. Fla. 1997).

Robin v. Espo Eng. Co., 200 F.3d 1081 (7th Cir. 2000).

Sims v. Brown & Root Indus. Services, 889 F. Supp. 920 (W.D. La. 1995).

Ugalde v. W. A. McKenzie Asphalt, 990 F.2d 239 (5th Cir. 1993).

U.S. v. Acosta-Martinez, 106 F. Supp. 2d 311 (D.P.R. 2000).

U.S. v. Esparza-Mendoza, 265 F. Supp. 2d 1254 (D. Utah 2003).

U.S. v. Galvan-Torres, 350 F.3d 456 (5th Cir. 2003).

U.S. v. Kole, 164 F.3d 164 (3rd Cir. 1998).

U.S. v. Montero-Camargo, 208 F.3d 1122 (9th Cir. 2000).

United States v. Noriega, 746 F. Supp. 1506 (S.D. Fla. 1990).

U.S. v. Perez, 658 F.2d 654 (9th Cir. 1981).

U.S. v. Zapata Rodriguez, 2001 WL 194758 (N.D. Tex. 2001).

Wheelcox v. Phillip Morris, 1997 U.S. Dist. LEXIS 1292 (E.D. La. 1997).

Zamora v. Local 11, 817 F.2d 566 (9th Cir. 1987).

Other Cases

Carrollton Farmers v. Edgewood I.S.D., 826 S.W.2d 489 (Tex. 1992).

Chavarria v. State, 2000 WL 567072 (Tex. App.—Dallas 2002, pet. ref'd).

Edgewood I.S.D. v. Kirby, 777 S.W.2d 391 (Tex. 1989).

Edgewood I.S.D. v. Kirby, 804 S.W.2d 491 (Tex. 1991).

ISD v. Salvatierra, 33 S.W. 790 (Tex. Civ. App.—San Antonio 1930).

Ovalle v. State, 13 S.W.3d 774 (Tex. Crim. App. 2000).

People v. Almendarez, 639 N.E.2d 619 (Ill. App. Ct. 1994).

Ruiz v. Hull, 957 P.2d 984 (Ariz. 1998).

Union Pacific R.R. Co. v. Loa, 153 S.W. 3d 162 (Tex. App.—El Paso 2004).

Wagment v. State, 67 S.W.3d 851 (Tex. Crim. 2001).

Cases Mentioned

General Index